Healing Through Deliverance

The Biblical Basis

Peter J. Horrobin

Hon. Director
of
Ellel Grange
Centre for Training and Ministry
in Christian Healing and Counselling

Sovereign World Limited

Sovereign World Limited
P.O.Box 17
Chichester
England, PO20 6YB

British Library Cataloguing in Publication Data
Horrobin, Peter J (Peter James) 1943-
        Healing Through Deliverance

        ISBN 1-85240-052-8

Printed in England by Clays Ltd, St Ives plc

To
Mum and Dad
who taught me so much,
gave me such a solid foundation for life
and,
above all,
have given me a Godly heritage.
I thank God for them and pray that they will
see this book as part of the harvest from
their years of sowing.

This book is also dedicated
to the team of people at Ellel Grange
whom God called together to establish and
nurture a special ministry of evangelism,
healing and deliverance.

Contents

Preface

The contents of this book have been contributed to by many people. Although the book bears my name, it could not have been written without the determined commitment of all those who have shared in the work that God brought into being at Ellel Grange.

Neither could it have been written without the many thousands of people who have sought God's help at Ellel Grange, and, in so doing, have trusted members of the team to minister Jesus into their lives. I want to thank every single one of them for the living contributions they have made.

When, in 1986, Ellel Grange was acquired, in a quite amazing way, none of the pioneering team could have anticipated the pilgrimage that was to follow. It has not been easy. Joy and pain have both been experienced, as the fruit of the ministry has slowly matured. No-one expected that deliverance ministry would be such a strategic part of healing. Perhaps if we had known, the team would never have come together!

Time and again members of the team have been thrown on the Lord in difficult personal ministries and scripture has come to life under the anointing of the Holy Spirit. On occasions the dramatic thrill of the Gospel stories has been experienced first hand. At other times we have been more conscious of the long list of pressures and problems that Paul described to his friends in Corinth (2 Corinthians 11:22-29)!

Neither had we any idea then, that God would take the teaching and ministry to areas far removed from our roots in the North of England. So much so that we are now on the verge of opening a centre in the South of England and pioneering a special ministry to Pastors and Leaders in Hungary and Eastern Europe. The opportunities God has given for teaching and ministry, both in England and abroad, have served more to demonstrate the relative ignorance about healing and deliverance that there has been in the Body of Christ at large, than draw attention to there being anything special about the ministry of Ellel Grange.

For those who are not familiar with Ellel Grange, the work is administered by a registered charity, *The Christian Trust*. The objectives and basis of faith of the work are as follows:

Objectives:

To fulfil Christ's command to preach the Gospel, make disciples and heal the sick in the widest sense. This is achieved through prayer, teaching, preaching, personal ministry to individuals and by training others to be involved in this ministry, especially in their local churches.

Basis of Faith:

God is a Trinity. God the Father loves all mankind. God the Son, Jesus Christ, is Saviour and Healer, Lord and King. God the Holy Spirit indwells Christians and imparts the dynamic power by which they are enabled to continue Christ's ministry. The Bible is the divinely inspired authority in matters of faith, doctrine and conduct and the basis for teaching.

At the present time there is a full-time team of about forty people and nearly fifty part-time Associate Counsellors. To date some 7,000 people have received personal ministry from members of the team and about 20,000 people have attended the various training courses and teaching conferences that have been conducted over the years.

Those in need are usually ministered to on Healing Retreats where Jesus's practice of *"welcoming the people, teaching them about the kingdom of God and healing those in need"* (Luke 9:11) is the normal basis for ministry. After the welcome, teaching and ministry always go hand-in-hand.

Many people need to really hear and understand the basics of the Kingdom of God before they are able to receive ministry. Often, the reason why they are still in need is directly related to not having applied in their lives vital foundational principles such as forgiveness, acceptance, etc.

New training courses are in a constant process of development. Those currently available through Ellel Grange are as follows:

One Day Courses:
Getting Acquainted with the Healing Ministry
Ministering to the Sexually Abused
Spiritual Warfare
Setting Captives Free
Claiming the Ground
Called to Counsel?
Counselling the Terminally Ill and Bereaved
Ministering to Children
Learning to Pray
Emotional Wholeness

Residential Courses (3 to 5 days in length):
Healing
Inner Healing Counselling
Dynamic Praying
Deliverance Ministry
Ministering to the Sexually Abused
Moving Under the Anointing of the Holy Spirit
Worship
(in cooperation with the musicians of Wellspring)
Leaders' Retreats

Teaching Conferences
The Battle Belongs to the Lord
> *A comprehensive four or five day conference on:*
> *How to minister evangelism, healing and deliverance*
> *in the power of the Holy Spirit*

Healing and Wholeness
> *A training conference designed to help local fellowships*
> *establish the ministries of healing and deliverance in their*
> *church community*

Also under preparation is a residential *School of Evangelism, Healing and Deliverance* which will embody the main teaching elements from all the above courses. This will be especially suitable for those coming from overseas or those who are able to set aside a few weeks for a more concentrated time of teaching and practical experience.

The school will last for two months. The first month will be devoted primarily to teaching the foundations and the second (optional) month to the application of the teaching in personal ministries.

Full details of the current programme of courses, events and ministries, as well as books and teaching tapes, are available on request from:

> Ellel Grange,
> Lancaster,
> LA2 0HN,
> England.

I am tremendously grateful to the various members of the team, and other friends and colleagues, who helped so generously with the preparation of the manuscript and made many helpful suggestions. I thank them all for their help and encouragement. I apologise to the many others who have lovingly endured my lateness for meals, lack of immediate response to letters, and apparent likeness to a hermit at critical stages of the writing process!

This volume covers the scriptural basis for healing through deliverance. A further volume will be a more practical work providing teaching and insights that will help Christians bring healing and deliverance to those in need.

My prayer for each person who reads the book is that their commitment to Christ will be deepened and that they will respond afresh to the calling God has put before each and every believer, to preach the Gospel, heal the sick and cast out demons.

Peter Horrobin
Ellel Grange
May 1991

Chapter 1

Introduction

When Jesus told the disciples to heal the sick and cast out demons, I believe he intended the disciples to do just that - heal the sick and cast out demons! In common with most of my contemporaries, however, who were nurtured and reared in the post-war church, I was taught nothing about the deliverance ministry.

References to demons being cast out in the Gospels were hastily passed over, and assumed to be of little relevance to Christians in the twentieth century. Vague stories of missionaries encountering dark forces on the mission field were only acceptable because they happened so far away, in lands that had supposedly not been civilised by the impact of Western Christianity.

Truth, however, cannot be suppressed for ever. Deep down there were questions that were fighting for my attention. The real nature of the questions was so elusive though, that many years passed before the circumstances of life and a calling of God forced them into the light of day. The circumstances revolved round a small handful of people in whom were forces and powers which were definitely not of God, but yet were dangerously real. The calling of God was to pray for the sick.

But this was not the first time that I had encountered a calling from God. As a child I sensed a call upon my life to full-time ministry from an early age. It was not until many years later, however, that this general calling became more specific, and I knew beyond any shadow of doubt what my major calling in life was to be.

Jane had come for help in very deep need. Through prayer she received a measure of help, but as she walked away,

God spoke very clearly into my heart. I was being encouraged to establish a ministry centre where the Janes of this world could receive the help they needed and the Body of Christ could be trained to minister effectively in the local church. It was not a word that could be easily welcomed, however, for one is tempted, by human reasoning, to focus on the apparent impossibility of fulfilling such a calling!

There then followed ten years of lonely praying before God spoke further into the vision and I knew that the time for its fufillment was drawing near. Two years later, by a miracle of God's grace, the doors of Ellel Grange were opened in November 1986. Close on half a million pounds had been needed by October 31st, the date set for completion of the property purchase.

We started off with nothing and had been allowed six months to find the money by the vendors. On that never to be forgotten completion day we had just £6 too much! God had provided, through his people, an astonishing amount of money and affirmed the vision in a quite dramatic way. The full story of how God brought the vision into being, in a remote corner of northern England, will have to be told on another occasion.

The small, but dedicated, team that God brought together to initiate the work had little concept of what lay ahead. They knew something of the three principle dimensions to the healing ministry - physical healing, inner healing and deliverance. None had any concept, however, of the particular pilgrimage that would have to be followed in the ensuing days, as it became increasingly clear that deliverance ministry had a far more significant role to play in healing than any of us had previously believed or imagined. Some of the elusive questions of earlier years began to be answered.

As powers of darkness were encountered and dealt with, we began to see long-term infirmity in some people being healed, childless couples conceiving and giving birth to children, crippling fears being dealt with, emotional problems (which were previously thought to be only in need of inner healing) being resolved, women who had been devastated by sexual abuse coming through to wholeness, etc. We realised afresh that the commission Jesus gave to the disciples to cast out demons was, indeed, a vital part of the Great Commission for the whole church for the whole of time (Luke 9:1-2 and Matthew 28:19-20).

There was much to learn, and right from the beginning we began to teach what we had learned to others, so that they could benefit from our experience. Some local churches began to extend their healing ministry to include deliverance, sometimes with remarkable consequences. People began to travel quite long distances, even from abroad, both for the training courses and to bring those in need on Healing Retreats. Before very long requests began to come in for written material to help those who were treading a similar pathway in their local church.

This book is an attempt to meet that need. I pray that those who read it will not, however, do so just because they are fascinated by deliverance ministry, but because they wish to see the whole ministry of Jesus firmly established in the Body of Christ - preaching the Gospel, healing the sick and casting out demons.

Deliverance Ministry in the History of the Church

There are many well-documented accounts of deliverance being a normal part of Christian ministry throughout the history of the church. Tertullian, for example, writing about 200AD, comments in his De Spectaculis, *"We have the case of this woman - the Lord himself is witness - who went to the theatre, and came back possessed. In the outcasting, accordingly, when the unclean creature was upbraided with having dared to attack a believer, he (the evil spirit) firmly replied, 'And in truth I did it most righteously, for I found her in my domain!'"*

Origen, in his work Against Celsus (about 250AD), says, *"It is not by incantations that Christians prevail over evil spirits but by the Name of Jesus . . . and by the use of prayers and other means which we learn from Scripture, we drive them out of the souls of men, out of places where they have established themselves, and even sometimes from the bodies of animals; for even these creatures often suffer from injuries inflicted upon them by demons."*

Lactantius quaintly adds in the Epitome of the Divine Institutes (about 315AD), *"As He Himself, before His passion, put to confusion demons by His word and command, so now, by the name and sign of the same passion (the cross), unclean spirits, having insinuated themselves into the bodies of men, are driven out, when racked and tormented, and confessing themselves to be demons, they yield themselves to God, Who harasses them."*

Throughout the centuries, there have been many well-documented accounts of the demonised being set free in the name of Jesus. In more recent times, stories of prophetic characters, such as Smith Wigglesworth, have increased faith for the impossible among ordinary believers. And the diaries of a less well-known, but nevertheless truly remarkable woman, Maria Woodworth-Etter, have dramatically demonstrated the power of the name of Jesus over the works of darkness. She ministered at the end of the nineteenth and the beginning of the twentieth centuries, largely in the USA, but also in England, and was mightily used by God as a healing evangelist with a remarkably fruitful deliverance ministry.

Throughout the history of the church there have always been those who have practised the deliverance ministry. In these days the Holy Spirit is now restoring the ministry of deliverance to the wider Church, in what is a natural extension of the process of renewal.

Reactions in the Church Today

Many misconceptions, and the lack of good teaching, have kept most of the church ignorant of the enemy's devices, in total contrast to the policy adopted and recommended by Paul (2 Corinthians 2:11). Within the church it has been popularly assumed that evil spirits are only very occasionally encountered, and that there is no way they could possibly affect believing Christians. The church, therefore, has been seduced into deception and error by believing that deliverance from evil spirits is not a ministry that is worthy of any attention by the average church attender.

Indeed, it has been argued by some theologians that we should adopt a healthy disregard for the enemy. Those who have adopted this stance, however, have usually failed to recognise the enemy and his influence and are denying hope to the masses who have been ensnared by the demonic and seem powerless to get out of the enemy's clutches.

The responsibility of Christian leaders not to mislead the flock is considerable. Ezekiel warned the shepherds of Israel in these devastating words, *"You have not taken care of the weak ones, healed those that are sick, bandaged those that are hurt . . . because the sheep had no shepherd, they were scattered, and wild animals killed and ate them"* (Ezekiel 34:4-5 GNB). Denying a primary means of healing (deliverance) to the flock in our care is undoubtedly misleading them.

This supposedly healthy disregard for the enemy is, in reality, far from healthy, and because the church has, in general, been totally ignorant of the way the enemy works, Satan has walked all over the Body of Christ unchallenged, unrecognised and unperturbed. I believe that unless deliverance is accepted as a key part of the armoury that is available to, and used by, God's people, then the church will be severely limited in its effectiveness.

Those who have been willing to take the Scripture at face value, and seek to minister deliverance to those in need, have often been treated with a great deal of suspicion by their fellow-churchmen. For some their isolation has on occasions led to extremism, which has further isolated them from the main body of the church.

Many Christians tend to ignore or reject deliverance ministry because they cannot accept that Christians can possibly have demons inside them. They ask 'How can the Holy Spirit and an evil spirit co-exist inside the same person?' Others, usually with a liberal theological perspective, prefer to reject all evidences of supernatural power, whether it is claimed to be of God or Satan. The whole idea that demons are real is, therefore, firmly rejected. Some theologians try to argue that Jesus only talked about a personal devil and demons because his medical understanding (or lack of it) was limited to that of his own generation.

At the other end of the scale are those who naively think that deliverance is the answer to every problem people suffer from and seem to thrive on demon hunts, even when it is manifestly obvious that other healing needs are more relevant and important. Almost every author of books on this subject has quoted C.S.Lewis's warning not to either ignore the devil or give him too much attention. The warning is only of such universal acceptance and relevance because of the profound truth it contains.

Somewhere in the middle, there is a concerned body of Christians, who believe that the commission Jesus gave to the church includes the ministry of deliverance and are seeking to build an effective and credible deliverance ministry into the life of the Body of Christ. It is possible to do so and I pray that this book will be of significant help to those who want to take seriously both Jesus's injunction to *"cast out demons"* and the commission to build the church.

A word that is frequently used by critics of the deliverance ministry is *"balance"*. They advise you not to go overboard on demons, or take too much notice of them. In ministry to individuals they tell you to concentrate on more important aspects of the person's life.

As you read this book, however, you will find that in order to cast out demons both a truly balanced and a dramatically radical ministry is required. Balanced, in that the whole range of Christian foundational truths (such as repentance, forgiveness, acceptance, etc) are essential ministry tools; and totally radical in that if a demon is encountered in a person's life during ministry then we have a responsibility to remove any rights it may have, cast it out and teach the individual how to live before God so that it can't get back in.

I believe Jesus's ministry was totally balanced, which in practice meant that he taught with radical authority on the whole range of life's issues. *For Jesus, balance did not mean middle of the road compromise,* but decisive teaching and action which was sufficient to meet the needs of all who came to him.

When he encountered the rich young ruler he was able to answer his penetrating question about inheriting eternal life with an equally penetrating answer, *"sell all that you have . . . and come, follow me"* (Matthew 19:16-22). Jesus cut right across Nicodemus's tentative theological comments by telling him that he needed to be born again of the Spirit of God (John 3).

To the Pharisees, who wanted the woman who was caught in the act of adultery stoned to death (John 8:1-11), he said, *"if any of you is without sin, let him be the first to throw a stone at her"* (NIV). And in the case of the epileptic boy (boy with the deaf and dumb spirit), whose father was deeply distressed, Jesus recognised a demon and ordered it out (Luke 9:37-43). In the man whose arm was paralysed, he raised his faith level by telling him to stretch out his hand. The man tried, found he could, and was healed (Luke 5:6-11).

Each of these, and many other, illustrations from the life of Jesus demonstrate radical and decisive thoughts, words and action - but overall one can say that because Jesus was radical in the way he treated each and every individual who came to him, his whole ministry was, as a result, balanced.

There was no compromise whatsoever in how Jesus dealt with any situation. He was always loving, but always radical. Balance and compromise are not the same thing. Sadly, many of those who thought they were proponents of balance in the healing ministry have, in reality, become proponents of compromise and become, as a result and through ignorance, opponents of the deliverance ministry.

A balanced healing ministry is one that uses the whole range of ministries that Jesus commissioned us to practise. A balanced ministry is not one that takes a "middle course" with each ministry so as not to offend or, perhaps more significantly, to avoid shaking theological foundations that may be inadequate for the task!

For Jesus, and those being discipled by him, deliverance ministry was normal and natural. People expected Jesus to deal with evil spirits, and he did so. But today's prevailing world view (Christian or otherwise) would say that we have more medical knowledge and better terminology to describe the conditions that in Jesus's day were attributed to evil spirits! Such a world view, however, is just as deceived as the rationalism which discounts the supernatural.

In some sectors of the church the sovereign will of God is sometimes given as the reason why people are not healed. Out of this has come mistaken doctrines of 'suffering for the sake of the Gospel'. This viewpoint, however, is inconsistent with the ministry of Jesus, for there is no record of him saying to anyone that they can't be healed because it is God's sovereign will for them to suffer! Whilst some aspects of suffering will always be an enigma, I believe that in many cases people are not being healed because the church is praying for the wrong thing. It could be that the person needs to forgive from the heart, or confess some sin, have a curse on their life broken, or, even, be delivered of an evil spirit.

That is not to say that God is not sovereign, nor is it to say that there are circumstances when his will seems to run contrary to our desires and even expectations. But it is to say that God expects us to conduct our ministries in accordance with his instructions, and if a person is sick because they have a demon, it is hardly honouring to God to blame his sovereign will for our disobedience in not casting it out, and then spiritualise the problem with a misguided doctrine of suffering!

Many sick people have lost hope. They are like the woman with the issue of blood - they have exhausted themselves in looking for healing. For them, life holds little purpose when health has given way to long term infirmity. Whilst deliverance ministry is not the total answer for those in need, for those who are sick 'because they have a demon' it has to be the key part of the answer when the underlying cause is demonic.

The Gospel of Hope

The Gospel is, supremely, a Gospel of hope - a hope that is not a vague wish, but an absolute certainty, backed up by the guarantee of God's faithfulness. For each person who comes to him there is the assurance of eternal life. Eternal life begins the moment we are born again of the Spirit of God (John 3) - and is not just something that is waiting for us when we die.

Some preaching has so majored on the offer of life after death that many are unaware of the wonderful blessings God has for us in the present life also. Many people today are in such personal crisis that they are now asking 'Is there life before death?' We do not need to wait for death before we can enjoy the benefits of the cross! The Christian's hope includes the offer of healing and deliverance during our passage through time.

Most Christians recognise that healing flows from the cross. It was the prophet Isaiah who first said that *"by his stripes we are healed"* (Isaiah 53:5 NKJV). Healing, therefore, is a central part of the atonement, and part of the Christian's hope. Deliverance, also, flows from the cross. For on the cross *"Christ freed himself from the power of the spiritual rulers and authorities; he made a public spectacle of them by leading them as captives in his victory procession"* (Colossians 2:15 GNB).

Jesus was not killed by Satan when he went to the cross. If that had been the case Calvary would have been a celebration of Satan's victory. Jesus chose to lay his life down, and whilst he was betrayed by a human being and actually killed, physically, by men, they only had the power to do so because he chose to be obedient to the will of his Father. Matthew reminds us that even at the eleventh hour Jesus could have summoned twelve legions of angels to effect a rescue (Matthew 26:53).

When Jesus rose again from the dead, therefore, it was a mighty statement to all the powers of darkness that their king, Satan, had done his worst, and that Jesus still reigned. When Paul said to the Galatian Christians *"I have been crucified with Christ and I no longer live, but Christ lives in me"* (Galatians 2:20 NIV) he was illustrating from his own testimony the amazing fact that Christians are in the same position relative to Satan as Jesus himself was when he rose from the dead! That is, in a place of victory over all the demonic realms. Jesus demonstrated at Calvary that he truly did have the authority to give his disciples (both then and for all time) the power and authority to cast out demons.

There is no question, therefore, that, according to the Scriptures, deliverance is also central to the atonement, and that deliverance ministry is part of the Christian's hope. For outside the victory of the cross we would have no power or authority over the powers of darkness. It is for this reason that Satan did his very best to deter Jesus right at the beginning of his ministry during the wilderness temptations - see Chapter 7.

Jesus has entrusted to his church the task of ministering both healing and deliverance to those in need. I have come to see that a church which does not minister healing and deliverance is partially disabled and is only offering a limited salvation. It cannot fully represent Jesus's ministry as the Body of Christ on earth. It is denying to its members some of the hope which is their right as children of God.

Those churches which pray for healing but are unwilling to consider deliverance ministry, for whatever reason, are also severely limited in their effectiveness. In our experience, unless a church is ministering deliverance as well as healing, the effectiveness of their healing ministry will probably be less than 20% of what it could and should be. Not to minister deliverance can mean depriving some Christians of God's best for them.

Overview of the Book

In this book I will seek to establish that deliverance ministry is a rightful ministry for Christians; that God intends Christians to be naturally supernatural in their life and ministry; that demons are certainly real and have to be reckoned with; that in Christ we have the power and authority to deal with them, without capitulating to fear; and that by being obedient to what Jesus told us to do we can play a strategic role in setting captives free from the powers of darkness.

Throughout the book there are many illustrations of what God has done in the lives of people through deliverance. In every case, names and some incidental details have been changed so as to protect individuals from personal identification. The essential details are, however, the same. There is nothing within this book that has not been hammered out, often at great cost, on the anvil of experience and tested many times in ministries to others.

Whilst this book is not the history of Ellel Grange, it could not have been written without the experience that has been gained in ministry to several thousand people since the opening of the centre in November 1986. The small team that God brought together to begin the work had no expectation that such a significant part of the ministry would involve deliverance. Nor of the amazing, and sometimes dramatic, consequences of ministering healing through deliverance.

It needs to be said, however, that whilst deliverance ministry is a strategic part of the work of Ellel Grange, it is only one part of the total armoury that is available to the church in being obedient to the Great Commission. But it must not be left off the church's ministry agenda. If it is, there will be many needy and hurting people who will not receive the help that God has provided for them.

In this book I frequently refer to "we" when talking about aspects of deliverance ministry. In doing so I am referring to the ministry team at Ellel Grange who have shown such determination in seeking answers from the Lord for those who have knocked on the doors for help. We do not pretend to have all the answers. But I do believe that if the church applies itself diligently to the application of God's Word into the lives of hurting and broken people, there will be a dramatic increase in the number of people who are actually being healed, as opposed to just being prayed for without any noticeable result.

I would ask you to read this book with an open heart and mind - a heart that is open to listen to the voice of the Father and a mind that is not closed, through prejudice or earlier training, to new understanding. This book presents the scriptural foundations for the healing and deliverance ministries. A subsequent volume will be a practical manual on deliverance for those involved in the ministry of healing.

A Final Word

Finally, may I suggest that no-one should get involved in deliverance ministry unless:

a)   Their own faith in Jesus is well-founded;

b)   They are willing at all times to be an evangelist (for many people they seek to help will be outside the Kingdom of God when ministry is first considered);

c)   they are willing, if it proves necessary, to receive
        ministry for themselves;
d)   they have a deep compassion and love for people;
        and
e)   they are operating under the secure cover of
        Christian leaders.

The experience of the Sons of Sceva, who attempted
deliverance ministry, but were not committed to Jesus,
should be a salutary warning. They finished up running
down the street stark naked! (Acts 19:11-20). Deliverance
ministry must never be separated from the ministry of the
whole Gospel of Jesus Christ. It is an inseparable part of
the Good News, and to attempt to minister deliverance
outside the remit of Scripture is a dangerous practice with
potentially dangerous repercussions for both the minister
and the person receiving help.

There is only one safeguard and that is to know Jesus as
Saviour and for him to be Lord of your life. It is only
through knowing him that the Holy Spirit can flow through
us in power. And it is only through the power of the Holy
Spirit that we have any authority over the powers of
darkness.

What should we do then? Peter's answer at Pentecost to
this very telling question has stood the test of time. *"Each
one of you must turn away from his sins and be baptised in
the name of Jesus Christ, so that your sins will be forgiven;
and you will receive God's gift, the Holy Spirit"* (Acts 2:38
GNB).

When Jesus said, *"I am the way, the truth and the life;
no-one comes to the Father except through me"* (John 14:6
NKJV), he was either supremely arrogant or supremely
right. This text is certainly unpopular with those who
would say that 'All roads lead to God' or words to that
effect. But we have seen it demonstrated time and time
again that when Jesus said these words he was
proclaiming truth. It was not Jesus who was the arrogant

one, but Satan, who sought to elevate himself above the status of God himself.

Satan is a defeated enemy, but the victories of the cross and the resurrection can only be experienced by those who have come to faith in God through his Son. John proclaimed in his Gospel that as many as receive Jesus have the power to become the children of God (John 1:12). These words are being dramatically fulfilled in the latter days of the 20th century as the children of God are exercising the power and authority that is, indeed, their right through faith in Jesus Christ.

Chapter 2

Mankind - God's Special Creation

Mankind is unique within the whole of creation. God made him in his own image (Genesis 1:26 and 9:6). Full understanding of what it means to be made in the image of God will have to wait until the final appearing of our Lord Jesus Christ, when, as Paul says we will no longer see as if through a darkened glass, but face to face. (1 Corinthians 13:12).

In the meantime there are some very clear keys in the scripture to guide us in our understanding, which are of special relevance to the healing and deliverance ministry. Just as doctors begin their training by dissecting a body so that they will understand its workings, so those who minister healing and deliverance should begin by understanding what is in the scriptures about the nature of man.

God is Spirit

When Jesus was speaking to the woman at the well (John 4), he not only exposed her sexual history with a word of knowledge, but went on to share with her some profound theology. At first glance it seems as though Jesus should have been sharing such truths with a theologian, such as Nicodemus in John 3. For surely this woman, with such a questionable past, would have benefited more from what Jesus actually did tell Nicodemus - *"you must be born again"!* (John 3:7 NIV).

Perhaps, however, there is something of a clue here to Jesus' attitude to the religious leaders of his day, who had such supersensitive minds when it came to the letter of the law, but were quite insensitive when it came to discerning spiritual matters! Isaiah chapter 1 tells us something of what God thinks of religion for religion's sake. *"It's useless to bring your offerings. I am disgusted with the smell of the incense you burn. I cannot stand your New Moon Festivals, your Sabbaths, and your religious gatherings; they are all corrupted by your sins"* (Isaiah 1:13 GNB).

There are many ordinary people I have known and know (some, like the woman at the well, with pasts that are best forgotten), whose power and authority in Christ has made them extraordinary warriors for God. Their Spirit-filled lives have been a powerful defence against the evil one and they are living demonstrations of the potential there is, under God, in every human being.

In spite of her previous relationships and sexual history the woman at the well must have understood something of what Jesus was talking about, for she went back to the village rejoicing and became an evangelist. She gossiped the Gospel and told the villagers *"Come and see the man who told me everything I've ever done!"* (John 4:29 GNB). As a result half the village later gave testimony and said, *"We believe now, not because of what you said, but because we ourselves have heard Him, and we know that he really is the Saviour of the world"* (John 4:42).

The truth that Jesus proclaimed to her was simple, but incredibly profound - *"God is Spirit, and those who worship him must worship in Spirit and in truth"* (John 4:23 NKJV). If God has made us in his own image, whatever else this amazing phrase means, man must also have a spirit with which it is possible both to worship God, who is Spirit, and have a relationship with him.

The Trinity - of God and Man

A further clue to the nature of man can be seen in the Trinitarian nature of God. There is only one God, but within the Godhead there are three *"persons"* - God the

Father, God the Son and God the Holy Spirit. It is not surprising, therefore, that man, who is made in the image and likeness of God, should have a reflection of this trinity in his own being.

It was Paul who, when writing to the Thessalonians, most clearly defined the trinity of man. He prayed that they may be whole in spirit, soul and body (1 Thessalonians 5:23). By so doing he directly implied that not only does man have three distinct dimensions to his creation, but also that it is possible for fallen man to be less than whole (sick) in any one (or more) of these three dimensions.

Not even the angels, as spiritual beings, were given the capacity 'to come in the flesh' and be at one and the same time, beings with a spirit, a soul and a body. That capacity, 'to come in the flesh' is unique to God and to those who are made in his image. That is why the phrase 'He came in the flesh' is such a crucial statement in the major Christian creeds. It is a statement of devastating authority and significance as far as the powers of darkness are concerned.

In the scriptures there are numerous examples of angels appearing in human form. But there is a world of difference between appearing as a person and actually becoming a creature of flesh. Satan, as a fallen angel, has the power, as do the angels when given permission, to manifest as a human being. But no spiritual being, be it angel or demon, can actually become flesh. That capacity is unique to God and his special creation, man.

We have seen on numerous occasions that to give a command to a demon *"in the name of Jesus Christ of Nazareth, who came in the flesh"* has been especially powerful. Those last five words have demonstrated before our very eyes the truth of James 2:19, where the demons are described as trembling with fear because of their belief in God. Their recognition of who God is, and of the authority of believers who minister deliverance in the name of Jesus, reminds the demonic powers that their

ultimate end is spelled out in Revelation and that their
time is limited.

With regard to the angels Paul states (1 Corinthians 6:3)
that we shall judge them, and the writer of Hebrews
(Hebrews 2:5-10) adds that it is only for the time being that
man is lower than the angels. The Psalmist (Psalm 8:4-8)
declares that man was made inferior only to God himself.
The wonder of the incarnation was that Jesus, the very
Son of God, submitted himself to being lower than the
angels for his allotted span of thirty-three years, and
appeared on earth as a man with a body, a soul and a
spirit.

There is so much that we do not know or understand, but
there is sufficient evidence in the scriptures to encourage
us that, one day, those who believe will be restored to their
position in the created realm above the angels. The
capacity 'to come in the flesh' appears to be a special
hall-mark of the pinnacle of God's creation.

The Spirit

Before Jesus came in the flesh he existed in the spirit
(John 1). At the incarnation, from the moment when the
child was conceived in Mary's womb, Jesus was limited
to the frame of a man. At conception, he took upon
himself the nature of man and became flesh as well. The
Spirit of Jesus pre-existed the flesh of Jesus.

In the same way one dimension of each person born into
the world is spiritual and mankind is not primarily flesh,
but spirit - a spirit that was created by God with which to
enjoy fellowship in a relationship with himself.

Broadly speaking, in the western hemisphere we live in a
flesh dominated society. Eastern culture is far more
sensitive to 'the spirit world' and is spirit dominated. Both
concepts are wrong. The dominating western philosophy
of life is sadly mistaken for it largely ignores the spiritual
nature of man. But the dominating eastern culture is

equally wrong, for it has been deceived into fear and worship of a spirit realm that is in rebellion against God.

Satan has no fear of spirit conscious people, provided spirits under his command are in control! So both extremes, eastern and western are deceptive lies that Satan has sold to the world. It is only when man recognises his true spiritual nature, and is restored to a right relationship with the Father through repentance and forgiveness, that Satan has any reason to fear. And it is only then that, we as human beings, can be truly fulfilled and realise something of the potential that God in his love planned and purposed for us. Man truly is a spiritual being.

Sickness of the spirit is not a condition that the medical profession can recognise and quantify, but the consequences of such sickness walk through the doors of doctors' surgeries every single day. For where the spirit is out of harmony with God, who is Spirit, it is inevitable that there will be consequences, some of which will manifest themselves psychologically or physically with clearly measurable symptoms.

Paul declared that outside of Christ our spirit is dead to God because of our sin (Ephesians 2:1). My understanding of someone who is declared to be dead is that their sickness is very severe! The only remedy for a dead spirit is to be born again - hence the importance of evangelism being closely allied to the ministry of healing and deliverance.

In the ministry of Ellel Grange we have seen many, many hundreds of people come into the Kingdom of God through being born again of his Spirit. Many of these would not have had the opportunity of becoming Christians if we had not explained to them that the most important healing that any of us can ever experience is to receive Jesus into our lives as Saviour and Lord. The very word salvation in the Greek of the New Testament means wholeness and healing, and it is translated in various

ways according to the context. Salvation is healing and
healing is part of the ministry of salvation.

In addition to the sickness of spirit that comes from being
dead to God, there is the sickness which is a consequence
of being involved with the wrong sort of spirit realm - the
supernatural world that is under the control of Satan and
in rebellion against God. Satan is no respecter of persons
and whoever we are, if we put down the welcome mat for
the enemy we will suffer the consequences - more about
this later.

The Flesh - Soul and Body

In some versions of the scriptures there is confusion over
the correct translation of the words for soul and spirit, in
spite of the fact that there are perfectly good Greek words
for both soul and spirit which make the distinction clear.
In various places the same Greek word is translated as
either soul or spirit according to the understanding of the
translator.

The writer of Hebrews (4:12) emphasises the distinction by
saying that *"the word of God is living and active and
sharper than any two-edged sword, and piercing as far as
the division of soul and spirit"* (NASB). The spirit and the
soul are not one and the same thing. The soul is very
much part of our flesh life. Failure to recognise this and
distinguish between them leads many people into
condemnation, and leaves them wide open to Satan
coming as the 'accuser of the brethren' and undermining
the security that they should have in God.

Without this understanding, those who are alive to God in
the spirit, following conversion, are tempted to discount
the reality of their new life in Christ because of problems
they are experiencing in their soul. Satan loves to have us
confused on this issue and keep us in defeat.

The Body

The body is the easiest part of our created realm for us to understand and define, primarily because it is a solid and visible reality. Medical practitioners have made huge strides in their ability to treat physical disorders. But the body is so incredibly complex that even with the enormous advances that scientists have made there are still huge holes in our understanding. Only the sheer genius of God could have conceived and put together hundreds of mutually dependant and perfectly balanced organs to create the human body.

This is not the place to get too involved in the whole evolution/creation debate, except to say that the more I learn about the intricacies of the created realm, and the more I see of a decaying world in the latter part of the 20th century, the less credible are the highly theoretical and totally unproven arguments of the evolutionists.

They calmly state that the evolutionary process has resulted in a steadily improving world, through the survival of the fittest. The theory of evolution has, however, in these past ten years come under severe criticism, from within the scientific world which originally gave it birth, and from scientists whose comments are not prejudiced by any particular religious viewpoint.

The conflict, for example, between the earliest date for the creation of the world proposed by the geologists, and the time scale that evolutionists indicate would have been necessary for man to have evolved, is so huge as to make the whole theory of evolution less viable now than it has ever been since first propounded by Darwin.

With regard to the survival of the fittest, history would seem to indicate that the fittest, in terms of power and wealth, have only in very rare instances been those who are fitted for the exercise of such power. The survival of the fittest has all too often meant persecution, and even attempted genocide, by those who are at the top of the allegedly evolutionary pinnacle!!

This is a doctrine of man which is hardly commensurate with the ministry of Jesus to the downtrodden and the poor, and his scant regard for those who abused their power and influence. The judgment executed by angels upon Herod (Acts 12:22), when he was eaten by worms and died, could be seen as an interesting commentary on how God perceives those who elevate themselves, and abuse their power, at the expense of the masses.

However one interprets the various theories of the origin of man, God is ultimately the Creator, and I stand by the scriptural assertion that *"in the beginning, God created"*. The body that each of us has is an incredible commentary on the wonder of the created realms. However, as everyone knows, the body does not always function perfectly and irrespective of how God created man in the first place his body is now subject to sickness, disease, malformation and accident and is often in need of healing.

The body itself is made to protect itself from invaders and be healed of its own accord. It has its own built-in defense systems, such as the antibodies in the blood stream which fight invading organisms; and first-aid kits, for example when a person cuts the flesh, immediately a substance in the blood called fibrinogen reacts with oxygen in the atmosphere, changing its nature and forming first a healing mesh (or clot) and then a scab, which eventually falls away when new flesh has regenerated beneath the protective layer.

It is only when the built-in systems fail, or the injury is so bad that additional help becomes essential, that most people think in terms of medical treatment. Sadly, it is only when this fails that most Christians will seek personal ministry from those who believe in healing and deliverance. God, as it were, becomes the last resort!

It is at that point that the one who is ministering healing needs to be especially alert to God in the spirit, for many of the conditions that afflict people have an origin that lies outside the physical realm. Unless one understands something of God's creation of man it is not always easy to pinpoint the source of the problem and bring healing and/or deliverance to the sufferer.

The Soul

When it comes to the soul one is venturing into territory that cannot be measured by scientists, but can only be understood in the light of scripture and experience. When God created the human race he gave to each person a living soul. The soul is that dimension to our flesh-life which is eternal. When our body dies it will rot, or be cremated. The physical part of our being is unarguably temporary, limited to a tiny span - a time capsule within the realms of eternity.

When the body dies its period of usefulness is over. The soul, however, is not restricted to the dimensions of time and the limitations of three score years and ten. And it is our eternal destiny beyond the grave which gives urgency to evangelism and point to the conversation Jesus had with Nicodemus about the need to be born again. Each one of us is a spiritual being, to whom God gave a soul, and together they reside within the body and are the person (personality) that we are.

Most commentators would agree that the soul itself has three principal dimensions - the mind, the emotions and the will, all of which need to be clearly understood if we are to have a doctrine of man which is an adequate foundation on which to build a theology of healing and deliverance. There are several good books which teach this area in depth, but for the purposes of the present work, it is important to realise that the mind, the emotions and the will are not physical organs (they cannot be given pills or cut out in an operation!), although clearly the body can be given medication and treatment which can, in turn, have a profound effect on the soul.

The Mind

The mind is that part of the soul which processes all incoming information through the physical senses, thinks and provides a rational basis on which to make the day to day decisions of life. The mind is not the brain. The brain is simply a large physical organ which acts very much like a computer, storing much information and carrying out many routine functions which control the body, without the mind having to think about what needs to be done next.

The mind can, however, over-ride some of the brain's standard bodily instructions (such as breathing - for a limited period of time it is possible to hold one's breath and suspend the intake of oxygen), but fortunately most of the brain's functional control of the body is totally involuntary - we cannot choose, for example, to make our heart stop beating. Voluntary control of such vital mechanisms was not programmed into the computer by its designer!

With the mind we can choose whether or not to store important information in the brain, and then we can recall (remember) the information as and when we need it. With the mind we can think through ideas, create pictures, generate schemes and work out plans of action without moving our body an inch. The ability to conceptualise and be creative is one of the strongest evidences that man truly is made in the image of God, who is the Creator.

When a person's mind and brain are dislocated, so that no longer are there rational thought processes or consequentially sane bodily behaviour, we say that a person is mentally ill. Although what it actually means for a person to be mentally ill can, I believe, only be truly understood in the light of spiritual truth. Without such understanding one is permanently limited by the observable and measurable.

Notwithstanding the Greek origin of the word 'psychiatrist', which means 'doctor of the soul', modern psychiatry depends heavily on drug treatments which affect chemical processes in the brain (the body). These are undoubtedly effective in suppressing behaviour which is both anti-social and damaging, both to the individual who is unfortunate enough to be suffering, and those who have to care for and live with them. But few psychiatrists would go so far as to claim that such medication is a cure, and many would freely admit that they have little idea as to why the chemicals they give act in the way they do!

Unfortunately the side-effects of much medication are considerable and in psychiatry a balance has to be maintained between destroying either the quality of life of the patient, or that of those who would otherwise have to cope with their bizarre extremes of human behaviour.

I am not in any way questioning the integrity or commitment of the psychiatrists. I believe that most of them are dedicated individuals, who are operating to the very best of their ability and within the parameters that have been laid down for them by their profession. But these parameters inevitably exclude the spiritual and demonic dimensions to mental illness. Indeed, we know of some patients who have been specifically told that in order to receive psychiatric help they must lay aside their religious beliefs.

Without doubt, just as the body can be sick, so can the mind and in any ministry of healing or deliverance we must be aware that the root cause of a person's condition could lie in this area of their being. The presenting symptom and the root cause are often radically different. When someone asks for prayer their presenting symptoms are what I call 'their agenda for God', whereas the root cause is 'God's agenda for them'.

Unless we are dealing with God's agenda, any ministry
that is given to any individual will have limited value, and
may, in the end, turn the individual away from the
healing and deliverance ministries and even away from
God himself. I believe the most common single reason
why an individual is not healed through prayer is because
the minister of healing is praying for the wrong thing -
dealing with man's agenda instead of God's.

The Emotions

Emotions are feelings that we experience inside ourselves
as a response to events that are going on around us.
Those events may affect us through our bodily organs -
such as a sudden loud noise to which our response may
be fear; through our minds - the satisfaction of creative
thought can give us pleasure; through our wills - a bad
decision can lead to anguish and distress; or through our
spirits - there are many spiritual experiences which can
result in deep and lasting joy. Indeed the highest
expression of our emotions is, I believe, experienced when
our spirit, soul and body are working in perfect harmony
and in relationship with God.

Much of the church has despised emotional experience as
being irrelevant to real spirituality. But that attitude
denies the fact that God created us with emotions for a
purpose. Instead of denying a precious part of God's
creation it would be far more honest to recognise
emotional reality and bring our emotions to the Lord for
healing. Indeed, if damaged emotions are not healed, the
potential for making shipwrecks of our lives, and those
who we relate with on a day-by-day basis, is enormous.
Emotions need healing as much as physical wounds.

It was perhaps a reaction against this possibility that
made some people equate sensitive and responsive
emotions with superficiality and produced accusations of
emotionalism against all evangelical initiatives. There is
a world of difference between a genuine reaction in the

emotions to being in the presence of God and whipped up feelings that bear no relationship whatsoever to the real thing. For most people, the experience of conversion, being born again, is a rightfully emotional moment, and I would never want to deny people the privilege of responding to God with their feelings when he comes into their lives, or on any other occasion in their spiritual pilgrimage.

Similar comments apply to many of the experiences that a Christian can go through in their personal pilgrimage. The damage done to countless Christians who have been forced to bury their emotions in a morass of pain has left us with a generation that is scarred and hurting in this area. There are few people whom I have counselled in recent years who have not needed deep emotional healing, in addition to ministry for the obvious presenting symptoms that prompted the original request for prayer.

There are many different sources of emotional pain - experiences such as sexual abuse or physical violence that have so damaged emotional responses that people have chosen to hide their real feelings and survive as emotional cripples. Mankind has become quite expert at putting on a mask to hide these real feelings. Nowhere more so, it seems, than in the Body of Christ, where 'feeling fine', irrespective of the real situation, is almost a hallmark of certain brands of stoical Christianity!

I thank God that he is not only in the business of healing the more obvious conditions of men, but of bringing healing to the emotions also - those areas of our lives which have been damaged by the cruelty, lack of consideration or even plain ignorance of those we have had to associate with in the past.

Clearly the emotions can be sick, very sick. Equally clearly God does not intend his people to remain sick in any area of their lives. Jesus died, not only that we should inherit eternal life, but also that we might be saved - which means healed and delivered as well. This is very,

very good news for the many, many people who are
nursing emotional damage and are longing for release.

The Will

The third principal aspect of the soul is that with which
we make decisions - the will. Scripture talks about the
spirit being willing, but the flesh weak. The meaning of
this phrase, which has become part of the language of
temptation, is simply that if the flesh has not been
crucified, then the will gets out of control.

Satan will use every trick in the book to make our wills
subject to the flesh, instead of the other way round. A
person who is walking in wholeness and obedience before
God is one whose will is under the Lordship of Jesus
Christ, and whose flesh life, as a consequence, is under
his control. This is not an area which many people will
freely talk about - for if the real truth about all our lives
were made public there would be some very embarrassed
and red faces sitting in church each Sunday!

Crucifying the flesh is not the most popular of Paul's
graphic spiritual phrases, but it is a road to wholeness
(holiness) which, if followed, will have enormous benefits
in every dimension of our lives. The key is control of the
will.

There are many people who are so sick in this area of
their lives that they are incapable of making rightful
decisions - temptation is always too strong for them. One
of Satan's major tactics with all Christians is to gain
control of this area. If he wins here, he has won
everywhere. Healing for a sick will is possible, and
deliverance will often be necessary, but it does require a
determination and obedience on the part of the Christian
which only the Holy Spirit can give.

In Conclusion

Man has three principle dimensions to his creation and one of these, the soul has three specific aspects to it. Whilst man is an integral whole, and the different dimensions cannot be separated from each other, it is clearly possible for man to be sick in any of these dimensions.

Because man is an integral whole, it is likely that if he is sick in one area other areas will also be affected. For example, a person who has been physically ill for a long time may also be emotionally sick as a consequence and could also be in rebellion against God because of the sickness, causing damage to the spirit. Conversely, a person who is sick in the spirit through bitterness or unforgiveness may become sick physically as a result. For example I have seen many people healed physically as they have come to terms with the need to forgive others!

Finally man can also be sick in any one of the areas outlined above through the presence of an evil spirit, deliverance from which is the main topic of this book.

Chapter 3

The Realm of Angels

Angels are real! Western rationalistic man may find it hard to cope with the idea of spiritual beings floating around the world that can be neither seen nor heard, but the scripture writers had no such difficulty. For them angels were a natural and real part of spiritual life. There are some 300 references in the scriptures to angels.

Lucifer, before he was renamed Satan, used to be part of the Angelic hosts. He was one of the highest angels in rank and authority equal only to the Archangel Michael. In order to understand more of how Satan is likely to operate, it is helpful, therefore, to study the power, objectives and abilities of the angels, about which there is quite a lot of information in the scriptural accounts.

The demonic realm is directly opposed to the work of God, so if we see how angels operate and function under God's control, we will, by contrast, understand something of how demons do the work of Satan. For the demonic realms appear to be organised and deployed in much the same way as the angels.

In making such a study I am not saying that Satan is equal and opposite to God (that is the heresy of dualism). Satan is a created being who fell from his place in glory, but he does try to deceive people into thinking he is an alternative God, however, and once people have swallowed such lies they become wide open to the demonic, who will hold them into the bondage of false belief.

The first chapter of Hebrews, which majors on the nature and character of Jesus as being greater than the angels, concludes with a question which the writer immediately proceeds to answer. *"What are the angels, then? They are spirits who serve God and are sent by him to help those who are to receive salvation"* (Hebrews 1:14 GNB). In other words, angels are spirit beings whose principal responsibility at the present time is to serve God by helping Christians! That means they are on our side!

The Ranking of Angels

Only angels of the highest rank are actually named in scripture. Michael, the archangel (or chief angel) and Gabriel (who appears to be the chief messenger angel) are the only ones whose names and roles are illustrated or described. The angel Raphael is referred to in the Apocrypha as one of seven holy angels. (Tobit 12:15).

There are many references in the scriptures to a heavenly order of spiritual beings implying that angels have varying degrees of power and authority. Paul states that *"God created everything in heaven and on earth, the seen and the unseen things, including spiritual powers, lords, rulers and authorities"* (Colossians 1:16 GNB, see also Ephesians 1:21, and 1 Peter 3:22).

There are also references in the scriptures to other winged angelic creatures - the cherubim (Genesis 3:24, Ezekiel 1 and Revelation 4:6-9) and the seraphim, whom Isaiah saw during his life-changing experience of seeing into the presence of God and realising the extent of his own uncleanness (Isaiah 6:1-8).

Michael and the Warrior Angels

There are three major references to Michael. It is clear from these that Michael is a warrior angel. The first of these, in Daniel 10:21, describes Michael as *"Israel's guardian angel"*. The one who is responsible for watching over the interests of God's chosen people.

The earlier part of Daniel 10 describes how the angel that was sent in answer to Daniel's prayer (presumably Gabriel who had made previous visitations to Daniel), ran into heavy opposition and had to do battle with the 'angel prince of the kingdom of Persia'.

This angel prince was not an angel in the service of God, but a fallen angel who had joined Satan's rebellion against God and who had been stationed there by Satan as the spiritual ruler over the nation. There is much we can learn from this about ruling spirits over nations and regions which is highly strategic to an understanding of spiritual warfare. The battle was so severe that Gabriel had to send for reinforcements and it was Michael who came to his aid. However high in ranking the prince of Persia was, he was no match for Michael.

Our next major reference to Michael, in Revelation 12, describes how he did battle with Lucifer in heaven and expelled him, along with all the other angels who joined in the rebellion against God (including the angel prince of Persia). *"He was hurled to the earth, and all his angels with him"* (Revelation 12:9 NIV).

So when Michael, the mighty warrior angel, who had already defeated all the hosts of Satan (Lucifer), appeared on the scene over Persia the outcome was a foregone conclusion. After the battle was over Gabriel was then free to complete his task and meet up with Daniel. Gabriel began his message by apologising for the delay! Daniel had been fasting and praying for 21 days - exactly the same time span that it had taken for Gabriel to get through to him. None of us have any idea what may be happening in the heavenlies when prayers seem to be slow in being answered!

The only other direct reference to Michael is a somewhat obscure one in Jude 9. Here, even Michael, in an argument with the Devil, is described as showing him proper respect - not daring to insult him, but leaving God to do the rebuking. Christians who are dismissive of the Devil's power often demonstrate amazing naivety, arrogance and pride when talking about Satan and consequently make themselves vulnerable to his devices. Even Paul had to admit that Satan interfered in his ministry (1 Thessalonians 2:18) and would not let him return to his friends at Thessalonika!

The actual argument with the Devil was over the body of Moses. Some commentators assume that even though Moses himself (spirit and soul) was securely part of God's Kingdom, because of his sin (as a murderer and someone who was disobedient to God when put to the test), Satan had laid claim to the body as a prize.

I wonder if Satan's objective here would have been to see Moses' body being used as a religious relic, so that people would venerate his remains and take their eyes off God. Satan is very subtle, and I believe it is he who is the chief proponent of the use of religious artefacts, knowing that if people can be deceived into putting their faith in them, they are well on their way to worshipping demons and, ultimately, Satan himself.

To some, this may sound an extreme view, but having delivered many people from spirits of religious bondage that had controlled their lives, I am very concious of the dangers. Having watched, also, people in slavery to idols and those who believe that venerating icons, statues and religious relics is an essential part of Christian living, I know the depths of Satan's bondage from which many will need deliverance.

The angel that appeared at the resurrection was undoubtedly a high warrior angel, if not Michael himself. First, he rolled the stone away, and when the Roman guards saw him they *"were so afraid that they trembled and became like dead men"* and *"his appearance was like lightning and his clothes were white as snow"* (Matthew 28:3-4).

Whilst ministering deliverance we have, on occasions, been conscious of what could only have been angelic help. Demonic powers, which had been so desperately hanging on to their footholds in the person's life, have screamed in fear at the scriptures describing angels. And when we have prayed to the Lord to send angels to help us, in accordance with Hebrews 1:14, the demons have cried out 'No, not them!'. There have also been occasions when the person being delivered has had his or her eyes opened to see into the supernatural and described both the angels and the battle that ensued. This has always resulted in a mighty deliverance taking place.

Gabriel and the Messenger Angels

Gabriel appears to be the chief messenger angel, commissioned by God to communicate directly with his people on exceptional occasions and sometimes personally manifesting himself before the individual concerned. His usual introduction in the scriptures is *"Fear not"* - a mercifully comforting command to those who might otherwise be in a deep state of shock!

In Daniel 8 Gabriel interprets a vision for Daniel, and in chapter 9 he brings understanding to him on difficult matters. In Daniel 10 it is presumed that it is Gabriel who comes in response to Daniel's prayer.

In the New Testament, Gabriel is entrusted with telling Zechariah that he is to be the father of John the Baptist (Luke 1:11-20), and then telling Mary that she is to be the mother of Jesus (Luke 1:26-38). Clearly these are major events in God's timetable, requiring a totally unmistakeable visitation leaving the recipient of the message in no doubt whatsoever that God has spoken.

There are numerous other instances in the scriptures of messenger angels appearing to communicate with believers in this way. For example, an angel appeared to Samson's mother, advising her that even though she was childless she was now going to conceive (Judges 13:3).

In Genesis 18, two angels warn Abraham about the impending destruction of Sodom and Gomorrah and then go on to warn his nephew Lot. In Judges 6 an angel appears to Gideon and commissions him as the Lord's agent for the rescue of Israel from the Midianites. And in

Acts 10 Cornelius sees a vision in which an angel of the Lord tells him that his prayers have been answered.

Clearly messenger angels have a strategic role in the direction of God's people and in answering their prayers. I suspect that their intervention in response to prayer, and in speaking guidance to our hearts, is somewhat greater than any of us might imagine!

On one occasion whilst I was preaching, I had inadvertently missed a key part of the teaching. One of our team began to pray hard and was utterly amazed, for as she looked up she became aware of an angel gently tapping me on the shoulder! I remember nothing, except that at that moment I looked down, saw the item in my notes I had overlooked and started to tell a story which fully illustrated the missing point!

Ministering Angels

Immediately after Jesus had endured 40 days of fasting and prayer in the wilderness, during which Satan tested him severely, angels came and ministered to him (Luke 4:11). In 1 Kings 19 an angel is seen providing sustenance for Elijah in the wilderness. It seems that ministering angels have a specific purpose in bringing encouragement and personal blessing to God's children. There are many ways in which they function.

As Christians we face much spiritual opposition and angels play a strategic role in encouraging us and lifting our spirits at these times. I am reminded of the story in Bunyan's Pilgrim's Progress when Christian, at the House of the Interpreter, is amazed at a fire which continues to burn brightly in spite of cold water being poured onto it. The key was the 'man' round the other side of the fire who was pouring on oil.

On one occasion, when I was teaching, there was a particularly heavy anointing of the Holy Spirit and God was ministering deeply into people's lives. After the meeting one of those present said that half way through

the teaching her eyes had been opened into the
supernatural, and she had seen a ring of angels all round
me. In turn they would come forward and pour 'oil' into
me to give out to the people. It was a very humbling
experience, but one in which I rejoice. The angels truly
ministered the Lord to people on that night.

The Job Functions of Angels

In addition to the three broad categories of angelic
function described above, we can deduce from the
Scriptures a number of aspects to the character of angels
and understand something of the various roles which
they fulfil.

1.   They are always worshipping God (Matt 18:10,
        Revelation 5:11-14)
2.   They rejoice in the works of God (Job 38:7)
3.   They always execute God's will (Psalm 103:20)
4.   They have influence over the affairs of nations
        (Daniel 10, 11:1 and 12:1)
5.   They watch over the interests of churches
        (Revelation 2 and 3)
6.   They assist and protect believers (Hebrews 1:14, 1
        Kings 19:5)
7.   They are used to punish God's enemies (Acts
        12:23. 2 Samuel 24:16, Isaiah 37:36)
8.   They perform extraordinary acts on behalf of God's
        people (Acts 12:6-10, Exodus 23:20-23)
9.   They minister personally to each one of God's
        children (Matthew 18:10)

By contrast with the above, and knowing that the demonic
powers will always oppose what God is doing, we can see
that demons will act in the following contrary ways:

1.   They are always serving and worshipping Satan.
        The worship they offer Satan, however, is not that
        which is willingly given, but that which is

extracted from them through a reign of fear and terror. They are puffed up with pride and seek to dominate and control through fear. Punishment and retribution are hallmarks of Satan's Kingdom.

2. They rejoice in the works of Satan, because they have a vested self-interest in Satan achieving his objectives. They gain more power as a result.

3. They always execute Satan's will and wishes, which means they are totally committed to:

    a) attacking God's special creation - human beings,

    b) keeping them out of God's Kingdom, and

    c) radically opposing committed Christians, especially those with a heart for being obedient to God's will.

4. They are strategically involved in the affairs of nations via ruling princes whom Satan has positioned in control of specific territories throughout the world.

5. They oppose the interests of churches. Many Christians naively believe that inside their churches they are free from Satan's attack. In reality that is the place where Satan has a major influence, continually undermining the work of the Holy Spirit who is moving the fellowship forward to do the works of the Kingdom.

6. They oppose and attack believers. Wherever believers are seeking to be obedient to the will of God, and to move forward under the anointing of the Holy Spirit, demons will seek to undermine what God is doing through them. Satan is not particularly concerned, however, about those who are just religious, whatever their particular brand of religious expression may be. Religion which is outside the anointing of the Holy Spirit is no particular threat to Satan's Kingdom.

7.   They will do all they can to attack God's children
        (Satan's enemies). The personal attacks may
        include sickness, accidents, financial problems,
        relationship breakdown etc. Indeed, they will take
        advantage of any weakness in the defences, or
        unhealed past, to gain, or strengthen, a foothold in
        the Christian's territory.

8.   They perform extraordinary acts on behalf of Satan
        and his kingdom. Even the Egyptian magicians
        were capable of duplicating some of the signs that
        Moses did in front of Pharaoh. There are many
        deceptions operating in Satan's kingdom which
        the people of God need to be discerning about.
        Scripture says that in the last days even the very
        elect may be deceived (Mark 13:22).

9.   They "minister" personally to each human being.
        But their style of ministry is not that which we
        would want to encourage! Just as God would give
        to each child an angel (Matthew 18:10), so, it
        seems, Satan would try to put on each child an evil
        spirit - what the spiritualists would call a guiding
        spirit, but which we would recognise simply as a
        demon. The job function of such a spirit is to do
        everything possible to turn a person away from
        God and to deceive them into actions that are
        contrary to God's will and purpose.

In Conclusion

It is clear that angels have a very important role to play in
this world and that, just as they are deployed on the face
of the earth in accordance with the will of God, the
demonic powers are also deployed so as to achieve Satan's
objectives.

Demonic power will always be seen to be opposing the
work of angels. Much more about the tactics of the evil
one and his demonic agents will be said in later chapters.

Chapter 4

Satan and his Kingdom

The Origin of Satan

Satan is real! He is a fallen angel who sought to elevate himself above his angelic status as an archangel. His original name was Lucifer and as such he was a splendid and very beautiful creation of God.

Most commentators interpret Isaiah 14:12-15 as describing how Satan (portrayed as the King of Babylonia) vowed to *"make himself like the Most High"* (NIV). As a result there was rebellion in the heavenly hosts and there was no way in which this angel, who had chosen to use his free-will to oppose his creator, could be allowed to remain. Ezekiel 28:12-17 is a similar passage in which Satan is portrayed as the King of Tyre.

Revelation 12 describes the ensuing war in heaven when Michael, the Archangel and chief warrior angel, was deployed with his warrior forces against Lucifer and his angels *"and the great dragon was thrown down, that serpent of old who is called the devil and Satan, who deceives the whole world; he was thrown down to the earth and his angels were thrown down with him"* (Revelation 12:9 NASB). From then on Lucifer was no longer called Lucifer, meaning light, but Satan, meaning the Adversary, or one who is hostile to and opposes God.

Jesus adds his own personal account of Satan's expulsion from heaven in Luke 10, when talking to the 72 who returned full of joy because they found the demons were subject to their commands. It was important that Jesus should put their exuberance into a right context and remind them that he had all power and authority in the first place, as was demonstrated by the fact that he was there when Satan was expelled from heaven, and that he, therefore, had the authority to delegate his power and authority to those whom he chose.

Those whom Jesus chose to receive this power and authority are all those who *"received him, (for) to them he gave the right to become children of God, even to those who believe in his name"* (John 1:12 NASB). As children of God we have delegated rights. Therefore he was able to say to the 72 that he had given them authority over *"serpents and scorpions and over all the power of the enemy"* (Luke 10:19 NASB).

However, he reminded them that it was far more important that they should rejoice because their names are written in heaven, for they only have power and authority over the enemy because their names are written in heaven. This is a salutary reminder to all those who would seek to be obedient to the commission to cast out demons. Our first and foremost priority is to be evangelists and never to forget that outside of the Kingdom of Heaven we are nothing.

Satan, therefore, with all his angels, was thrown down to earth where he took up residence and began to exercise his own spiritual authority in a domain which, for the time being, is under his control. Jesus referred to Satan as the *"ruler of this world"* (John 12:31) and Paul stated that the *"god of this world has blinded the minds of the unbelieving"* (2 Corinthians 4:4 NASB). Both Jesus and Paul, therefore, recognised the present position that Satan holds in the hierarchy of earth's spiritual powers and we err badly if we are disparaging or dismissive of the reality of Satan and his kingdom, or his power and areas of authority.

I am not advocating that we should pay him any respect in the sense of offering homage, for believers have been *"delivered from the domain of darkness and transferred to the Kingdom of His beloved Son"* (Colossians 1-13 NASB), but we place ourselves in grave danger if we are not aware of the wiles of the enemy for, as Paul says in Ephesians 6:12 *"our struggle is not against flesh and blood, but against the rulers, against the powers, against the world forces of this darkness, against the spiritual forces of wickedness in the heavenly places"* (NASB).

One of Satan's temptations to Jesus in the wilderness was the offer of the world on a plate. *"He led Jesus up and showed him all the kingdoms of the world in a moment of time. And the devil said to him, 'I will give you all this domain and its glory; for it has been handed over to me, and I give it to whomever I wish. Therefore if you worship me it shall be yours'"* (Luke 4:5-7 NASB).

The amazing thing about this particular temptation was that Jesus did not deny that Satan had the right to make him such an offer! Jesus recognised that it was a genuine offer which Satan had the right to make and which he could have accepted - but the price would have been high, very high. Total role reversal, with Jesus bowing down to Satan, instead of every knee bowing to Jesus (including Satan's) as seen by Paul and described in Philippians 2:5-11.

Ultimately, the force of this temptation was to offer Jesus the chance of winning back the world without going to the cross, a superficially attractive proposition. There are many people who would like to achieve great spiritual objectives and make a name for themselves without visiting Calvary, but Jesus knew that without the cross there would be no eternal hope for redeemed sinners. So he rounded on Satan with the second of three devastating quotes from the book of Deuteronomy, *"It is written, You shall worship the Lord your God and serve him only."*

Understanding the position that Satan currently holds with respect to this world, aids us considerably in our understanding of the incarnation, death and resurrection of Jesus. By living for thirty-three years in a world that is in the control of Satan, without sin, Jesus established the eternal and solitary precedent of independence from the power and grip of Satan. If Jesus had sinned once his mission would have failed!

The wonder of salvation is that through belief in Jesus we benefit from his sinlessness. When Christ is in us (through being born again of his Spirit) we are in the same position before God as Jesus himself. Our sin is covered by his glory. The shed blood of Jesus through his sacrifice on the cross is sufficient and we are redeemed out of the hand of the devil! What amazing grace!!

The Character of Satan

Names in the Bible have enormous significance. There are many different names for God - especially in the Old Testament - each one of them showing us something different and special about his character. This Jewish custom also enables us to understand something of the character of Satan. Many different names are used in the scripture, many of which are dramatically expressive of his nature.

However glossy the wrappings round the temptations Satan puts in front of us, the real character of the tempter will always eventually be exposed. In that extraordinary film 'Chitty-Chitty Bang-Bang' the obnoxious 'child collector' tricks children into a decorated cart which offers all sorts of fancy and exciting attractions. The moment the children enter the cart, however, iron gates slam shut and the children find themselves, not inside a children's wonderland, but in a prison on wheels that rushes them off to the dungeons.

Satan is a bit like that with his temptations. People become victims of their own desire and then the gate slams shut! James comments that *"evil desire conceives and gives birth to sin; and sin, when it is full-grown, gives birth to death"* (James 1:15 GNB). People only find out what the real character of Satan is like when it is too late. There is only one who is able to deliver us out of the hands of the enemy, Jesus.

The scriptures are there for our instruction, and looking at the names of Satan (and their meanings where that is not immediately obvious) should alert us to his real character. Many of the names clearly indicate the filth, depravity and evil intent of this prince of demons.

Abaddan or Apollyon	The destroyer, Revelation 9:11
Accuser of the Brethren	Revelation 12:10
Adversary	1 Peter 5:8
Angel of Light	2 Corinthians 11:14
Angel of the Abyss	Revelation 9:11
Antichrist	Alternative to Christ, 1 John 4:1-4, 2 John 7
Beelzebul	A dung god of the Ekronites, Matthew 12:24,27 (Lord of the flies)
Belial	Worthless, perverse, 2 Corinthians 6:15
Condemner	1 Timothy 3:6
Deceiver	Revelation 12:9, 2 Corinthians 11:3
Devil	Accuser, slanderer Matthew 4:1, John 8:44
Dragon	Revelation 12
Enemy	Matthew 13:39
Evil One	Matthew 13:19

God of this World	2 Corinthians 4:4
King	Revelation 9:11
Liar	John 8:44
Murderer	Destroyer of life, John 8:44
Oppressor	One who dominates, Acts 10:38
Prince of the Power of the Air	Ephesians 2:2
Roaring Lion	1 Peter 5:8
Ruler of the demons	Matthew 12:24
Ruler of the World	John 12:31, 14:30 and 16:11
Satan	Adversary, one who opposes, Matthew 4:10, Zechariah 3:1
Serpent	Snake, Genesis 3:1, Revelation 12:9
Tempter	Matthew 4:3
Thief	John 10:10
Wolf	John 10:12

Satan's Objectives

Satan has always been in rebellion against God, and he
has sought to attract worship to himself and turn people
away from God. His tactics have not changed since the
beginning of time. He still uses the age-old well-tried
temptations that have so effectively led men and women
into sin generation after generation.

Power, sex, wealth or false religion are at the heart of most of his tactics, however subtly they may be dressed up for public consumption! In fallen man are things such as self-pleasing, greed and lust for power - all of which make fertile ground for Satan to sow his seeds of rebellion.

In serving any of these false gods people are unwittingly bowing the knee to Satan. He does not mind that people are ignorant of what they are really doing, although he does, clearly, get great satisfaction out of the rituals of Satanism where people knowingly worship him - especially when he is paid the ultimate 'honour' through the sacrifice to him of a human being.

Deception is his stock in trade, for once people have been deceived and, as it were, have taken the bait, the progression of temptations that can follow is endless. James' advice to *"resist the devil"* is downright practical guidance for everyday living (James 4:7). For if we do not resist, we lay our lives wide open to the demonic.

Satan hates to see people live long, fulfilled lives in the service of God. The sooner a person's life is terminated, the less opportunity there is for salvation to be accepted. At a recent meeting I asked the body of Christians present how many of them had ever contemplated suicide, however fleetingly. Over 60% of them admitted to having had suicidal thoughts. The progression to self-destruction is down a well-worn path which begins with deception.

Once people are walking in deception they become vulnerable to being disturbed, for conflict arises inside between our God-given sensitivity to the Lord and the desires that we are giving way to in the flesh. Depression is sometimes the consequence with the whole range of sicknesses, which can ride in on the back of a depressed personality, following on. Distress is the next stage of the downward spiral with the need for heavier medication to keep individuals on an even keel. At this point the person's life is so controlled, by their condition and the consequential medication, that life begins to lose its purpose.

For some, despair sets in, and this is but a hair's breadth away from attempts at suicide. Satan is a filthy fighter, he is no respecter of persons and he hates God so much that he will stop at nothing to destroy those whom God created. But God loved people so much that he sent his Son to die for them. Satan has never forgotten the defeat of Calvary and is working to the limits of his capacity to keep people away from finding out the truth, that in the name of Jesus people can be set free. No wonder Satan works overtime to discredit the deliverance ministry!

Evangelism, healing and deliverance are urgent commissions to be fulfilled by the church of Jesus Christ. They are not optional extras that we might occasionally practice. If we cease from evangelism we cease from following Jesus. If we fail to minister healing and deliverance we leave people in a bondage from which Jesus died to set them free. And we ignore a command which Jesus gave to the church within the great commission of Matthew 28:18-20.

Before moving on it is worth noting five significant contrasts between Satan and God.

1.   God is the Creator - Satan is a created being
      (Ezekiel 28:13-15)

2.   God is omnipresent - present at all times and in all
      places. Satan is limited in both time and location
      (Job 1:6-7). He can only, therefore, carry out his
      work through the agency of demons and evil spirits
      who are under his command.

3.   God is omniscient - there is nothing that he does
      not know. Satan and his forces are limited in
      knowledge (Acts 19:15).

4.   God is omnipotent - his power is unlimited.
      Satan's power is limited and restricted within the
      confines which God has allowed (Job 1:6-12).

5.   God is eternal - there is no beginning or ending to
      God's kingdom. Satan's time is strictly limited.
      One day Jesus is coming again as King of Kings

and Lord of Lords. At that time Satan's rule and reign will come to an end and the scenario of Revelation will commence. Satan and his demons know the scriptures well and the prophetic words in the Bible which tell of the end for Satan and all his angels are feared and hated by the demonic powers.

Revelation 20:7-15, Hebrews 2:14-15 and Matthew 25:41-46 are all very encouraging reading for God's people and very effective passages of scripture for undermining the supposed rights of demonic powers! Sadly demons have a greater appreciation of the truth and authority of these scriptures than do most Christians.

Satan's Kingdom

Satan reigns as the ruler of this world. He is not omnipresent and his reign is extended via a hierarchy of demonic power. Presumably those angels who fell with him from heaven who were in the higher echelons of angelic authority have now taken up equivalent positions as princes over nations under Satan's world system.

Recently, when travelling from one country which has had a severely oppressive history, into a neighbouring country which has seen a great deal of religious freedom I was immediately conscious in my spirit of a change in the 'atmosphere' - something which could not have been measured, but which was certainly felt. There was a different ruling spirit in operation.

Similarly, within a nation one can move from one region to another and be conscious of discernible spiritual changes. And every minister who has had to move about the country during his ministry will be able to recount stories of the different prevailing spiritual climates in the towns in which he has ministered.

An American couple we minister with from time to time recounted their experience, in Scotland, of a dark foreboding 'presence' while driving through a certain valley. Several days later, while they were enjoying an accurate Scottish historical novel, they realised they had been passing through the place where the Campbells had massacred their "guests". The curse on the land was perceptible to them even though, at the time, they knew nothing of the history of the area.

The extent to which demonic powers can continue to hold sway in a country, a region or a town is directly related to the commitment (or otherwise) to intercessory prayer of the Christians in that territory. The freer country referred to above has had a body of intercessors interceding for the nation for close on forty years. The effect was noticeable.

Satan also attempts to rule on a much more local level by placing ruling spirits over churches, schools, companies, organisations etc. When taking teaching weekends in local churches around the country we have sometimes seen dramatic differences in the ministry take place immediately after doing battle with the ruling spirits that Satan had placed over the churches concerned. The consequences in terms of church life and evangelism are sometimes so dramatic as to lead to a doubling of the congregation inside twelve months!

At the human interface Satan will always seek to oppress, afflict and, preferably, occupy human beings with evil spirits (demons) who are constantly working to fulfil Satan's objectives.

In Conclusion

For the time being Satan is god of this world. But his time is limited, as are his various abilities. He is not worthy of our worship, but he continues to deceive much of the world to follow after him.

Christians can have victory over him and his forces in the name of Jesus, but they must be constantly on their guard for, as Peter says, *"the devil, prowls about like a roaring lion seeking someone to devour"* (1 Peter 5:8 NASB).

Chapter 5

The Fall and God's Rescue Plan

No-one could doubt man's capacity to sin. I have never met an individual who has not been conscious of both the capacity to do wrong and the fact that they have done wrong in their life! The reality of the fall is all around us. The potential man has for depravity is ably demonstrated by every single day's news bulletin.

Whilst writing the last paragraph I broke off to watch the Television News and was confronted in those few minutes with the murder of small boys who had been caught in a sexual abuse nightmare, the deaths of two women who had first been raped, and in the world of business, accusations of gross malpractice at board level in a major UK company.

All society has to endure the effects of other people's sin. Whilst it is only a very small percentage of the population who becomes directly involved in the extremes of depravity referred to above, I will never cease to be astonished at the varied, and sometimes bizarre, experiences of very ordinary people whose problems tumble out in the counselling room.

Stories of unfaithfulness, perversion, deception, theft, sexual abuse, come pouring out once the lid has been lifted off the defences of respectability and the plastic face has been removed. I recognise now that when Paul stated *"all have sinned and fall short of the glory of God"* (Romans 3:23 NASB), he was not only stating a theological precept, but was commenting directly on life as he, also, must have seen and experienced it.

Rebellion and the Fall

Man as he now is, is not as he was first created. God is holy and righteous and he made man in his own image, so somewhere, at sometime, something must have gone sadly wrong. However one interprets the story of Adam, Eve, the Garden of Eden and the Serpent, the consequences of the fall are exactly as Genesis relates. The evidence is there for all to see, both in our own lives and in the lives of others - man is a creature of sin and is in rebellion against a holy and righteous God.

As soon as we mention the word rebellion we are reminded of what happened in heaven when Lucifer tried to take for himself the glory which belonged to God. Rebellion in the heavenly ranks could not be tolerated and Lucifer was expelled and thrown down to earth. Rebelliousness had become part of Satan's character and having been frustrated in his first endeavour, to dethrone God himself, Satan set about destroying what God had made. He targeted on Man, the pinnacle of God's creation, made in the image of God himself, and his primary tactic was to sow the seeds of rebellion; to infect mankind with Satan's own spirit.

Rebellion is like a contagious disease for which there is no cure - once caught you have it for life. The essence of all sin is simply rebellion and the heart of the Genesis account of the fall of man is simply that - rebellion against instructions that God had given.

The greatest, but most risky gift that God gave to man was his free-will. At no time has God ever over-ridden this capacity for us to choose and do our own thing. Adam and Eve had free-will to choose. As long as there were no seeds of rebellion sown in their hearts the concept of choosing anything else but obedience to God's loving direction would never have entered their head. Up to that point they had used their free-will wisely.

The Nature of the Fall

In the Genesis story Satan is portrayed as a serpent. A picture which is consistent with Jesus's comment to the 72 - *"I have given you authority, so that you can walk on snakes and scorpions and overcome all the power of the enemy, and nothing will hurt you."* (Luke 10:19 GNB). Here Jesus was making a statement about the authority that those who are believers in him have over Satan and all the works of the enemy.

The serpent's tactic was simply to make Eve question whether or not she would die if she did eat of the forbidden tree. The question was enough to make Eve doubt. But she had free-will to choose whether to believe the serpent's doubts or continue to trust in the God she knew and who loved her. God did not create a race of automatons who had no alternative but to be obedient to him.

At this point Eve had not sinned, but she was contemplating an act of rebellion. The moment she took of the fruit, rebellion was no longer a thought in her head, but an action which had been carried out. Sin had entered the race and the rebellion which began with Satan in heaven had contaminated mankind. Adam followed Eve's example and the disease of sin became endemic. Man had fallen from his primary state.

God had planned that man, who is primarily a spiritual being, should always live in total harmony and fellowship with him. There is nothing in the scripture to indicate whether that was to have been eternal life on earth, or in heaven. But what is clear is that just as Satan was deprived of fellowship with God by being expelled from heaven, there was no way that man, who had joined in Satan's rebellion against God, could continue in fellowship with God without some very radical action on God's part.

Genesis 3:15 tells us that even at that earliest moment of man's history a prophecy was made that one day the offspring of woman would actually crush the head of the serpent.

Early in the ministry of Ellel Grange we were ministering deliverance to a man who had, whilst in prison, sold himself to the devil. Subsequently, in solitary confinement the only thing he was allowed to have was a Gideon New Testament. He read this and finished up giving his life to Christ. He came out of prison a changed person, but still with horrendous problems stemming back to his earlier days.

For him deliverance was a vital part of the ministry he needed. The day came when we had to deal with the spirit that had come into him when he had sold himself to Satan. The deliverance was violent and awesome, and his body was severely tormented by the demon as it left.

When it was all over, the man was clearly in a state of shock and joy at the same time. I asked him what he had sensed happening. In his very northern accent he described what he had 'seen' in the spirit as deliverance took place. *"It was a great snake,"* he said, *"grey, with black bloody blotches all over, and its 'ead was all bashed in."*

Up to that point he had never read the Old Testament and knew nothing about the prophesy of Genesis 3:15, but what he described was an exact image of what Genesis had prophesied that Jesus would do to Satan - crush his head. Experiences like that significantly help one's appreciation of the authenticity of scripture!

The Consequences of Sin

For Satan, God had chosen immediate expulsion from heaven and the promise of eternal punishment in the lake of fire for him and all his angels (Revelation 20:7-15 and Matthew 25:41-46). Having once dealt with rebellion so justly, firmly and finally, there was no way that God could deal with similar rebellion in man any less justly, firmly or finally. As Paul says (Romans 6:23) *"the wages of sin is death"* and as through Adam and Eve sin entered the world, so, also, was the judgment of God brought upon the world.

By joining in Satan's rebellion against God, man also contracted to share in the judgement that had been meted out to Satan. That may sound hard, but it is fair. God's heart must have broken when he saw what man chose to do with the free-will that he had been entrusted with. In English law an accessory to a crime is as guilty as the man who commits the crime. Adam and Eve may only have been accessories to Satan's 'crime' but they, and all after them, were, and are still, guilty of complicity.

The Beginnings of Demonisation

Adam and Eve were affected by a spirit of rebellion and the Genesis story goes on to illustrate how the sins of the fathers are not just restricted to the fathers. Exodus 20:5 (GNB) says that they are visited *"on those who hate me and on their descendants down to the third and fourth generation"*. The word hate, in this context, implies far more than the emotion of hatred. It is assumed that the fact of disobedience is evidence of hatred in the heart, even if the person may not feel that they hate God. In a similar way, in the New Testament, Jesus assumed that those who were not for him were against him. Cain and Abel were affected by the rebellion of their parents and when Cain had cause to be angry with Abel the thought of murder entered his heart.

Genesis 4:7 says that *"sin was crouching at the door"*. An ancient Babylonian text of this verse reads *"a demon waiting to get in"*. By acting on the thought of murder, and actually killing his brother, Cain further opened himself up to Satan's ploys and a spirit of murder will have entered.

In ministry we have had to deal with several people who have been involved in murder - usually the murder associated with willingly having an abortion. Frequently we have had to cast out a spirit of murder from the person who chose to have an abortion. At other times we have encountered a spirit of murder which has been given the right to enter because of hatred towards someone in the heart. No wonder Jesus, who brought such insight and spiritual understanding to the law, implied in the sermon on the mount (Matthew 5:21-24) that wrongful anger in the heart was as damaging to the person spiritually as the act of murder itself.

It is easy to see that, once rebellion is in the heart of man, the continuing practice of sin provides a stream of entry points through which Satan can deploy his forces (evil spirits) against man directly, and, therefore, against God. Demonisation of man is a natural consequence of Satan's original rebellion against God. The more mankind is demonised the more internal opposition he has to the things of the Spirit and the less likely he is to turn back to God.

Consequences for Mankind

The ultimate consequence of the fall is death. God did not create man with any imperfections and I cannot believe it was God's intention that man should be subject to sickness and disease and physical death through the failure of the bodily systems, followed by eternal spiritual death through endless separation from the God who created and loved him. But it is, nevertheless, a fact of experience that mankind does get sick, there are countless diseases which ravage the human body and conditions which control the mind. In his life and death man is a victim of his own rebellion.

The immediate effect of the fall was man's spiritual separation from God (who is Spirit) - an inevitable consequence of rebellion. At that moment, when man used his free-will to rebel against God, man became dead (to God) because of sin. In the Old Testament, under the covenant that was established through Moses between

God and his chosen people (the Jews), provision was made for the forgiveness of sin through repentance followed by animal sacrifices.

Wonderful though that was for the Jews, it was of limited value to the Gentiles! And the establishment of a law meant that for many Jewish people obedience to the letter of the law became far more important than responsiveness to the Spirit of God that was behind the law. Hence Jesus's antagonism towards the Pharisees who weighed people down with the fine details of interpreted laws, but whose hearts were in spiritual disarray.

He also exposed this sort of hypocrisy by his comments on things such as adultery. He saw into men's hearts and knew that men looking at women lustfully was as sinful (as far as the person who is thinking about illicit sexual stimulation is concerned) as actually committing the act. Indeed, the perverted imaginations of the mind would probably far exceed any performance that was actually achieved.

Yet men thought they were sinless because they hadn't actually had intercourse with the objects of their lustful desires. People used the law to their own ends and when their heart was not right with God the law became a limit which must not be exceeded as opposed to a principle that must be followed.

During the centuries that preceded the coming of Christ vital lessons were being learned by mankind. Precious understandings about the nature and character of God were painstakingly recorded by prophets, historians, poets and commentators on society. People who were acting under the inspiration of the Holy Spirit wrote down what we have come to know as the Old Testament. For them they were recording their experiences of life, but at the same time God's greater purposes for the whole of mankind were slowly being fulfilled.

Once man had sinned, no longer was there that intimate spiritual communion between God and his creation. No longer could man understand what was in the heart of the Father, or the Father speak to his children through unblocked channels. The lessons were hard learned over centuries of time. Slowly, as the scriptures were written and accumulated into the Old Testament, the character and love of God were being revealed for the whole of mankind - not just the Jewish people.

The Jews, however, were the vehicle through which God chose to reveal himself to the world. The fact that the Jews have not always been impeccable witnesses to the glory of God is not to be held against them. They are part of a sinful race, and any other people that God might have chosen would have been equally unworthy recipients of God's amazing grace.

Periodically God's Spirit would reveal to some of the Old Testament authors prophecies about the future which hinted at a greater salvation than was possible through the provisions of the law. Veiled references which the authors are unlikely to have understood, such as *"not a bone of his is broken"* (Psalm 34:20) and *"the stone the builders rejected has become the chief cornerstone"* (Psalm 118:22 NASB) abound in the scriptural records. There are, also, very specific and detailed prophecies from people such as Micah, Isaiah and others who foretold the coming of Jesus.

But when the time for Jesus to come finally arrived, the Jewish people were under the domination of a Roman occupying power and the only Messiah most of the people were looking for was someone who would rid them of this tyranny. Only a handful of people were actually ready and alert in their spirit to welcome Jesus into the world.

Joseph and Mary had been warned by angelic visitations. They must have been totally dazed by the enormity of what was happening to them. How encouraged they must have been, when they took the baby Jesus up to the temple, to find there two very elderly people, Simeon and Anna, who

---

knew exactly who this baby was and whose lives were totally fulfilled by that brief encounter with Messianic destiny. Whilst visits of angels are very special, the assurance and encouragement of human beings is also very, very precious.

How Joseph and Mary must have rejoiced when Simeon came out with those beautiful words, said and sung all over the world as the Nunc Dimittis, *"Lord, now lettest thou thy servant depart in peace, according to thy word; for mine eyes have seen thy salvation which thou hast prepared in the presence of all peoples, a light for revelation to the Gentiles, and for glory to thy people Israel"* (Luke 2:29-32 RSV).

Simeon knew then that he could die in peace. The child that God had told him about had finally been born. He had delivered his word of affirmation and encouragement to the parents. His life's work - just a few minutes of eternally precious time - was over. God had indeed fulfilled his word. And at that very same hour along comes Anna, 84 years of age, but still fasting and praying and never ceasing to worship God. What a lady! And how precious of the Lord to send both a man and a woman to Joseph and Mary - two witnesses affirming each other's testimony.

God's Rescue Plan

Joseph had been told by the angel to call the baby Jesus, for he would save the people from their sins (Matthew 1:21). But they were told nothing of how Jesus would achieve this objective. As Jews they will have known about the promise of a coming Messiah, but it is unlikely that they would have understood that their son would die a cruel death for the sins of the world.

Jesus states quite simply, in his conversation with Nicodemus (John 3:16), that God loved the world (the people he had created) so much that he gave his only Son, that whoever believes in him will not perish but have eternal life. That scripture is perhaps the most quoted and best loved verse in the Bible.

The implication of these words, however, is not free pardon for all, come what may, but pardon for those who believe. If a person chooses not to believe, the result is inevitable - a share, with Satan, in the consequences of rebellion, which, according to Matthew, Hebrews and Revelation means the lake of fire and the second death!

It was as soon as man sinned, at the very moment when time began to run out for the human race, that God put into effect his plan for a way of escape. He chose to send his Son to earth to live and die as a human being but remain without sin. As such Jesus could take upon himself the punishment for our sin - but should he sin, the plan would fail. For it was only by not joining in Satan's rebellion that the way would be open for those who are trusting Jesus to be saved from the consequences of their own rebellion.

The temptations in the wilderness, indicative of the pressure that Satan himself placed on Jesus, were very real. Had Jesus chosen to use his divine powers for selfish ends (make bread when he was fasting), or accepted Satan's offer of all the Kingdoms of the world without going to the cross, or jumped off the pinnacle of the temple to impress people with the aerial expertise of the angels in protecting him from harm, or succumbed to any other temptation that Satan threw at him, then his mission would have failed. Even the Son of God would have been seen to be no better than mankind in coping with the attacks of Satan.

The sinless Son of God was the only possible threat to Satan's rule over mankind. Several times Satan tried to kill Jesus prematurely. When he was a baby, Herod did his best in Bethlehem. Spirits of murder, probably given a right by pride, fear and jealousy in Herod, will have been used to manipulate Herod's thoughts and actions. Herod had already established himself as a murderer by disposing of his wife and mother-in-law!

At Nazareth the congregation (spirits of anger operating in the people) rose up at the end of his sermon and tried to throw him over a cliff (Luke 4:28-30). On Galilee, it seems that a spirit of the air whipped up a storm on the lake and tried to drown him - Jesus spoke to the storm (the spirit behind the storm) and immediately there was calm (Luke 8:22-25).

No-one was going to take Jesus's life from him. It was only when the time on God's prophetic calendar finally arrived, and Jesus voluntarily chose to lay down his life, that He finally faced death. This time there was to be no miraculous escape to Egypt, or supernatural rescue act such as on Galilee. And Satan was definitely not pleased, for he knew that he was beaten.

For Jesus to die willingly, and at the appointed time, meant that God was going to snatch back from the hands of the enemy countless millions of people who would otherwise have been lost in Satan's rebellion. Jesus was the sacrificial lamb, not just for the Jewish people, but for the whole world. He chose to lay down his life and therein lies the heart of the story of the cross and resurrection.

Three days later an angel rolled away the stone and Jesus burst out of the grave. Not only had Jesus been the sacrificial lamb, but he had conquered death and the greatest consequence of the fall had been overcome. Satan and all his demons were placed firmly under the feet of Christ and the greatest victory in the history of the world had been staged, played out and proclaimed on the fields of first century Palestine.

Jesus came to earth, or as John so graphically expressed it, *"The Word became flesh and dwelt among us"* (John 1:14 NASB). He came as a man but remained totally sinless. He ascended to glory and now sits at the right hand of the Father having achieved everything the Father had asked of him.

The way was open for people to enter Heaven wearing a spotless robe of righteousness that had been won for them on the cross. And the offer has been open ever since to all who would come and *"as many as received him, to them he gave the right to become children of God"* (John 1:12 NASB). No wonder Jesus underlined in his ministry that he was the only way to the Father (John 14:1-7).

The rescue plan was complete. On the cross Jesus defeated Satan and overturned all the curses that he had put upon mankind. *"Jesus became curse for us"* (Galatians 3:13). Included among those curses was sickness and demonisation.

Isaiah prophesied *"by his stripes we are healed"* (Isaiah 53:5 NKJV) and in Isaiah 61:1 Isaiah looks forward to the coming of Jesus. Hundreds of years before Jesus was born he wrote words about the ministry of Jesus which Jesus applied to himself when speaking in the synagogue at Nazareth. There Jesus proclaimed to the people, *"The Spirit of the Lord is upon me, because he has anointed me to preach the Gospel to the poor (salvation), He has sent me to proclaim release to the captives (deliverance), and recovery of sight to the blind (healing), to set free those who are downtrodden, to proclaim the favourable year of the Lord"* (Luke 4:18-19 NASB).

What a claim that was, to be the one who would bring the Gospel of salvation, deliverance, healing and restoration to those who are in need. It was only Jesus who had the power and the authority to make such a claim, and Satan knew it! Healing and deliverance are integral parts of the ministry of Jesus. They are implicit in the cross and included in the great commission that Jesus gave to the church. God's rescue plan was detailed and comprehensive.

The Way In

The essence of the Gospel is incredibly simple. The way is open for all who enter into the Kingdom of God to be born again. There are no restrictions and it is totally free - it is indeed a Gospel for the poor! But for the rich young ruler the cost was too great. Even though salvation is free and only has to be accepted, for many the cost is still too high. For it costs us everything to follow Jesus. And for the rich young ruler his money had become his god.

Many people who seek the ministry of healing are wanting God to deal with their symptoms, but are ignorant of the need to make Jesus Lord of their lives. It is clear, however, that if their symptoms have an origin which is spiritual rather than physical, there is very little one can do for them unless they are willing to be healed spiritually first.

For this reason evangelism has to have a high priority in the minds of all those who would seek to minister healing and deliverance into people's lives. The agendas can switch from healing to evangelism very quickly. It's amazing how much more willing people are to listen to the Gospel when they are pressurised by their own circumstances! Whilst God is not the author of sickness and suffering, he certainly uses it to get our attention when other channels have failed.

In Conclusion

The Fall is real and has resulted in man's separation from God through rebellion. God's love is such that he sent Jesus so as to open up a way for the relationship between God and man to be restored. That way is open for all who believe in Jesus. The victory of the cross is such that not only is the free gift of eternal life available to us, but we are then, also, in a position of victory over Satan and his works since healing and deliverance are implicit in the work of the cross.

Chapter 6

The Character and Work of Evil Spirits

The Powers of Darkness

Already we have seen how Satan is Prince of the powers of darkness and that he has under his control all the angels that joined in the rebellion in heaven, and were thrown down to earth by Michael. We have established that Satan is not omnipresent and that without the assistance of other powers of darkness he is extremely limited in what he is able to do.

Unfortunately, however, he has at his disposal a very large number of fallen angels. Most commentators assume that Revelation 12:4 indicates that one third of the heavenly beings rebelled with Satan and followed him out of heaven. But just how many is a third of the heavenly beings?

The size of the heavenly host is referred to in Revelation 5:11. Various translations of this verse refer to *"myriads of myriads and thousands of thousands"* (RSV and NASB), *"ten thousand times ten thousand and thousands of thousands"* (AV) and the more graphic, but equally imprecise *"thousands and millions of them"* (GNB). What is clear is that a countless host of angels is involved and if they represent the angels that were left after a third had been expelled, then we are talking also about a very, very large number of fallen angels who are serving Satan in rebellion against both God, and his creation, man.

Fallen Angels

Paul strongly implies that the fallen angels, who rebelled with Satan, have now been carefully organised into a hierarchy of Satanic power around the world. He describes, on several occasions, in real though imprecise terminology, a supernatural heavenly structure that was the real enemy he faced in his day-to-day ministry.

The most specific of these references (Ephesians 6:12 NASB) highlights the spiritual battle lines. *"For our struggle is not against flesh and blood (human beings), but against the rulers, against the powers, against the world forces of this darkness, against the spiritual forces of wickedness in the heavenly places."* Paul was under no illusion. He believed that even though his ministry was very much an earthly one to human beings made of flesh and blood, the reason why the battle was tough could be attributed far more to the spiritual powers in the heavenlies than the mere resistance of the human mind to the truth of the Gospel. He warns us, therefore, to take up the full armour of God that we may be able to stand firm against whatever Satan and his heavenly powers throw at us.

Paul's comments are certainly consistent with Daniel's experiences recorded in Daniel 10. Daniel, who, as a prisoner serving the emperors of Persia, came before God in fasting and prayer. Three weeks passed after he began to pray, when, suddenly, he was confronted with an angel who came in answer to his prayers.

The angel accounted for the 21-day delay in coming by describing something of the battle that took place in the heavenlies on the way! The 'angel prince of Persia' was only overcome with assistance from the Archangel Michael, the guardian angel of Israel (verse 21). Daniel's prayers initiated the aerial combat and his consequential experiences 'on the ground' were undoubtedly a result of what was happening 'in the air'.

Demons and Evil Spirits

In addition to the occasional references to Satan and his angels, the Gospel writers seem to use different Greek words, almost interchangeably, to represent the spiritual powers that are under Satan's control and which have invaded man. These are *daimon* or *daimonion* (demon), *ponera* (evil spirits) or *akatharta* (unclean spirits).

Demons, and evil or unclean spirits appear to mean the same thing to the Gospel writers (they are described as having similar effects in the lives of the demonised) but these spiritual powers also appear to be distinct from fallen angels. Luke, for example, (in Acts 23:8-9) seems to distinguish between angels and spirits. In general therefore, it is assumed that when we are talking about deliverance ministry we are dealing with demons and/or evil spirits.

However, if one tries to be too specific over these various definitions, one is in danger of trying to define what is scripturally indefinable. Nevertheless one is forced to ask a very obvious question. If Jesus cast demons and evil spirits out of people, and these spiritual beings are not fallen angels, then what are they, where did they come from and who created them?

In the Ephesians passage (6:16) Paul refers to the *"flaming arrows shot by the evil one"*. Just what are such flaming arrows? Are they in fact evil spirits that are sent by the evil one against man? Or are these merely temptations that arise because we are creatures of flesh?

Whatever they are Paul uses the analogy of a Roman soldier's shield, which is pictured as a shield of faith, with which one will be able to fend off these spiritual attacks. Pictorial language maybe, but the picture is one of protection from something that is likely to penetrate our defences unless dealt with effectively. Paul was an accurate writer and he is unlikely to have used a descriptive illustration such as this if the obvious interpretation would lead the reader into misunderstanding or error.

There are many questions on which scripture is either non-specific or silent, but that does not mean we should assume an attitude of arrogant indifference over what are nevertheless very important considerations. There are many major issues on which scripture is silent, but that does not mean we should suspend our intellects over these issues and imply that it is sin to attempt an answer! We can smile now at the early astronomers who were branded as heretics for proposing that the world was round, but for them the taunts and threats of current day theologians were painfully real!

Another question that is often asked is, *"Can demons multiply, can they breed?"* By way of comment on this difficult question, though by no means a comprehensive answer, is the obscure reference in Genesis 6:1-4 to the product of sexual intercourse between heavenly beings (sons of God) and the beautiful daughters of men. The wickedness of this conduct would seem to have been one of the major factors in God's decision to send the flood, and destroy life from off the face of the earth, excepting for Noah and his family.

Clearly the capacity for 'breeding', of a sort, is implied in this passage. Some commentators believe that evil spirits and demons were added to Satan's forces as a result of this further rebellion against God's creation, in which forbidden sexual relations were entered into.

Some commentators also link this obscure passage with Paul's instruction to the Corinthian ladies (1 Corinthians 11:2-16) to ensure that their heads are always covered when at worship or in prayer. In verse 10 he tells us this is 'for the sake of the angels', the implication being that when entering into the spiritual realms through prayer a woman is indicating to the angels, through the wearing of a head-dress, that she is protected by being under the cover of either her husband, or, for the unmarried, her father or other male member of the family or fellowship.

This was clearly an important issue in the Corinthian Church for Paul to have taken 14 verses of his letter to explain himself. There are no other scriptures that offer any help in this respect and all other information that is available in any sourcebook is extra-scriptural.

The majority of commentators believe that head-covering was a significant local issue, which the Corinthians had asked Paul about, and not an issue which was intended to provide detailed spiritual instruction for ladies throughout time. The fact that they are in the majority does not mean, however, that these commentators are necessarily right, for the style of Paul's writing in this passage is that of strong spiritual instruction.

As to any possible distinction between demons and evil spirits, it would certainly appear that the powers of darkness have varying size, power and authority. I understand that Satanists, whose daily stock-in-trade is the acquisition, manipulation and use of demonic power for their own end, recognise a definite difference in power and potential between demons and evil spirits, though not in their basic nature and character. Some would say that a demon is a collection of evil spirits that are grouped together for a specific purpose and with a corporate objective and, as such, has greater potential as a servant of Satan.

If this is the case then the Gospel writers would be quite accurate in using both words interchangeably, for whether one is dealing with a single evil spirit, or a group of them, it is still an evil spiritual power that is being confronted and expelled. Certainly in our own ministry we have encountered evil spirits that just lift off easily without too much of a fuss, and we have regularly encountered those who seem much stronger and have many more footholds in a person's life. Sometimes we have wondered whether or not we are dealing with a single demon or a collection of spirits, that is bound together, and is, therefore, able to hold on more tightly to the ground they have taken in the person's life.

Whilst questions like this are interesting, and on occasions important in actual ministry, the bottom line is that because Satan was defeated at Calvary no spiritual power that is under his control, be it demon, evil spirit or fallen angel, can ultimately stand against the power of the name of Jesus and whatever opposition they put up, they have to submit to the authority Jesus has given to his church!

And that is good news - indeed it is the message which is at the heart of the Gospel. The scripture *"Christ in you the hope of glory"* (Colossians 1:27 NASB) becomes dramatically expressive of the position we adopt, when we become Christians, with respect to the powers of darkness. Under their control and domination our only 'hope' is one of eternal separation from God. But because Christ is in us we are beneficiaries of his victory and have a rightful share in the glory that is to come. And because we are 'in Christ' we no longer have to be subject to 'the elemental spirits of the universe' (Galatians 4:3-5).

The Characteristics of Demons

Whilst there are many unanswered questions about the origin of demons, we do not need to be in such ignorance about their characteristics. There are many scriptural references to these, as well as observations that have been made, and which are common to those who have been involved in deliverance ministry right across the world. Some dismiss experiential theology as being extra-scriptural and, therefore, suspect or, even, irrelevant. But where such experience is consistent with scripture, and also consistent between different observers in different countries at different times we dare not dismiss its relevance.

Indeed, we must recognise the converse, that if our theology is inconsistent with the reliable experience of committed Christians who are ministering under the Lordship of Jesus Christ, and whose work is not in conflict with scripture, then we must reassess the understanding we thought we had about such matters!

Demons are Alive!

Demons are not just ideas or indefinable forces that operate from within the mind of man. They are living, functioning, spiritual beings with a mind, personality and will of their own that are dedicated to the service of Satan. All of this is directly implicit in the Gospel accounts of the encounters Jesus had with demons. (see Chapter 8 for a more detailed analysis of each of these incidents).

Jesus never treated a demon as anything else but a living entity who was in opposition to the interests of God and man. He was not surprised when they spoke out through the lips of a demonised person (Luke 4:34). He was not taken aback by their challenging him with either statements or questions from an obviously knowledgeable and intelligent mind, such as, *"What do I have to do with you, Jesus, son of the most high God?"* (Luke 8:28)

He himself said that *"when the unclean spirit goes out of a man, it passes through waterless places, seeking rest, and does not find it. Then it says 'I will return to my house from which I came'; and when it comes, it finds it unoccupied, swept and put in order. Then it goes and takes along with it seven other spirits more wicked than itself, and they go in and live there, and the last state of that man becomes worse than the first"* (Matthew 12:43-45 NASB).

In this comment Jesus is admitting that the demon is alive (it chooses to live somewhere); it has a will of its own (it chooses to do things of its own volition); it has enough intelligence to think that the place it has just come from might still be vacant and worth going back to; and enough innate wisdom to curry favour with higher demonic powers (more wicked than itself) by introducing them to a new home!

Their knowledge, however, is limited. The demon that spoke out to the sons of Sceva (Acts 19:15) said, *"I recognise Jesus, and I know about Paul, but who are you?"* All demons recognise and know about Jesus. Many times in ministry demons have recoiled in fear when they have seen Jesus in those who have been in our ministry teams. They cannot stand either his love for the person in need, or the authority that believers have because they have Jesus in them. But the demon's knowledge was limited as to who the sons of Sceva were. Some demons seem to be very knowledgeable, whilst others would seem to be almost totally ignorant! Their intelligence and knowledge vary enormously.

As to the emotions, demons definitely have feelings of their own. James tells us that *"the demons also believe and tremble with fear"* (James 2:19 GNB). By saying that the demons believe, James was not saying that demons trusted in God, but was recognising that demons are well aware of the truth about God.

This passage highlights the need not only for belief which is a mental assent to the truths of the Gospel, but also for belief which includes personal commitment to Jesus Christ. Many people are deceived into thinking that because they believe in God, then they are part of his kingdom. Without heart commitment and personal trust, belief in God is no different than the belief which demons have in the reality of God. The demons tremble with fear because they know that they are on the losing side.

In ministry we have seen demons express the whole range of emotions that people can also feel, sometimes deep anger at being exposed. At other times they whimper pathetically at the thought of being cast out of a home they have occupied for such a long time! We have come to realise that many people whose emotions are out of balance, or even out of control, are like that because of demonic control of their feelings.

The fact that demons are living spiritual beings does not give us any reason to be sympathetic towards them, or take any notice of their entreaties when they plead for permission to stay, sometimes even promising to be good if we will only not cast them out!

Demons are Disembodied

Demons do not have bodies of their own. Whilst they can exist outside a body, as do the ruling territorial spirits, they can express themselves most effectively through occupying the body of, preferably, a human being, or, an animal. Whether or not they ever had bodies of their own is another of those theological questions that will have to remain unanswered until that day when we will see all these spiritual mysteries in the light of eternity.

Some believe that such is their desire to occupy a body, that they must, at some time, have had one of their own which they are now deprived of. Be that as it may, when they take up residence in a human being (or an animal) they are contravening God's intentions for his creation.

A Roman legion contained up to 6000 men. It is generally assumed that the ruling spirit calling itself Legion probably had that number of spirits in its control. It is not surprising that the Gadarene demoniac had problems (Luke 8:26-39)! When it was clear that Jesus had won the battle, and the whole army of demons under Legion's control was going to have to leave, it was the demons who asked for permission to enter the pigs. It is presumed that out of sympathy for the man, whose prime need was to be free of the demons as quickly as possible, Jesus granted their request. I do not think the demons had anticipated, however, that the pigs would be such a short-term home as was occasioned by the whole herd being catapulted into the sea of Galilee!

Being disembodied creatures, however, introduces a dimension into the understanding of deliverance ministry which is absolutely vital and about which more will be said later. When people die, demons don't. They are completely unaffected by the death of their host! They have to leave the body, yes, but they are then free to carry on their work in someone else whom they will try to occupy. The whole subject of transference at death is such an important one that it will be dealt with extensively later in this book.

They Are Able to Speak

There are numerous examples in the scriptures of demons speaking out through the mouths of those people whom they are occupying. At Capernaum, right at the beginning of his ministry, the man stood up in the synagogue and shouted out at Jesus, *"What do we have to do with you, Jesus of Nazareth? Have you come to destroy us? I know who you are, the Holy One of God!"* (Luke 4:34 NASB).

This is a classic case of a demon overstepping the mark and so exposing itself that it got expelled from its host. The effect on the gathering at Capernaum that day was certainly electric, for after Jesus expelled the demon from the man (who was thrown down onto the ground by the demon during the actual deliverance) the crowd were amazed and said, *"With authority and power he commands the unclean spirits, and they come out."*

Their amazement was not at the fact that Jesus commanded the unclean spirits, but at the fact they actually came out when he commanded them! They were used to the Jewish exorcists who would attempt to expel demons with much noise but with very little success! The demon's precocious behaviour gave Jesus an important teaching opportunity.

There was a time, some years ago, when I was preaching in a fairly typical Anglican Church. I was five minutes into my sermon and beginning to teach about the power of the Name of Jesus over all the powers of darkness, when a lady stood up on her pew, started shouting at me, *"Shut up! Shut up! Shut up!!"* The demons within her could not stand what was being said.

She tried to tear a Bible up into small pieces to throw at me, but then the Holy Spirit fell upon her and she, like the man in Capernaum, was thrown down to the floor and finished up lying between the pews, with her head on a hassock, before she was delivered of an evil spirit! That church has never been the same since! Her deliverance marked a major turning point in the life of the church, which has since become a focus for renewal, personal counselling and healing ministry in the district.

Later that day there was a somewhat challenging discussion in the church about whether or not Christians could have demons. In the middle of the debate this lady got up, came to the front, took over the microphone and ended the discussion with one of the most profoundly brief statements on the subject I have ever heard. *"Now listen"* she said, *"I'm your church secretary. I've been born again five years, and I didn't think I had a demon, but I did. And now I don't, so there!"* With that she returned to her seat and saved the whole meeting hours of fruitless theological discussion! Christians certainly can, and do, have demons.

Most people who have any experience of healing and deliverance would admit that demons can and do sometimes speak. Indeed, the scriptural accounts make this very clear. A more contentious aspect of this subject, though, is whether or not you should talk to demons as part of the ministry. There are some who say you should never talk to demons, for all demons are liars and you will only be deceived. The problem with this viewpoint is that it is both unscriptural and untrue to the experience of many workers in this area.

True, there is only one (of the eight) major deliverance cases referred to in the Gospels in which Jesus did enter into conversation with the demons - that of a very severely demonised man, the Gadarene demoniac. (This whole story is looked at in greater depth in Chapter 8). But in this case, where there is at least an eight part conversation recorded by Luke, it seems to have been necessary. It is only, in our experience, with some severely demonised people that such conversation has sometimes become a necessary part of ministry.

As far as the demons speaking truth or lies is concerned, yes, they do attempt to deceive with lies, but it is usually easy to tell when a demon is lying. That is part of what the gift of discernment is all about. The demon should be placed under your authority and ordered to *"speak the truth which Jesus Christ of Nazareth would confirm as truth"*. As far as the scriptures are concerned there is no record of any demon speaking a lie when faced with either Jesus, or someone ministering in the name of Jesus. The demons always, in these circumstances, spoke the truth!

There have been some cases where it would have been impossible for us to proceed with ministry, had we not been able to order the demon to speak the truth and reveal how it got in. This information has sometimes proved absolutely vital. For you can then minister to the person in that area, deal with the sin (if that is what was revealed) and thus undermine the demon's right to be there.

Most times the person you are ministering to has an inner witness in their own spirit, from the Holy Spirit, as to whether or not the demon is speaking truth. The main caution I would add here is that one should never seek information from a demon for any other purpose than its own eviction. To seek information unrelated to the process of deliverance is bordering on mediumship.

There are times, also, when demons will try and hold the floor with conversation. They will try and distract, for example, with out of place humour and use any delaying tactic they can think of to try and avoid expulsion. The difficulty sometimes is not to laugh, for, on occasions, some of the things that are said are so bizarre as to be genuinely funny. I will never forget the demon that would not be silenced. It kept on coming out with delaying comments such as *"You are only doing this (deliverance ministry!) because you can't get a proper job!!"* and *"you only want to get me out so you can put me in the book!".* In a perverse sort of way that demon did achieve notoriety by getting in the book. But it was also cast out of the person concerned, and not just so as to get it in the book!

They Have Job Functions

The primary function of all demonic power (fallen angels, demons and/or evil spirits) is to serve Satan in the fulfilment of his rebellion against the living God and his creation, man. We saw in Chapter 3 how their mode of operation can be understood as being the reverse of that of angels. In summary this was:

1. Serve and worship Satan
2. Rejoice in Satan's works
3. Execute Satan's wishes
4. Negatively affect the affairs of nations
5. Undermine the work of the church
6. Specifically oppose and attack believers
7. Punish Satan's enemies
8. Perform extraordinary acts to advance Satan's cause
9. Attack personally each and every human being

The specific means by which these objectives are fulfilled are many and varied. As you read on through this book you will see how subtle and devious demons can be in the ways they infiltrate every part of the human being and oppose the work of the Holy Spirit in pointing people to Jesus.

The hatred that demons have for God's people has to be experienced to be believed. But it can be seen in the intense hatred that is sometimes expressed by people who have been taken over totally by the demonic, especially in their active opposition to, and persecution of, God's people. The pursuit of the Jews by the Germans during the holocaust is a prima facie example of this.

The demons sometimes have particular job functions. For example, it appears that the work of some is to bring sickness generally (spirits of infirmity), causing all manner of sickness and inciting vulnerability to 'whatever's going around'; on the contrary, however, some spirits of infirmity are highly specific to particular conditions, only causing, for example, arthritis, cancer, paralysis or some other condition.

It is quite common to come up against spirits that have come down a family line, causing the same symptoms in generation after generation. Doctors usually ask a patient who has a serious illness if there is any history of the condition in the family. Whilst there are good medical reasons why that is an important question, there are equally good spiritual reasons why it is a question that must be asked when counselling those in need. Deliverance from a spirit of infirmity that has travelled down the family lines can have far reaching consequences for the future generations and not just for the present-day victim!

Other spirits have a specific effect on the mind, controlling the thought processes of individuals so that they cannot function as God intended. Paul seems to be commenting on this when in Romans 12:2 he encourages Christians *"not to be conformed to this world, but be transformed by the renewing of your mind, that you may prove what the will of God is, that which is good, acceptable and perfect"* (NASB).

It is certainly hard for those who are affected by mind-controlling demons to understand spiritual truth. For example, those who have been involved in freemasonry, or who are children of freemasons often suffer in this direction. It is perhaps significant that I know of no active freemasons who are moving forward powerfully under the anointing of the Holy Spirit. Neither

do I know of any spirit-filled ministry which is headed up
by a freemason minister.

The emotions are another area where demons can have
highly specific roles, holding people in bondage to
experiences of the past. Most women who have been
seriously abused, sexually, have deep emotional problems
and many of these are prevented from being healed by the
presence of the demonic. Without deliverance ministry,
for many of them emotional blockage and bondage is a life
sentence.

Very often the specific job function of a demon is governed
by the entry point it was given into the person's life. More
understanding of this complex area will be given in the
consideration of demonic entry points in the next volume.

Once a demon has entered a person with a specific job
function it generally remains loyal to that job function
throughout its term of occupation. Part of the ministry of
deliverance can involve establishing what right the
demon had to enter in the first place, and undermining
that right, so that the person is not only delivered but is
also in a position of victory so that they, and their
children, can remain free.

They Know Their End

One thing that many Christians could learn from demons
is their understanding of the truth of scripture! Scripture
really is, as the book of Hebrews describes, *"living and
active and sharper than any two-edged sword"* (Hebrews
4:12 NASB). The demons hate scripture, for it has a divine
power over them which they cannot withstand. The
reason for this is not because scripture has any magic
quality, but because the spirit behind scripture is the Holy
Spirit.

Unfortunately many Christians have attributed to words
of scripture the qualities of a magicians toolbox, and use
it, often out of context, to justify their own desires and
ends. If we are not in fellowship with God through being

filled with the Holy Spirit, we will be prey to every wrong understanding the enemy might throw at us. We will not have the discernment to recognise when we move out of the Spirit, or the desire to do anything about it when someone else shares with us what they see happening.

In Matthew's account of the deliverance of the Gadarene demoniac (8:29) the demon cries out *"Have you come to torment us before the appointed time?"* Clearly this is a question loaded with understanding. The demon knew that its days were numbered and that a time has been set when Jesus will come again as King of Kings and Lord of Lords, and the destiny then for the devil and all his angels (and demons) is to be the lake of fire of Revelation 20 and 21.

On one occasion during ministry I was reading aloud from Revelation 20, which talks about them being tormented in the lake of fire, day and night, for ever. The demon in the person suddenly rose up, took over her body, and she lunged forward. In a moment of time she tore those particular pages out of my Bible! Such was the hatred expressed by the demons at the truth of God's word.

It is only truth that would make a demonic power behave in such a way. Another lady had six Bibles or New Testaments in her possession - all six of which were minus the whole of Revelation! Her demons would not let her keep a Bible in the house unless these incriminating pages had been removed!

Sometimes, when ministry has been difficult, and for some reason a demonic power has held on determinedly to ground in a person's life, I have read passages from the scripture about the final judgment and the effect has been dramatic in undermining the demon's power. The Word of God and the truth of scripture are indeed powerful weapons in our ministry armoury.

Many times I have seen peoples' attitude to the truth of scripture be completely changed, as in ministry the power of the Word of God has been applied. One cannot but be influenced by such experiences and recognise how right the reformers were to restore to the church a dependence and trust in the inspiration and accuracy of the Scriptures.

They Can Have Supernatural Strength

The accounts of the Gadarene demoniac in Matthew, Mark and Luke (one of the few healing stories that appear in all three synoptic Gospels) all give testimony to the fearsome strength of the man. They tell of how he would break the chains that were used to hold him down (Matthew 8:28-34. Mark 5:1-20 and Luke 8:26-39).

This was a perfectly ordinary man who was highly demonised. Of himself he had only the ordinary strength of a man, but when the demon manifested itself and empowered his muscles it was quite a different story. The strength he had was totally supernatural and utterly astonishing. No-one could hold him down.

Not everyone who is demonised manifests with such supernatural physical prowess. In the Gospel accounts only one (out of eight) of the specific deliverance ministries described is of this nature. In our own experience it is only a relatively small proportion of those people in need of deliverance who manifest in such a way. But when they do we have found that even a slender young girl, who would normally struggle to lift a couple of bricks, can acquire a physical strength which heavyweight weightlifters would envy!

How this phenomenon works, I have no idea, other than to think that the demon must be operating directly on the adrenal glands which pump 'power' into the muscles in the form of adrenalin. The fact that the adrenal glands sit on top of the kidneys, and this is the area of the body which, in Hebrew understanding, is the location of the heart of man (as opposed to the blood pump in the chest) might have some relevance.

In ministry one must always be aware of the possibility of this sort of manifestation occurring. For this and other reasons we would never enter deliverance ministry alone, and in the case of severely demonised people the ministry team might need to be three or four strong, or even more on occasions when continuing in ministry to someone whose track record is known! The first time that something like this happens it can be a little off-putting (some would say frightening!), but pressing on in ministry, notwithstanding the manifestations will lead to victory.

The son of a close friend of mine greeted me at the door of their church (after I had preached) with the words, *"It's a good job you stopped preaching when you did, if you'd carried on much longer I would have come up and thumped you."* And he wasn't joking! That afternoon I counselled him and discovered that he had been listening to heavy metal music and through this he had become demonised with spirits of violence. At the same time he was moving away from the Lord and had little desire to follow Jesus, in spite of an earlier commitment he had made.

I asked him if he wanted to be set free. He chose to repent of his involvement with heavy metal music and recommit his life to the Lord. I then took authority over the powers of darkness which were controlling his life and for a while it seemed as though *"all hell had broken loose"* as this strong young man developed an even greater strength, which was totally supernatural. But, in the name of Jesus, he was set free, and his life was totally transformed as a result. Just twelve months later this young man, who had been rapidly running away from God, was at Bible College training to spend his life as an evangelist. Without deliverance his life would have quickly descended into violence and despair.

They Are Well Organised and Are Under Higher Authority

Some people say that Satan's kingdom is a kingdom of chaos and therefore we should not expect to find any order in it. They use arguments such as this to oppose any teaching which might indicate that Satan's kingdom is organised in a hierarchy of demonic power. They forget, however, that Satan himself was part of a well organised hierarchy of angelic power before the fall, and in organising his own troops he is only imitating the angelic realms.

Our experience is that Satan's kingdom is certainly a kingdom of chaos, but it is chaos which is highly organised and designed to inflict the maximum harm on the saints of God. The ruling spirits over a nation are well-organised with a hierarchy of control over different regions, cities, towns and districts. In some towns, for example, you can actually 'feel' the difference as you move from one area to another. Peter Wagner, of the Fuller Theological Seminary, has just edited a major work on the whole subject of *Territorial Spirits* (See Bibliography).

In addition to territorial ruling spirits we are also aware that there are functional ruling spirits over both countries and towns, with specific job functions of inciting particular forms of behaviour which are contrary to God's purposes for man. For example, spirits that encourage sexual abuse, homosexuality, pornography, violence, greed etc, etc. It doesn't take much imagination to think about what spirits rule over certain areas of London, or any other major city in the world with well-defined business areas, red-light districts etc.

I was once told by a man who was being freed of a homosexual spirit that he could go into any town in the world and without asking anyone for directions be in the centre of the gay community in a matter of minutes. He was always, unerringly, led by a spiritual force to the area he was looking for. Drug addicts are led like this to the pushers of drugs. Others have told me similar stories of how clear demonic directions encouraged them in the pursuit of sin. Satan has organised himself very carefully so as to produce maximum chaos.

Within the lives of individuals there is often a well-organised structure of demonic control, especially with those who have been demonised a long time, even from earliest childhood. What Satan has claimed for himself he does not lightly give up. Bill Subritzky, in his book *Demons Defeated*, talks about three strong men (demonic powers) which he has found are often in control, namely Jezebel, Death and Hell, and Antichrist. We have certainly ministered to many people who have been under the control of these particular demons, but we have also encountered other 'controlling demons' that have been the 'strong men'.

In many cases we have found it necessary with severely demonised people to unpick carefully the demonic structure and loose the demons from each other's control before they could be loosed from the individual. Some people question why this should be necessary when there is little evidence in the scriptures about ministry procedures such as this.

In the next volume will be found much more information which will help the reader to understand this. For the time being remember Jesus's advice about deliverance when he said that if you want to plunder a man's house, first bind the strong man (Matthew 12:29). Sometimes there is a whole series of 'strong men' who have to be dealt with one at a time.

It seems that very few demons operate on their own. They are allowed to use their 'initiative' within the bounds of their instructions. But each one is under the authority of a higher power, until, ultimately, one reaches Satan himself - the pinnacle of the structure of the powers of darkness. Lesser demons also seem to be in great fear of those above them in the hierarchy.

We have seen many times how Satan's kingdom is built on fear and what the consequences will be (to the demon) if it steps outside its instructions. We have seem them whimper with terror at the thought of being cast out of their host, because they would have to report their mission as a failure to a higher authority. Especially is this the case if they had managed to gain a foothold in the life of someone on whom the anointing of God was resting for major ministry.

It is clear from the scriptures that a mantle of spiritual authority and special anointing rested on certain people whom God had chosen for specific tasks. Read the stories of Samuel, David, Samson, Daniel, Jeremiah etc, if you wish to pursue this theme in the scriptures. It seems as though such a mantle is recognisable by the spiritual powers on both sides of the war, so that the enemy targets those people, especially, with temptations and diversions which are designed to prevent the calling of God upon their lives being fulfilled.

One may ask why God allows such testing for one has to remember that every such test has been allowed by God. Remember the story of Job (Job 1:6-12). Without testing we will never know just how strong we are and where our weaknesses lie. To be tempted, and fall into sin as a result, and then rise up again, knowing the weakness and how to combat it, is often a preparation for a major ministry or greater testing, in the very area of life where the weakness is.

Simon Peter is a prime example of this. Through fear of what might happen to him he fell into sin three times by denying Jesus just before the crucifixion. After the resurrection Jesus personally ministered to Peter (John 21:15-19) and in spite of the failures commissioned Peter to feed the sheep. Then Jesus warned him that one day he would suffer martyrdom. Because of his failure, and the healing that Jesus gave, I believe Peter's fear of death had been dealt with so that one day he would be strong enough to face martyrdom without having to deny his Lord again.

Demons are Legalistic

It's interesting that Jesus was so condemnatory of those who were adamant about the fulfilling of the letter of the law, but were totally blind when it came to understanding the Spirit that is behind the law. The conflict between law and grace has kept the minds of theologians occupied for untold centuries!

Whilst obedience to the will of God is one of the pre-requisites for moving under the anointing of the Holy Spirit, Jesus made it very clear that obedience to the will of God and blind obedience to the law were sometimes, perhaps often, in conflict! It almost seems, from the Gospel accounts, that Jesus took particular pleasure in healing people on the sabbath in front of the Pharisees! Their reactions indicated the legalistic hardness of their hearts.

When the traditions of men become more important than sensitivity to the Spirit of God the church is in a bad way. I have often seen this being worked out in the dictates of denominationalism. Time and again I have sensed the Spirit wanting to move in a particular way in the life of a church, but it is as if the church is solidly anchored to hundreds of years of denominational concrete and if God wants to move in a way that is contrary to 'our tradition' then it certainly can't be God! And even if it is God, the people seem to say 'he had better think of ways to work in our church which fit in with the way we do things round here!'

It's amazing how the hidden Pharisees come creeping out of the woodwork. This may sound like a bad parody of the worst of churches. Unfortunately it is neither a parody, nor are such attitudes restricted to the worst of churches!

Even churches which have been instrumental in moving forward in renewal, under the leading of the Holy Spirit, can easily get themselves locked into their particular brand of charismatic experience, with the result that they

look with grave suspicion on any church which claims to
be charismatic, but whose experience is different from
their own!

What is happening is that religious spirits are
legalistically holding the church in bondage. Unless they
are dealt with through deliverance of the whole church
fellowship, the building and especially of the leadership,
legalism will eventually be a controlling influence on the
church.

The most effective church based ministries we have been
associated with have been in churches where the ruling
spirits have been dealt with effectively by the leadership,
leaving the fellowship free to respond to the Holy Spirit
without their understanding being clouded by the
legalism of religious spirits. Deliverance from religious
spirits is a significant and important aspect of
deliverance ministry.

In the Pharisees I believe that Jesus was facing religious
spirits. At Nazareth I believe it was religious spirits that
rose up in anger when Jesus proclaimed he had come to
set captives free. Similarly I believe it was religious
spirits that motivated the priests when they sought to use
the technicalities of the law against Jesus, so as to
establish a water-tight case for disposing of this
individual who so threatened their hold on the people.

Demons are given rights by man through sin. Unless that
sin is repented of, demons will legalistically hang onto the
ground they have been given. For example, no amount of
shouting at a demon of lust will effect deliverance, if the
person receiving ministry is continuing in an adulterous
relationship and unrepentant about his or her sexual sin!
The demon has a legal right to stay.

One of the commonest reasons why demons do not leave
Christians is the fact they have a right to be there which
they will legalistically hang on to. On many occasions we
have struggled to bring a person to freedom, but it has
only been when the legal right to be there has been

exposed, and that right dealt with at the cross, that deliverance has eventually been effective.

In churches it is often the sins of the leadership of the church in previous generations that have given demons a right over the fellowship. For example, there are many Anglican churches whose foundation or dedication ceremonies included masonic rituals, sometimes as an acknowledgement and thanks to the local freemasons who contributed money towards the building of the church.

The practise of freemasonry is idolatry. Idolatry is an anathema to the living God. The commandments warn us (Exodus 20:4-5) that the sins of the fathers in this respect will be visited on the children for three or four generations. And if during those four generations there is, for example, further masonic sin a new line of demonic control is established.

Spirits of freemasonry will legalistically exercise their right over whatever congregation is gathered in that church for all of time. They will hold the fellowship into the bondage of the past, unless the matter is properly dealt with through repentance for the sins of the ancestors (the Nehemiah principle of Nehemiah 1:6-7, see also Leviticus 26:40) by the present-day leadership of the church and by effective spiritual warfare against the ruling spirits through praise, worship and deliverance ministry. Effective cleansing of both churches and individuals requires specific ministry to deal with the legalistic rights that a demon has.

At one time the Lord gave me a word of knowledge about sexual sin that had taken place in a person's life some 17 years previously. After the meeting a woman came forward to a member of the team and confessed that she and her husband had commenced intercourse some three months before the wedding date. Having confessed her sin of so many years previously the spirit that came into her through her sin was then addressed and ordered to leave. It's legal right to be there had been dealt with through repentance. Immediately she convulsed on the floor into what was a *grand mal* epileptic fit. Ten minutes later she had another one as another spirit came out of her.

The symptoms we observed were just like those described in the scripture, when Jesus ministered deliverance to the epileptic boy (Luke 9:37-43). After it was all over she got up completely whole proclaiming she was healed of epilepsy. We then learnt that she had commenced with epilepsy shortly after her marriage and that she had been a sufferer for all of those seventeen years.

It appears that in her case, her sexual sin had given a spirit of epilepsy a right either to enter, or be activated if it had been lying dormant after being inherited generationally. We have sometimes seen people, who had not yet developed particular diseases, be delivered of spirits of infirmity whose job function was to induce the disease when released to do so, either by the sin of the person or through the working of a curse on the generation line. When these particular demons left the manifesations were typical of the disease in question!

This lady had been prayed for many times in the past, but it was only when, through repentance and forgiveness, the sin was dealt with, and the demon's legal right made void, that she could be delivered and healed. When asked how she knew she was healed, she said that normally, after a fit, she has to be three days in a darkened room, and suffers intense pain and other symptoms.

After those two fits, which were manifestations of the demons leaving, she had no side effects whatsoever and got up off the floor completely whole and in her right mind. In consultation with her doctor she came off all drugs over a period of time and eighteen months later she had shown no signs of epilepsy.

There is no doubt that demons are highly legalistic, both with respect to their own hierarchy of demonic power and the instructions they have been given and also with respect to the rights they were given to enter the person concerned. I believe that the paralysed man in Luke 5 was delivered by Jesus of a spirit of infirmity, for it was only after Jesus had dealt with the sin in the man's life (Luke 5:17-26) that Jesus was able to heal him of the paralysis. Three times I have seen people become paralysed as a particular demon has surfaced and manifested its character during deliverance.

Some Demons Have Animalistic Character

The manifestation of Satan as a serpent in Genesis 3 is the first scriptural illustration of a 'demonic' manifestation in the form of an animal. It is interesting to note that when Jesus talked with the 72, after they returned full of joy at being able to cast out demons, he told them *"I have given you authority to tread upon serpents and scorpions and over all the power of the enemy"* (Luke 10:19 NASB).

I do not believe that in this instance Jesus was referring solely to the actual creatures that snakes and scorpions are, but also (or possibly exclusively) to the manifestations of demons as snakes and scorpions. For in the same breath Jesus includes victory over all the power of the enemy, implying that snakes and scorpions are just two aspects of his power.

Certainly we have seen many demons manifest during deliverance as snakes or scorpions. People have finished up slithering across the floor in an incredibly snake like manner, or with their backs bent so far over that the tail of their spine resembled the sting of a scorpion. It seems as though these are the commonest animalistic manifestations, being part of the basic character of the demonic. In addition to these we have experienced almost every possible animalistic manifestation you can think of.

Innocent looking girls have suddenly become fierce tigers as the Holy Spirit has exposed hidden demonic power. Demonic lions, bulls, dogs, rams, goats, cockerels and many, many more have surfaced and been despatched in the name of Jesus. The Psalmist says (Psalm 91:13 GNB) *"you will trample down lions and snakes, fierce lions and poisonous snakes."* And just what was the monster Leviathan (Psalm 74:14)? On a few occasions we have encountered demonic beasts by this name!

One can rightfully ask just how do demons acquire such characteristics. In addition to the innate character of the demon, which can be animalistic, it also appears that a demon will acquire the characteristics of animals (and people) it has occupied previously. So if a demon has been in a goat then it has the knowledge and capacity to manifest as a goat.

Unfortunately we have had to deal with many people who have been caught in the web of witchcraft or Satanism, or are descended from people who have been involved. Some of the rituals involve the sacrifice of animals into which demons have entered. When the sacrifice has been made the demons then enter people who are involved in the ritual, bringing with them the character of the beast they have just come from.

With some religions the ruling spirit is an animalistic demon. Worshippers of the elephant God acquire a spirit which manifests as an elephant. All Sikhs have the name Singh, meaning lion. When Sikhs become Christians they need deliverance from all the controlling spirits of Sikhism, the ruling one often being the spirit of a lion. At one of our training courses recently an ex-Sikh, who had been a Christian five years, was still suffering from a lot of problems. He asked for prayer and deliverance from some of the things that were controlling him.

The moment I began to pray against the demons concerned, the ruling spirit of Sikhism surfaced, absolutely furious that some of its kingdom was in danger of being stripped away. It roared away in defiance and it took some ten minutes before the man, who was in a state of shock at the power of the beast that was in him, could recover control of his own body. It was a very important learning experience for the others present on the course, as they witnessed over the next couple of hours the complete demonic kingdom being stripped of its power and authority, through repentance from sin and the gradual establishment of the Lordship of Jesus in every area of his life.

He had no idea that his involvement in Sikhism was still ruling him demonically in his flesh, even though he was born again of the Spirit of God. At the end of the ministry the lion which had roared so fiercely earlier in the evening left without much of a struggle. Once it had lost all its support troops it was as weak as all the other demons.

We have also encountered many of the beasts of mythology. Beasts that appear never to have existed as living creatures, but which have a very real existence in the demonic realms. Beasts such as griffins and dragons, werewolves and other were-creatures (half-beast and half man), leviathan, the phoenix and the like.

Many of the ancient gods of the Greeks, the Romans and the Egyptians were worshipped because they had power, but the power which worshippers enlisted through their ritual worship, sacrifices and, often, sexual rituals was that of the ruling spirit of the shrine. As a result worshippers would receive a spirit with the characteristics of the ruling demon of the shrine. And that spirit would find its way down the family lines affecting the generations yet to come.

It sometimes comes as quite a shock to people to discover the echelons of demonic power they have been battling with over the years. It is hardly surprising that the physical conditions they have do not respond to conventional medical treatment!

In the psychiatric arena people who manifest grand delusions, and describe the character of these creatures (which the psychiatric profession would not recognise as demons), are far more sane than most people realise. For

many of them are under the control of demonic power
which has come down their family lines and, for some
reason has been given a right to manifest and control the
individual's life. More will be said about unseating these
powers and ministering to the heavily demonised in the
next volume.

They Work Together in Families

The spiritual strength we gain through working with
other people is well known. In the scriptures it is
expressed in the Old Testament with the words *"a cord of
three strands is not quickly torn apart"* (Ecclesiastes 4:12
NASB) and in the New Testament by Jesus, when he
talked about the spiritual power of agreement between two
or three believers (Matthew 18:19).

Demons have taken advantage of the same principle. For
it is commonly found that several demons work together
to support each other in their work. One of the commonest
examples of a family of demons is the group which
control rejection. The ruling spirit of rejection (which can
enter a person even when they are in their mother's
womb) is usually supported by a spirit of fear of rejection
and a spirit of self rejection as well.

The spirit of fear of rejection rides into the emotions to
prevent people who have been rejected going into
circumstances where further rejection might occur. That
is how the person is responding inside, but in reality it is
the demon who is afraid that the person might feel
accepted, for that would undermine the power of
rejection! So rejected people are made to fear further
rejection. They are then in danger of hating themselves,
and as soon as they give way to feelings of self-hatred they
open themselves up to a spirit of self-rejection which
ensures that the rejective cycle cannot easily be broken.

In their book *Pigs in the Parlour* (demons inside a person)
the Hammonds list out many of the demonic families they
have found working together. This is a helpful guide

which will give many clues to further ministry that some individuals will need. But I would add that the Hammonds' experience is largely based on ministry in the United States where there are different ruling and generational spirits in operation.

In Western Europe, for example, where there is a much stronger witchcraft influence, going back many generations, there are many other powerful groupings which are often encountered. Other regions will also have their own demonic groupings which are typical of the culture and religious background of the indigenous races.

In a person who has become demonised, a demon that is already in residence will attempt to strengthen its power base by inviting others to come in as well. For example, a spirit of lust, which enters through the eyes, might then encourage the person to get involved in sexual sin. As a result a spirit of fornication will enter. And once this demonic doorway is open it acts like a demonic tube down which the enemy can pour his workers!

They Will Try and Remain Hidden

Demons do their work most effectively when they are able to lie hidden. There are many, many people who are struggling with physical, emotional, mental or spiritual problems who are really struggling with demons and don't know it. And what is often more sad is that those Christians who have been trying to help them have not realised what the real problem has been either!

Satan always prefers to work in the dark. John 3:20 expresses very explicitly the attitude of demons to the light of Jesus that comes through the Holy Spirit. *"For everyone who does evil hates the light, and does not come to the light, lest his deeds should be exposed"*. Whilst John was talking about people, he was also describing precisely how people behave when they are driven by a demon who wants to remain hidden. Exposure to the light is the very last thing that a demon would want.

One of the reasons why those who minister deliverance are often spoken against by other Christians, is that they are such a threat to the hidden powers of darkness - often religious spirits that control those who are, apparently, so concerned! Those who would criticise deliverance ministries need to look very carefully at Matthew 12:22-32.

This whole section is about the deliverance ministry of Jesus and Jesus concludes his comments by saying that *"he who is not with me* (in this ministry of deliverance is implied) *is against me, and he who does not gather with me scatters."* Those who would stand against deliverance ministry need to examine their own hearts and see if there is not some hidden demonic power in their own lives stimulating the opposition. They need to recognise that opposing the work of the Holy Spirit, in empowering God's people to cast out demons, does, according to Jesus, make them scatterers! (Matthew 12:30).

One of the gifts of the Holy Spirit is the gift of discerning those spirits which are not of God. Christian leaders should not be standing on the sidelines questioning the validity of a major part of Jesus's ministry. Rather they should be praying that the Lord will develop in them the gift of discernment to its full potential, so that they can effectively expose and deal with hidden demonic power that would stand against the work of the Holy Spirit in the renewal of the church and the extension of the Kingdom.

They Have to Bow to Jesus' Name

No matter how much power a demon may think it has, it's master Satan was defeated at Calvary. Whenever a demon challenges my authority to cast it out I begin to undermine its arrogance by asking who its master is. Eventually they will admit that Satan is their master. At this point their resistance is broken. For once having admitted this they know that their power is limited.

Scripture very clearly expresses the truth that Satan was defeated when Jesus rose again from the dead, and that

Satan is firmly under the feet of Jesus. That means that for those who are in Christ, Satan is also under their feet. And if Satan is under our feet then every demon in hell is also under our feet!

Philippians 2:10 is an important victory scripture to read to arrogant demons, *"At the name of Jesus every knee should bow, of those in heaven, and of those on earth and of those under the earth"* (NKJV). There is no being that will not have to bow the knee to Jesus' name. It is only in his name that we do have power and authority over them, and the demons know that they have to submit to his authority when it is expressed through the lips of believers. When we minister deliverance in the name of Jesus we have all the authority of the courts of heaven to back up our legal claim against demonic power.

In Conclusion

The powers of darkness are real, be they fallen angels, demons or evil spirits. They are living beings with personality and the power of speech, but they are disembodied and have to live out their existence in someone else's body. They are all in the service of Satan and deployed by him against mankind.

When they occupy a person they inflict their character and presence on the victim. They will try and do this whilst remaining hidden so that the person will not seek out the ministry of deliverance, the only course of action that can ultimately help them. All demons have to bow the knee to Jesus, however, so it is only Christians who are able to bring healing to demonised people.

Demonisation can be carried on down the generation lines as a result of the sins of the fathers (Exodus 20:5, Leviticus 26:40 and Lamentations 5:7) which affect the children and the children's children. Much more will be said about this subject in the next volume when dealing with the practicalities of personal deliverance ministry.

Chapter 7

The Direct Encounters of Jesus with Satan

Jesus was a marked man. The moment he was conceived in the womb of Mary the whole of hell went on red alert. God's counter plan to the fall had been long expected. When it was finally revealed, and Old Testament prophecy was being fulfilled, Satan played every trick in his book to try and prevent Jesus voluntarily laying down his life for the sins of the world as the first ever totally sinless man.

The Gospels record the major physical attacks on Jesus's life. Herod's massacre of the babies in Bethlehem was the first, and no doubt there were others during the thirty years in which Jesus prepared for his ministry. Satan used Herod's jealousy and fear to prompt this act of infanticide. But an angel intervened who warned Joseph in a dream that they had to flee at once to Egypt. They did and Jesus escaped the consequences of Herod's plot (Matthew 2:13-23).

What a lesson this was in obedience. Nothing could have been more bizarre for Joseph, a rural carpenter, than to immediately get out of bed and, that night, put his wife and baby on a donkey and begin a journey into exile of many hundreds of miles. We don't know how long they were in Egypt, excepting that the same angel told them when Herod was dead and that they were back in Nazareth by the time Jesus was twelve, the next recorded event in Jesus's life.

The other specific physical attacks on the life of Jesus that we know about were at Nazareth, when the congregation from the local synagogue tried to throw him over a cliff

(Luke 4:28-29); on the sea of Galilee when what appears to have been a demonically induced storm threatened the safety of the boat (Luke 8:22-25); and at Jerusalem, where the crowd objected to the implications of his teaching about demons, and his claims to be 'I AM', so they tried to stone him to death (John 8:48-59). In addition to these demonically instigated physical attacks, however, there were other specific encounters that Jesus had with Satan himself which reveal much of Satan's tactics in the way he attacks Christians by using demons.

The Baptism of Jesus
(Matthew 3:13-17; Mark 1:9-11 and Luke 3:21-22)

When Jesus was baptised in the river Jordan by John the Baptist, it was against John's better judgment. He knew who Jesus was and found it incongruous that he, the forerunner of Jesus the Messiah, should be the one who was being used to baptise him! After all, wasn't John's baptism a baptism of repentance, and what did Jesus need to repent of? He could not have done anything wrong, for he was the Messiah!

What John could not have understood was the divine purpose in Jesus being baptised by John. The fact that John's baptism was a baptism of repentance was the critical point. For ultimately Jesus had come to die for the sins of the world. In submitting to a baptism of repentance it was his first public association with the sin of mankind. If he had not submitted to this baptism, and stood with sinners in an act of 'repentance' on behalf of all those who would believe and receive life through the cross, then he could not have gone to Calvary to die for their sins either.

No wonder his baptism gave such pleasure to the Father. For when Jesus went down into the river Jordan, God's rescue plan was finally being put into action. As Jesus came up out of the water the Holy Spirit came down from heaven and rested on him. So God chose this moment of

total obedience, in being baptised of John, to also baptise
Jesus with the Holy Spirit. Then a voice from heaven was
heard to say, *"You are my beloved Son; in you I am well
pleased"* (Luke 3:22 NKJV).

From this moment on Jesus was an active threat to Satan
and his Kingdom. Up to that point he was a potential
threat, but now, having been baptised in the Holy Spirit
the battle lines had been drawn up, for Jesus was now
equipped to start unseating demonic power from Satan's
strongholds. Concerted action from the powers of
darkness was now required. And this wasn't a task that
Satan would risk delegating, even to his highest aide in
the Satanic ranks. It was a job for Satan himself!

The Temptations in the Wilderness
(Matthew 4:1-11; Mark 1:12-13 and Luke 4:1-13)

Luke 4:1 records that Jesus returned from the Jordan full
of the Holy Spirit, implying that there was now something
radically different about Jesus. His life's work had begun.
The Spirit of God then led Jesus into the wilderness for a
40 day time of prayer and fasting prior to the
commencement of his public ministry.

This is an important spiritual principle. Major ministries
require major times of preparation. But let not the ardent
Christian think that in following Jesus's example he is in
for a wonderful time of endless peace and joy - whether
the fast is for one or forty days!

Whenever people withdraw from normal activities, at the
leading of the Holy Spirit, Satan is immediately on the
alert. He will do everything he can to attack at that time
and undermine the saint at the very point of his highest
spiritual endeavour. When God is dealing with a man or
woman of God 'the devil and his angels' are not usually
very far away!

I believe that Satan looked on this time in the wilderness
as one of his best, and last, personal opportunities to
divert Jesus from his mission. It is never easy to count

the cost of following God unconditionally. And sometimes the real cost can prove to be very high indeed. Satan knows this and will test us to the limit over what following Jesus will cost us. This is what he did with Jesus. On the other side of the balance is the potential blessing from God which will be the fruit of obedience.

The cost is real and measurable, the fruit is, at the outset, unreal and unmeasurable. Jesus warned us always to count the cost of following him (Luke 14:25-33). There are many Christians who at this point have done just that, but have found the cost to be too high and turned back from God's first plan for their life. They have done what the world would judge as eminently sensible and which most of their friends, Christian and non-Christian alike, would commend.

In looking at the specific tactics of Satan in tempting Jesus we see many lessons for the Christian in the way demons attack believers. What needs to be understood at this point is that to be tempted and tested is not sin. But that if we do fall into temptation, and sin, then we have made ourselves vulnerable to the agent of the attack. At that point we can become demonised, but scripture tells us plainly (in addressing Christians) that *"if we confess our sins* (that means agree with what God thinks about our sins), *God is faithful and righteous to forgive us our sins and to cleanse us from all unrighteousness"* (1 John 1:9 NASB).

If we do not take that course of action and receive the cleansing (as well as the forgiveness - they are two very different things) then I believe that at that point, whether we are Christian or not, we are vulnerable to demonic control and being demonised. That is a fact of both personal experience and of countless stories that have been unravelled in the counselling room.

Even before Jesus had come, Satan had successfully diverted many people from their God-given calling. I believe he will have rejoiced at the many elderly people who looked back with regret, and wondered what might have been if they had had the courage to say an unconditional 'Yes' to God. Satan's diversionary tactics had been effectively tested over hundreds of years of demonic experience. He had had plenty of practice before turning his attentions to Jesus to try and head off this ultimate threat to his earthly kingdom and his eternal fate.

The First Temptation
(Matthew 4:3-4, Luke 4:3-4)

"If you really are God's Son, order this stone to turn into bread" (Luke 4:3). The temptation would appear to be that of using his supernatural power to turn some stones into bread and meet his immediate physical needs. As anyone who has fasted for a reasonable period of time will know, that is a very real temptation.

But the subtlety of this temptation does not lie in the obvious, although using divine power for less than divine purposes is a real enough temptation, which we must be aware of in any area of Christian ministry. James comments on this aspect of the Christian pilgrimage in saying *"when you ask, you do not receive, because your motives are bad; you ask for things to use for your own pleasures"* (James 4:3 GNB).

No, the real test to Jesus of this temptation lay in the doubt introduced in the opening words of the temptation, *"If you are God's Son"*. Only days earlier Jesus had heard his Father's voice from heaven saying, *"You are my beloved Son; in you I am well pleased"* (Luke 3:22 NKJV). Satisfying Jesus's physical hunger was only the cover for a much deeper test. For Satan knew that the temptation for Jesus to use his own gifting for selfish purposes would be unlikely to throw him off course, even though it could be very effective indeed with lesser mortals!

Jesus believed he knew why he had come to earth. He expected there would now be three years of gruelling ministry, beginning with popularity but facing steadily

increasing opposition and ultimately crucifixion. He
believed his Father had called him from heaven for this
task. He believed that he was God's Son.

And yet, could he be mistaken? Were all those stories
about his birth, that Mary had told him, really true? If he
did go ahead with all that he believed was to follow, would
people really be saved from their sins? If he died, would
God really raise him from the dead? Satan must have
pounded Jesus's mind with countless such questions.
Questions that were designed to sow seeds of doubt, in the
hope that just one little seed might take root. For doubt is
deadly. Doubt is the forerunner of unbelief, which is the
opposite of faith and *"whatever is not from faith is sin"*
(Romans 14:23 NASB).

If only Jesus could doubt (disbelieve), even for one
moment, anything of what God the Father had told him,
then Jesus would have sinned and Satan's arrow would
have pierced his very heart and the rescue mission would
have failed. *"If you are God's Son . . . then why not prove
it? Just a few loaves of bread. See those stones? Turn them
into bread, then you will really know that everything God
said is true. Just a little test. Go on - then you'll never
need to doubt again."* So subtle, but also so deadly.

The voice of the serpent that floored Eve was heard again
in that wilderness experience of Jesus, *"Has God really
said . . "* (Genesis 3:1). Has God really said all those
things? Why not test your powers - and if they work then
you'll know its all true. It all sounds so innocent, but if
Jesus had for one moment entertained the possibility that
he needed to prove to himself that he was the Son of God,
doubt would have entered in. Satan so often uses doubt to
lead people into sin, and one sin would have destroyed the
glorious and eternal potential of Calvary.

Jesus saw through it all. He recognised the voice of the
serpent for what it was, deception, and using scripture
with devastating effect he reminded Satan of what he
already knew, *"Man shall not live by bread alone, but
man lives by every word that proceeds from the mouth of*

man lives by every word that proceeds from the mouth of the Lord" (Deuteronomy 8:3 NKJV). The words that Jesus had heard from the mouth of the Father were enough for him, and he did not need to turn any stones into bread to test his calling. God had spoken, and he had no intention of doubting one word of the Father.

Satan's first attack had failed and he was sent from the battle arena in disarray. But not for long. When one line of attack fails, Satan does not give up. He and his demons are well versed in the effectiveness of persistence. He would be back.

Before looking at temptation number two, a word of encouragement to those who have fallen into doubt and unbelief. Especially for those who are going through wilderness experiences and are struggling with doubt - doubt about God, doubt about the reliability or nature of their personal calling in life and self-doubt about their ability to cope with whatever calling God has given.

For Jesus, doubt would have spelt the failure of his mission. But not so for you! Because of the success of his mission and the potential there now is for forgiveness, you need not fear that because you have given in to Satan in this area in the past that there is no way back. There is - and from the consequences of any sin, so the same must be true of doubt. Forgiveness, cleansing and recommissioning are part of God's loving provision for all his children. The entrance gate is marked confession and repentance. Don't let the enemy keep you in defeat.

If God has called you to a work, and you have known the blessing of God on your ministry, but you are currently languishing in spiritual despair, get up, turn round, deal with the sin element in your present situation, go back to the point at which you began to falter and get moving again in the right direction.

Satan will hate it, he will do everything in his power to keep you where you are. He will throw fresh temptations and tests at you, and use others to speak words of discouragement. Ignore them all. God is for you. And he wants to do with you what he did with Simon Peter after the resurrection - forgive you, restore you and recommission you in his service.

Also, Satan still uses this temptation in its original format to try and encourage Christians, especially leaders, into proving their ministries in wrongful ways! He whispers words of doubt into their minds which often run like this, *"If God has really called you, why don't you do this, that or the other to prove it."* As a result many Spirit-filled and anointed leaders fall into the trap of unnecessarily defending themselves and always trying to prove themselves by spiritual performance.

One of Tozer's five keys to spiritual power in Christian leadership is simply 'do not attempt to defend what God has called you to do'. Some leaders have failed to perform adequately and subsequently have fallen for the ultimate lie, that they were never called in the first place and should resign from their ministry. Jesus knew that temptation well and is always ready to help us reject such Satanic undermining of a God-given calling and forgive us if we have already fallen into Satan's trap.

Satan takes some Christians further still down the slippery slide of doubt, so that eventually they cease to believe that they are even born-again children of God. They come to doubt their salvation and the reality of eternal life, and eventually cease to be part of the active church. No wonder James so forcefully attacked the castle of doubt which so often dominates peoples' lives.

The Second Temptation
(Matthew 4:5-5, Luke 4:9-12)

Satan tries again to get an arrow of doubt through Jesus's spiritual armour. This time he invites Jesus to prove he is the Son of God by jumping off the pinnacle of the temple in Jerusalem. The need for a hungry person to have bread is obvious, and to prove his divinity by making bread out of stones could have some logic about it. But what logical reason could there be for Jesus to find the idea of jumping off the temple in Jerusalem remotely attractive?

The Satanic mind is very devious, and in attempts to deceive mankind, Satan and his demons will often quote back to us things we would like to hear. Jesus had summarily concluded the first temptation by quoting scripture, so what better way to start than by quoting scripture back to Jesus? Perhaps, in that way, Jesus could be caught off guard?

Satan had done his homework well. He had found a scripture to support his devious cause. And he devised the temptation so that this time he had scripture to support the course of action he was recommending. Evidence indeed that not every use of scripture has to be listened to as if it is the law of the Medes and Persians! If Jesus had not listened to the spirit that was behind this use of scripture he might have fallen for the temptation. Satan did not attempt to argue with Jesus about the authority of scripture - that was assumed by both Jesus and Satan - only the interpretation of what both knew to be truth.

Jumping off the temple would certainly have been a dramatic gesture to entertain the holiday crowds, for whom death and bloodshed was very much part of life. They were cruel days. But what an ending to the story. How the people would have loved to see a detachment of angels swoop down from the clouds, and just before Jesus crashed to the ground, rescue him from the oblivion of a sudden death.

And the heart of the temptation? Put on a show, impress the people, let them see how great you are. They'll all follow you then. And you probably won't need to go to Calvary either. Just show them what you're made of, for you know what it says in scripture, don't you? *"He shall give his angels charge over you"* (Psalm 91:11 NKJV) as well as *"They shall bear you up in their hands, lest you dash your foot against a stone"* (Psalm 91:12 NKJV). So,

Jesus, you've nothing to fear. You've got scripture to back this one up! When are you going to do it?

I have no doubt that Jesus would have done anything not to have gone to the cross. Anything, that is, but swallow Satan's lies or be disobedient to his Father. Matthew 26:36-46 and John 17 record his agony before the Father as he longed for there to be another way. Nevertheless, he was willing to do what the Father had asked of him. Again, Jesus saw through the temptation and with another telling quote from Deuteronomy sent Satan on his way. *"You shall not put the Lord your God to the test"* (Deuteronomy 6:16 NASB).

The giftings God had given to Jesus were not to be used for his own ends. Nowhere in the scripture is it recorded that Jesus used his power for any other purpose than to fulfil the promises of Isaiah 61:1 in proclaiming the Gospel, healing the sick and setting the captives free. His whole ministry was directed towards those ends. Whilst the miracles he performed were certainly evidence of his Sonship, their primary purpose was not as a sign to prove who he was.

When the Pharisees came to him seeking a sign, they were demonically inspired and simply being used by Satan to repeat this second temptation in a different form. If Jesus could be persuaded to try and use God's power for any other purpose than the fulfilment of God's will then Jesus would have to submit to Satan, not the other way round. In that case Jesus would have become a sinner.

To the Pharisees Jesus was cutting in his criticism. *"An evil and an adulterous generation craves for a sign; and yet no sign shall be given to it but the sign of Jonah the prophet"* (Matthew 12:39 NASB). The word for adultery in both the Greek of the New Testament and the Hebrew of the Old has far more implications than just sexual sin. It also means spiritual apostasy - going after another *"lover"* than the one (God the Father) who had loved his people from the beginning. The Old Testament talks about their 'adultery' in worshipping false gods. Jesus was not polite to his accusers - even in front of others!

There was no way that Jesus was going to be trapped by these Pharisees into performing any supernatural sign for their benefit, not even jumping off the pinnacle of the temple. One day there would be a very special sign (represented by Jonah's three days in the whale), not just for the Pharisees but for all peoples and for all ages to come. Three days and nights in the ground - and then the resurrection. A prophetic fact that Satan knew only too well.

Those who minister in healing and deliverance are especially prone to this second temptation. They are moving in an area where evidences of the power of God are visibly demonstrated in their ministry, and there will be those who want to see a 'miracle'. Those who want to try and test you out - just to see if you can do the things you talk about.

At times I have been challenged with words such as 'see if you can get a demon out of me'. No matter how obviously demonised the person might be, you should always refuse all such challenges. Their origin is Satan who would want to boost your ministry in the flesh with wrongful pride in performance, or show you up by failure, or use the lack of results of such ministry to *"prove"* that the highly demonised person who issued the challenge doesn't have any demons after all! When we fall for such 'tests' Satan is the winner every time. There is a world of difference between this and Spirit anointed tests such as those that Moses and Aaron were told to do before Pharaoh.

Also, Satan will often subtly tempt us to be involved in a ministry which God is not asking us, or anointing us, to do. We need always to be discerning the spirit behind the request for help - is it from God or the enemy. Satan would love to exhaust the saints by wearing them down in ministry to people who are not serious about following

Jesus, but simply want rid of their symptoms so that they can carry on with a sinful life-style!

Another aspect of this temptation, with important lessons for each one of us, is the way we might be tempted to use scripture, out of context. Scripture is not to be used to hit people over the head with ideas that are not of God. It is only to be used by God's people to bring influence into the lives of others under the anointing of the Holy Spirit. An important lesson in spiritual growth is learning to discern the spirit that is behind someone who is quoting scripture to you.

As we have seen, Satan knows scripture well and is a master at using it against God's people. Some of the ways he trains demons to exploit the word of God are highly plausible, and we must be on our guard against deception in this area, for the demons know the scriptures as well as Satan.

I was once ministering to a demonised person and the Lord reminded me of a particular scripture which was relevant to the ministry. This particular demon had been arrogantly speaking out in defiance for some time. When I quoted the scripture to a ministry colleague, questioning what the reference was, it was not my colleague who gave me the answer, but the demon through the mouth of the counsellee! The chapter and verse that were given were precisely right! So watch out for Satan's attempts to blow you off course with scriptures quoted out of context and without the anointing of the Spirit of God.

The Third Temptation
(Matthew 4:8-10, Luke 4:5-8)

Subtlety had failed. This time Satan was far more direct. He played on Jesus's humanity. No human being, not even the Son of God, relishes the prospect of suffering. Ahead, for Jesus, lay the cross. God knew it, Jesus knew it, and Satan also knew it. It would be a cruel death, hours of pain and distress, harrowing experiences for

Jesus's family and all for what? Satan must have whispered something like this to the heart of Jesus, 'There is another way. Come with me and I'll show you.'

So Satan took Jesus to the top of a very high mountain and showed him all the kingdoms of the world. He arrogantly spoke the truth about his being in charge of planet earth and that all these kingdoms were at his disposal. (He declined to mention that the only reason this was the case was that he had been thrown out of heaven in the first place!) Jesus did not dispute the claim. It was a statement of fact and the only reason that Jesus was here was to rescue people from Satan's grip.

Many people are deceived by Satan when he speaks truth - as he always will if it can be used to serve his ends. It is not true that Satan and demons only ever speak lies. If all that they said was lies their deceptions would be too easy to detect. It is the subtle mixture of a few lies sown into a mass of truth that so often causes people to fall into temptation. The odd artificial fly, amongst a mass of real ones, is only noticed by the trout when it is too late, and the point of the hook has penetrated the skin and the barb has gripped him tight!

So Satan began this temptation by speaking truth. But then came the deception that he tried to ride in on the back of truth. 'All this can be yours. After all, isn't that why you came, so that you can win the world back. Let's strike a bargain, you can have the lot, no questions asked.'

The cross wasn't actually mentioned. But make no mistake, that was what this temptation was all about. If Jesus were to get to Calvary, and voluntarily lay down his life for others, it would be the beginning of the end for Satan and eternal freedom for all those who believed. Satan would do anything, absolutely anything, to keep Jesus from going through with it. Even, apparently, surrender control of his earthly kingdom.

"All this will be yours, if you worship me." Satan had not changed. Worship was what he craved for, the place of God was his goal. And Satan knew that Jesus and the Father (with the Holy Spirit) were one. So that if Jesus were to give in on this, then God himself would also come under Satan's dominion and control. Then all God's plans for Satan's future punishment could be overthrown. Satan did not relish eternal torment in the lake of fire.

Satan gave Jesus the chance of achieving his aim without going to the cross. The temptation was direct, very direct. Accept my offer and you can forget about Calvary. Worship me and you can have mankind. But Jesus knew that, far from achieving his Father's purposes, to accept Satan's apparently generous offer, would not only destroy the hope of salvation for mankind, but would also place the very Godhead under Satan's control.

Again Jesus used scripture to counter Satan's attack, this time with a third quotation from the book of Deuteronomy, *"You shall fear only the Lord your God, and you shall worship Him"* (Deuteronomy 6:13 NASB). Jesus's rebuke was short, effective and to the point. He did not enter into discussion with Satan, but concluded the matter unequivocally with the word of God.

This third temptation follows a pattern which Satan and his demons often use with God's people, offering them a route to achieve God's objectives that is different from the one the Father had planned. There is a cost in following Jesus, and Satan knows it. He uses that to devastating advantage on many occasions, leading God's people into thinking there are better ways of doing things than those which are given by the Holy Spirit. Ways which are not quite so costly, but, Satan would assure us, just as effective.

When individuals, or churches, begin to follow the demonised ways of the world in conducting the affairs of the Spirit they are on a downward spiral that can only lead to spiritual (and even physical) death and disaster.

They are heeding the same voice that spoke to Jesus, offering him the world without the cross. For example, Christians who are being called out of business may count too precious the retirement benefits of staying with the firm, thinking that, in the future, they can 'work for the Lord on the strength of a good pension'. But those extra ten years might well have been the very years that God would have used most effectively.

Ministers within the structure of a mainline denomination may have to weigh the benefits of towing the party line with an eye over their shoulder for promotion in the church, against being obedient to what God is calling them personally, or their church fellowship to be and to do in the Kingdom of God. Be on your guard that you are not deceived and finish up justifying disobedience!

Another aspect of this third temptation which needs to be guarded against often comes with the success of Christian ministry. Satan loves to attract worship to himself, and the moment we begin to take wrongful pride in 'our' achievements under God we are opening ourselves up to the very sin for which Satan was thrown out of heaven. If Satan cannot destroy a ministry by diverting the visionary from the cause, he will try again, later, to divert him at the point of greatest effectiveness and success by tempting him with self-glorification.

It sounds terribly obvious when talking about these things from a position of obscurity and no public image. But the god of this world does blind the eyes, and only a little elevation in public profile brings temptations of pride and self-glorification that can be hard to recognise by those who are used to being at the centre of what God is doing.

One final lesson from this and the other temptations: once Jesus had heard the temptation, given his response with a correct use of scripture, that was the end of the matter. No discussion was entered into. There are many people who have failed at this point, not because they didn't recognise the temptation, but because they tried to talk their way out of it. But discussion led to compromise and compromise, in dealing with the voice of the enemy, is sin. So deal quickly and effectively with temptation and move on quickly to continue doing the things that God has already given you to do.

Satan in Simon Peter
(Matthew 16:21-23 and Mark 8:31-33)

We all love Simon Peter. His humanity, courage, brash enthusiasm and sheer capacity to put his feet in it, all endear him to our own humanity. We love, also, his spiritual perception, especially when he was the first to blurt out what he knew to be the truth about Jesus, *"You are the Messiah, the Son of the living God!"* (Matthew 16:16 GNB).

What a moment in his life. Such revelation from God, and then such commendation as Jesus declared *"this truth did not come to you from any human being, but it was given to you directly by my Father in heaven"* (Matthew 16:17 GNB). Simon Peter had a direct word from God himself. He had a spiritual sensitivity that was tuned in to the supernatural and an openness to listen to God which exceeded that of all the other disciples, and Jesus commended him.

But Satan was watching in the wings. He, too, could use that supernatural sensitivity. He knew all about the spiritual realms. He could beam messages down that channel also. Even through Simon Peter? Well Satan knew that this uncouth, untrained fisherman did not yet have the maturity and discernment to sort out the wheat from the chaff. Satan grabbed his chance, sowed a seed (of pride?) in Simon Peter's mind, and waited his opportunity.

We have seen on many occasions how someone who can be mightily used of God on one occasion to bring a significant prophetic word, can, especially if unwisely elevated by those Christians around him, be equally used to speak a word which is definitely not of God. Because the word is spoken out of the same mouth through which God has genuinely spoken, people feel obliged to receive all that is said by that person, without testing it before the Lord. In this way Satan can act like a wolf and ravage the flock from within the sheepfold.

Jesus went on to talk about what must happen to the Messiah. He told the disciples that he must go to Jerusalem and suffer from the elders, the chief priests and the teachers of the law. He told them that he would be put to death, but that three days later he would rise again from the dead (Matthew 16:21).

The moment had come. Peter was still reeling from the shock. I don't think he could have heard the last phrase about rising again from the dead. He couldn't contemplate life without Jesus, or, perhaps, face the personal consequences of what it would mean to him if Jesus was to be crucified. He let his emotions rule and the seed Satan had sown rapidly came to harvest.

"God forbid it, Lord! This must never happen to you" (Matthew 16:22 GNB). The words came blurting out, as if he could tell God what must happen. That spiritual sensitivity was being used alright, but definitely not by God. And immediately Jesus recognised what was happening. Being filled with the Holy Spirit, and being sinless, he operated with perfect discernment, and he knew at once the source of the voice which was coming from Simon Peter's lips.

In a flash of time he was back in the wilderness. There was Satan with his sickly patronising temptations, offering him the world without having to go to the cross, 'just worship me, and it will all be yours'. And out of Simon's lips came the very name of God being used to endorse a path that would lead away from Calvary. This could only be Satan himself, persisting with his temptations.

Some have thought that Jesus dealt harshly with Simon at that moment. Couldn't he have been just a little more gentle in explaining to him where he had gone wrong? Couldn't he have been a little more sensitive to the presence of the other disciples who heard exactly what Jesus said to this man who had just received such commendation? Well couldn't he?

The answer is a short, and unequivocal, No! There could be no compromise with Satan whatsoever. There had been no compromise with Satan in the wilderness, and just because on this occasion there were a few other people around, he could not change his stance towards the great enemy of souls.

So he turned to Peter, but addressed Satan himself. *"Get behind me Satan! You are a hindrance to me, you are not on the side of God, but of men"* (Matthew 16:23 RSV). Jesus dealt with Satan directly, and immediately threw out the possibility of avoiding the cross. Satan had used the ideas of men (to avoid pain and death) to test Jesus once more with regard to obedience to his calling.

But what a rebuke this must have been to Simon Peter. To think that even he, the one whom Jesus had commended so highly, could be used by Satan himself. But we read elsewhere *"whoever thinks he is standing firm had better be careful that he does not fall"* (1 Corinthians 10:12 GNB). The potential in each one of us for sin is ever-present, and never more so than immediately following our highest spiritual achievements.

It is after those special moments that Satan rejoices to see us crash. The headiness of being so closely in touch with God affects our souls, and our very earthiness makes us vulnerable to the flesh. At that point the demonic can have easy access to us. Peter learnt the hard way, and I don't suppose he ever forgot the day when Satan used him to try and get at Jesus.

Those who are at the forefront of Christian ministry must be constantly on their guard against a demon using even a trusted member of the fellowship to speak lies into the heart. Attacks which come from obviously antagonistic sources can be easily recognised and countered - it is those that are spoken through the lips of those we trust that are the most deadly. Sometimes such attacks will be extremely subtle, such as suggestions for doing this or that, which are perfectly good ideas, but somewhere, deep down, you feel uncomfortable with what is being said.

Many times I have discerned the voice of the enemy speaking through Christian friends, who, nevertheless, meant well. Usually they brought suggestions that, in retrospect, would have been disastrous; or proposed good reasons as to why what we were doing, in obedience to what we believed God had told us to do, would be a big mistake! If we had listened to such advice, some of which even came from men of established reputation, right at the beginning of the work, the whole ministry of Ellel Grange would have been still-born!

Even when listening to the advice of mature Christians, we must not be deceived into following guidance which has its source in the flesh and is not anointed by the Spirit of God. If we are genuinely open to the Spirit ourselves we will be able to receive both positive and negative advice willingly, because we will be able to discern the mind of the Holy Spirit behind the advice being given. In this way we have also been prevented from making some very serious mistakes when the Spirit has spoken words of caution to us through anointed Christian friends.

Listen to the Holy Spirit and trust the discernment that God has given you. If there is a check in your spirit don't rush to accept the advice. Test what is being suggested carefully, and only proceed once you are convinced that the check in your spirit was God making you consider carefully the implications of what he is saying to you.

The good is always the enemy of the best, and if the enemy has proved from past experience that he cannot blow your ministry off course with outlandish suggestions, he will try and use good ideas! There are lots of good ideas around, but for you the only ideas that must matter are those which originate in the heart of the Father and which have the anointing of the Holy Spirit upon them.

Whilst not being encounters that Jesus had with Satan, there are two more lessons from the life of Simon Peter which will help us understand aspects of the demonic.

The Transfiguration
(Matthew 17:1-8, Mark 9:2-8 and Luke 9:28-36)

It was Peter's humanity that prevailed after the incredible experience of being present on the Mount of Transfiguration with Jesus, James and John. There he met Moses and Elijah face to face and heard the very voice of God affirming to them the divinity of Jesus, *"This is my Son, whom I have chosen. Listen to him!"* (Luke 9:35 GNB). And Peter's reaction? He was like so many of us, for he wanted to make permanent this high point of spiritual experience by building three dwelling places for Jesus, Moses and Elijah!

There must be countless churches and chapels around the world whose very names attempt to enshrine some great revival experience of the past, or great saint of God whose work must never be forgotten. But the spiritual experiences of past generations can become a curse on the present generation.

If any of us try to mimic the experience of others, or live out a pseudo-spirituality on the back of the genuine Christian experience of others, our best will simply be lifeless religion. Our experience of what we think is God can, sometimes, be the expression of a religious spirit that controls our lives and can even control our church.

God is always doing new things. We must always be looking forward and moving on with him into new territory. Our flesh likes to put down roots and remain at levels of spiritual experience where we feel safe. But such safety can be as death to real spiritual life, bringing with it the curse of rejection of anything which seems different or new!

I've lost count of the number of ministers I have prayed with whose spiritual back has been broken on the rock of *"nothing changes here"*. They have often needed deliverance from the spirits of curse unwittingly put on them by members of their congregations, who have opposed the life-giving work of the Holy Spirit. We must remember and learn from the past, yes, but not live in it. If we try and live on the back of past religious experience, we will make ourselves vulnerable to the demonic and will probably need deliverance from religious spirits as well.

At the Crucifixion
(Matthew 26:69-75, Mark 14:66-72, Luke 22:54-62 and John 18:15-27)

Peter had another major lesson to learn just before Jesus died. This time it was not caused by the headiness of spiritual triumph. No, it was the sheer fear of impending disaster that led him into denial of Jesus. He was very much a man of flesh as well as being a spiritual giant. The English poet Kipling wrote wise words when in his famous poem, *"If"*, he included the couplet,

> *"If you can meet with triumph and disaster*
> *And treat these two imposters just the same."*

Kipling knew that in triumph or disaster man is vulnerable to the extremes of emotional experience, and Peter was no exception. Satan also recognises that these are some of his greatest opportunities for undermining our spiritual lives. In these extremes Peter's weaknesses were laid bare and in disaster it was fear, which had lurked deep down in his life, that came to the surface.

Spirits of fear can have a devastating effect upon us, and it is sometimes in the extremes of life that they are exposed for what they are. Unless they are dealt with they will, from time to time, adversely control our lives and lead us into sin. They can have the effect of being Satan's fifth column lying dormant in the life of the Christian. Scripture tells us that *"perfect love casts out fear"* (1 John 4:18 RSV). Jesus is perfect love and in his name we have authority and power to deal with the bogey of fear which controls so many lives.

Often in ministry to a whole group I will deal with various fears and find that many people will experience complete release from the fear that had formerly gripped their lives and find healing from the presenting symptoms. Graham Powell's book *Fear Free* is a very helpful source book for information on how to overcome fear in the name of Jesus.

Satan in Judas Iscariot
(Matthew 26:14-16, Mark 14:10-11 and Luke 22:3-6)

There are many experiences that Jesus had with the demonic (which we will be looking at in the next chapter), but there is one more in the Gospels that the writers are quite specific about being an encounter not just with demons but with Satan himself.

Just as in the encounter with Simon Peter, the Gospel writers specifically record that Jesus addressed Satan himself, not just a demon, in Judas Iscariot at the moment of betrayal. It was Judas's sin in agreeing to betray Jesus that opened him up to being taken over. And at the moment of putting the sinful decision into action Judas became not just demonised, but the host for Satan himself.

Perhaps Judas had decided that the death of Jesus was inevitable. No doubt he was wondering what would happen to the disciples if Jesus were to be taken and killed. Local justice would inevitably come down heavily on those who were closest to him. Death for Judas might not be too far away either. How could Judas protect himself from the same fate as Jesus?

A plan was conceived - collaboration with the accusers. A secret visit was made to the chief priests. *"What will you give me if I betray Jesus to you?"* (Matthew 26:14-16 GNB). A price was agreed and Judas provided a way of escape for himself, in league with the accusers, in the event of a disaster. Thirty pieces of silver in his pocket - quite a significant sum - would certainly help him to start life all over again.

Self-seeking, greed and protecting one's own skin at the expense of others are all hall-marks of the 'Judas spirit'. Jeremiah's words about the deceitfulness of the heart were never more true than at this moment in the life of Judas (Jeremiah 17:9). In spite of having spent three years with Jesus himself, when the chips were down, selfishness came floating to the surface like a cork in a bucket of water.

Any Christian, even one who walks closely with the Lord as Judas did, can be used by demons to oppose the purposes of God, if his heart is not pure and his motives, therefore, become focused on selfish objectives. Satan loves it when the need for selfish gain in one person is used to destroy the purposes of God in another, and by the attitude of our hearts we give the demonic a right to act through us against fellow Christians.

In the story of Ellel Grange there have been numerous attacks on the work from many different sources, which have been aimed at undermining and destroying the ministry. Those from obvious sources, such as people involved in witchcraft and the occult or from sectors of the Christian scene that deny the authority of scripture, doubt the veracity of the incarnation, the resurrection and the healing and deliverance ministry of Jesus, are, in some ways, the easiest to cope with. At least they are to be expected.

Jesus was not at all surprised, for example, when the Pharisees opposed his work and nor was the early church surprised when magicians and occultists were used to oppose the Gospel when it was preached and practised by believers (for example, Acts 16:16-24). But the attacks that have been the most devastating to the team, and the hardest to cope with both emotionally and spiritually, have come from those whom we thought were walking with us.

The 'Judas spirit', the spirit of betrayal, is rampant in the Body of Christ. When those who have called you friend, whom you have walked with closely and shared with in the Lord, use their tongues to undermine the work that God has entrusted into your hands, the arrows seem very sharp indeed. In making such comments I am carefully distinguishing between honest doubts and criticisms shared directly with us, from those who are going in the same direction, and who are genuinely sharing what they see as the truth in love. That is not betrayal, but a hallmark of a courageous brother or sister in Christ - for *"faithful are the wounds of a friend"* (Proverbs 27:6 NASB).

What a difference there is between this and the murmurings and undercurrents set in motion by a contrary tongue that indulges in what can only be called malicious gossip. And sometimes it is even dressed up in the spiritual language of prayer, 'I'm just telling you this, so that you can pray about it!' Betrayal is sin. Satan's attack on Jesus through Judas must have been the most painful attack that Satan could have devised. For Judas became the betrayer. Every one of us must be on our guard against spreading the spirit of Judas in our churches. We must examine our hearts before God and rigorously root out every motive that could give access to the spirit of Judas.

Sadly, there are times when even those who bring the 'words of a faithful friend' are not content to leave the outcome of their words with God. So when they don't get the immediate response they think their words deserve, they fall into the temptation of giving God a helping hand by spreading words that are loaded with doubt and undermining rumour.

I have ministered to many heartbroken ministers whose work has been seriously undermined, and, in some cases, destroyed by members of their own congregation and family. Jesus warned his followers that loyalty to Him would separate with the sharpness of a sword, between them and some of the people they had been close to (Matthew 10:34-39).

Satan had tried to take Jesus's life on many occasions. The events of those days in Jerusalem were building up to a climax. Jesus would not be around much longer, that's for sure. Satan began to close in for the kill. Judas was easy game. His heart was greedy and jealous and I have seen how such emotions give rise to hatred of those who might stand in the way of immediate objectives. Hatred is a breeding ground for murder. And whilst betrayal of Jesus into the hands of other murderers was probably seen by Judas as only a small part in the whole scenario, he was as guilty as if he had personally nailed Jesus to the cross. The price had been fixed and the countdown to Calvary had begun.

Jesus was going to die, yes, but only because he had chosen to die. His time had come. And Satan knew that in these circumstances any victory celebration that the physical death of Jesus might initiate, would only be short lived. Prophecy, which Satan himself had read and knew only too well, was not on Satan's side! Three days after the crucifixion the party in hell was over and all the demons, fallen angels and Satan himself have been on the run from the people of God ever since.

For Judas it was a sad, sad day. The thirty pieces of silver became poisoned blood money in his hand. He realised he had betrayed an innocent man, threw the coins down on the temple floor and went out and hanged himself. Suicide is one of the objectives of the demonic.

Driving people into such tight corners, that to live seems worse than dying, is a trick that Satan and his demons have been playing on the mind since the beginning of time. To Satan, Judas was just another statistic. Another person, whom having used, he discarded on the scrap heap of life.

Even for Judas I believe there could have been a way back through repentance and forgiveness, but Satan did not let him live long enough to find out. There are many people who have been rescued from the edge of hell's precipice. Deliverance has been part of the ministry they needed from the spirits of death and suicide which had entered their lives. The Gospel is a Gospel of hope - even for those who have reached the very end of themselves.

In Conclusion

Jesus was Satan's prime target. It is not surprising that Satan himself chose to act against his supreme enemy, the very Son of God. Most ordinary human beings will never have a personal encounter with Satan himself. He is not omnipresent and has delegated to his demonic hosts the work of tempting and testing human beings.

When people say 'Satan tempted me', they are not saying that Satan himself was the tempting force, but simply admitting that the temptation came via an agent in the enemy's camp. Just as Jesus had to be constantly on his guard against the attacks from his personal enemy agent (Satan), so must we be constantly on our guard against the traps being laid for us by the demons who act against Christians in highly personal ways similar to those that Satan used against Jesus.

Satan has not changed his tactics. Jesus endured the attacks that he knew his people would have to endure down the ages. We need to pay careful heed to the lessons there are for us in the Gospels, and be constantly on our guard against all the enemy's devices. It is salutary to recognise that demons could even use us to devastating effect against the ministry of Jesus. We need to heed Jesus's warning and *"watch and pray, lest you enter into temptation. The spirit indeed is willing, but the flesh is weak"* (Matthew 26:41 NKJV).

Chapter 8

Encounters with the Demonic in the Gospels

Careful reading in the Gospels of the encounters Jesus had with demons, and of how he dealt with them, gives us much understanding of the whole deliverance ministry. Not every type of demonic power that exists is encountered in the Gospels, but the principles that can be learnt from this study are of general application to the whole ministry.

In this chapter we will look at each major encounter Jesus had with demons or demonic power and comment on the particular lessons we can learn from each such event in the life of Jesus.

In Nazareth
(Matthew 13:53-58, Mark 6:1-6 and Luke 4:16-30)

After his experiences in the wilderness, where he was tested by Satan himself, Jesus returned to his homeland, the territory of Galilee. On the Sabbath he followed his usual practice and went to the Synagogue to worship God.

But this time Jesus was different. It was his first visit to the synagogue since being filled with the Holy Spirit. He was now open to the full flow of the power of God and the anointing of the Spirit upon him was such that every demon in the place must have been aware of his presence!

He stood up to read the scriptures and, it seems, he deliberately found the passage from Isaiah 61:1 which tells about the work that the Messiah would do. He read out those amazing words, *"The spirit of the Lord is upon me to bring good news to the poor. He has sent me to proclaim liberty to the captives and recovery of sight to the blind; to set free the oppressed and announce that the time has come when the Lord will save his people"* (Luke 4:18 GNB).

The actual text of his sermon on that day is not recorded in scripture. But initially the people paid polite respect to his eloquent words and they marvelled at the way he spoke. As often happens when people are challenged and convicted in their spirit, and are looking for an excuse to ignore what is being said, they began to question his origins with such questions as, *"Isn't this the son of Joseph. How is it that a carpenter's son can speak like this?"*

Reading the scripture, and commenting on it in a sermon, was a normal and accepted part of synagogue worship. But Jesus did more than this. He read one of the well-known Messianic passages heralding the coming of the Christ and then told the people, including the Pharisees and teachers of the law who were present, that this passage of scripture was now being fulfilled at that very moment, and that was a very different matter indeed! For his claim to be the Messiah was either the ultimate blasphemy (if he was being serious), or the height of madness, unless, of course, he actually was the Messiah.

The normal reaction to religious maniacs is to dismiss them as being irrelevant. Mental hospitals contain many people (demonised and deluded no doubt) who claim to be Jesus, the Messiah, God or some other divine manifestation. No-one takes their claims seriously. But when Jesus made a claim which would normally have been the domain of the deluded and the insane, he spoke with such authority that the people realised he was serious. This was no ordinary madman.

Notwithstanding their polite respect for his eloquent words, hatred and murder lay just below the surface. Jesus knew, as did Paul who said that *"we are not fighting against human beings, but against the wicked*

spiritual forces in the heavenly world" (Ephesians 6:12
GNB), that the real battle was a spiritual one. Jesus will
have sensed the demonic beginning to incite the crowd to
action. John 2:25 (GNB) tells us that *"no-one needed to tell
Jesus about themselves, because he himself knew what
was in their hearts"*. On this Sabbath morning in
Nazareth, Jesus, who had perfect spiritual insight, could
see the battle in the spirit realm intensifying.

He knew that his claim to be THE prophet was being
questioned by the locals who knew his humble origins. So
he gave them Old Testament illustrations of how a
prophet of God is not respected amongst his own people.
The situation exploded. In a matter of minutes Sabbath
worship was transformed into a serious attempt on the
life of Jesus. Having failed in the wilderness to divert
Jesus from his life's work, Satan then chose murder as
his next direct line of attack.

How was it that superficially Godly people could suddenly
become an angry, murderous crowd of hooligans? It
seems that there was a direct power clash between the
Holy Spirit flowing out of Jesus and the demons who were
motivating the crowd. The demons recognised Jesus.
They knew that their very existence was threatened. So
they responded in the way that threatened demons
normally do - by making the people they are living in
believe that the thoughts and feelings of the demons
belong to them. Deception takes place and man then
chooses to respond, to what he thinks are his own
feelings, and enters into sin. It was as if Satan was the
conductor of an orchestra of demons who were lying
hidden in the congregation, but which were ready to
spring into action at the slightest hint of a signal from
their conductor!

The reason why suicides choose to take their own life is
because they have believed the lie of a demon. The reason
why people behave in ways that are totally irrational and
contrary to God's plans and purposes is because they
believe the lies that demons put into their minds. The

reason why superficially religious people can seem
completely unresponsive to the work of the Holy Spirit can
be because their minds are controlled by religious spirits
and have been closed to the truth by the demonic. James
says that the wisdom which does not come from a heart
that is pure before God is *"unspiritual and demonic"*
(James 3:15 GNB). Timothy, in addressing believers, says
that some people *"will obey lying spirits and follow the
teaching of demons"* (1 Timothy 4:1 GNB).

This encounter at Nazareth was not just a confrontation
between the man Jesus and the people in the synagogue.
It was a carefully orchestrated attack by the demonic
powers on the ministry of the Son of God. The only reason
that Satan could have mounted such an attack in God's
house is because of the extent of demonisation in the
worshippers. This is a lesson that we need to take very
much to heart in this day and age.

When it comes to renewal of the church, and obedience to
the Holy Spirit, church leaders are often opposed by a
demonic reservoir in the people, that rises up to oppose
the work of God. Unless they recognise this for what it is,
and take appropriate action through spiritual warfare,
they will exhaust themselves against walls of opposition,
without ever realising why they are tired and dispirited!

The Jews of Jesus's day were historically a Godly people.
But the generation in which we now live has little
Christian heritage on which to stand. If the problem of a
demonised 'church' was a curse on the ministry of Jesus,
how much more will this be a problem today with, for
example, the assault on the minds of ordinary men and
women through the media of every type of sexual
perversion; the use of television to bring visual images
into private homes that are beginning to reach the
extremes of corruption; and the demonic compulsion that
lies behind much of modern popular music. All these and
much, much more have, I believe, left us with a
generation of demonised people for whom the saving,

healing and delivering power of Jesus Christ is the only answer.

As I write this a historic court case is being fought in the United Kingdom. For the first time consequential damages are being claimed for people who were not directly involved in a tragedy. Relatives of the football fans who died in the Hillsborough stadium disaster, who were not even present at the match, watched it all happen on live television. They are suffering from the supposed psychiatric condition of post-traumatic stress syndrome caused by seeing members of their family die. I wonder how many of these people have actually been demonised through the shock of seeing those pictures in their own home and are in need of deliverance as well as medical care?

And how many people are demonised with sexual spirits because of the pornographic images that have poisoned their minds via cinema and television screens? People may smile and shake their heads in quaint disbelief at such suggestions, but they clearly have little experience of delivering people from demons that have gained access in this way.

Even though Jesus did not have to contend with demons that had entered people through the modern media, those that were there were just as vicious in their attack on his ministry. But it was not the time for Jesus to die. No-one (human or demon) would take his life from him, until the time when he chose to lay down his life willingly for the sins of the world and the prophetic meaning of his name would be fulfilled.

So, at Nazareth, the angels cleared a way through the crowds, and Jesus was able to escape from the attempt to throw him over a cliff. He was unscathed by the encounter, but there must have been some very angry demons who were so pinned back by the angels that the people could not press home the attack. As with this experience in Nazareth, there are many other encounters Jesus had with people that can only be truly understood in the light of what was happening behind the scenes in the demonic and angelic realms.

At Capernaum
(Mark 1:21-28, Luke 4:31-37)

At Nazareth the demonic powers had operated against Jesus without the people realising what was happening. But at Capernaum the reaction was overt, as demons made their presence in a man publicly known. Jesus was speaking in the synagogue with authority, and the demons could stand it no longer.

The man screamed out with a loud voice (hardly a polite comment from an attentive audience!), *"Ah, what do you want with us, Jesus of Nazareth? Are you here to destroy us? I know who you are: you are God's holy messenger!"* (Luke 4:34 GNB). Here we have a man (singular) screaming out words at Jesus indicating that he was plural! Evidently the man had more than one demon in him - or perhaps this particular demon was also acting as spokesman for all the demons that were present in the synagogue that day in other people also!

When Jesus responded to the situation, he initially ignored the man altogether and only dealt with the demon. He addressed it directly, telling it to be quiet and come out of the man. Notwithstanding these directions from Jesus, the demon first threw the man down to the ground before coming out of him. We must not be afraid of such manifestations when people are being set free. Jesus did not seem at all concerned that the demon had this affect on the man during the actual deliverance - neither must we be concerned.

Indeed, there is a strong argument for letting the people see what demons have done to others. It acts as a strong deterrent against sin and opens people up to the possibility of being set free themselves. Quite often I have sensed the demonic in people beginning to betray their own presence by displaying fear when others have been going through deliverance.

As already referred to in a different context, there was a time when I was preaching in an Anglican Parish Church when, five minutes into the sermon on healing and deliverance, a woman stood up and started to scream at the top of her voice, *"Shut up! Shut up! Shut up!"* Whereupon she tried to tear a Bible up into little pieces to throw at me! The effect on the congregation was electric. Morning worship had never been like this before!

The demons in her could not stand the threat to their security any longer. The teaching that was being given to the church had to be stopped at any price. But they overstepped the mark, revealed their presence and made it possible for that lady to begin to be set free. She was immediately set free from the demon that had cried out in church, and the Lord then began to show other areas of her life where the demonic had been exercising a strong hold.

Far from being a victory for the enemy, it was a tremendous victory for Jesus and the work of the Holy Spirit. For the incident was one of a number of strategic events in the life of that church which opened up the fellowship to a dynamic ministry in the power of the Holy Spirit.

It's significant that the lady involved is now a member of the ministry team in her church, and she with her husband are being used together to set other people free. This incident was a very powerful illustration of the fact that Christians can have demons. She had been converted some five years previously and was by this time the Church secretary.

This particular incident in the life of Jesus demonstrated to the people at Capernaum that Jesus had an authority over the demons which they had not seen before. No doubt they were familiar with the Jewish exorcists who would struggle with largely ineffective rituals, and much noise, to drive demons out of people. Their testimony to the authority that Jesus had, whereby with his words he drove demons out of people, must have been gossiped round the district like wildfire! For the needs of the people were great, and there were many in need of deliverance, just as there are today.

At Simon's House and After
(Matthew 8:14-17, Mark 1:29-34, Luke 4:38-41)

After leaving the synagogue at Capernaum Jesus went with his disciples to Simon's house, where his mother-in-law was sick with a high fever. Without antibiotics and modern medicines fevers were dangerous and potentially lethal. So Simon's question to Jesus, asking for help, was probably much more than a request for some spiritual medicine. It was far more likely to have been a life or death situation than a passing minor illness.

Social commentators also add that the situation was a difficult one for Simon in view of the conventions of the day. Jesus was an honoured guest. His friends had come back after the synagogue service and by custom the lady of the house should be waiting on them. It would certainly not have been right for Simon to have gone into the kitchen to prepare the meal. So the situation was double edged. Simon's mother-in-law was ill and in need of healing, but what was far more pressing, at that minute, was the fact that unless she was healed, and instantly, there was a social crisis on Simon's hands!

Could Jesus help?

Scripture tells us in specific detail just what Jesus did. The mechanics of this healing are particularly significant, having enormous relevance to the matter of physical healing through deliverance. Jesus clearly discerned that the illness was not just a bodily condition, but that there was a spiritual power behind the physical symptom of the fever. So, instead of healing her of the condition, Jesus rebuked the fever (addressed the spirit of infirmity causing the fever) and ordered it to go.

The scripture describes how the fever left her immediately and without further delay she got up to make the supper and waited on them! There was no recovery period - just deliverance and instant healing as a result. It is dangerous, however, to build a theology of healing out of one isolated incident and one cannot say that all physical symptoms are, therefore, demonic.

What seems to be the case is that some symptoms, such as this one, are demonically caused, others are straightforward physical symptoms without a direct demonic intervention and yet others are a mixture of the two - see the story of the woman whose back was bent double in Luke 13:10-17.

Whilst not all sickness is demonic, however, there are far more demonically induced symptoms around than the church would readily admit. And one of the main reasons why some people are not healed is because the demonic dimension is not being discerned, even by those who believe in and use the gifts of the Holy Spirit.

Indeed, amongst some charismatics I have sensed a certain amount of pride in the position they have reached. They don't want to listen to anyone who is moving in a dimension of ministry that is unknown to them. I have found it frequently easier to minister deliverance to people who, previously, had no charismatic experience of the Holy Spirit than those who thought they had all the answers! We know of many people, and even whole churches, who have come into totally new life in the Spirit when they have recognised the demonic dimension and seen the power of God bring wholeness through deliverance.

A woman on one of our training courses had a streaming cold which was clearly causing her some distress. When I asked her how long she had suffered from it, she shocked me with her reply, *"Twenty-five years!"* The condition was medically diagnosed as rhinitis, a chronic form of sinusitis, which necessitated her using two to three boxes of tissues every single day. Additionally she had to get up on two or three occasions every night so as to clear the sinuses, which quickly became blocked up again. The condition really was a curse upon her life. She had had prayer on several occasion for the condition and the doctors had tried every possible medication - all to no avail.

A few minutes counselling established that her aunt had died twenty-five years previously and that her aunt had also suffered from sinusitis. Clearly the spirit of infirmity that had afflicted the aunt had transferred to the niece at death. I addressed directly the spirit of infirmity that had come from the aunt, in much the same way as Jesus must have dealt with the 'fever' in Simon's mother-in-law.

Immediately the demon manifested itself and she began to blow out all the mess from her sinuses. Within a few minutes she was completely healed as the demon left her. That night she had the first uninterrupted night's sleep for twenty-five years and later in the year she wrote to me saying that her consumption of tissues had fallen from two to three boxes a day to just one in six months. Ample evidence indeed that she had been healed through deliverance.

There are many medical conditions that have a spirit of infirmity at their root. Whilst medication may minimise or even remove the symptoms, and whilst prayer for healing may bring about some reduction in, for example, pain, if the condition is demonic in origin, there will be no permanent healing until the demon has been cast out.

Medical treatment can and does, apparently, completely cure many demonically induced presenting symptoms. But often, within a short period of time, the patient is suffering from something else and there is a regular footpath between their house and the doctor's surgery!

Every doctor is aware of certain patients who, for no apparent reason, are always ill with something. Many such people are afflicted with a general spirit of infirmity and good general health will not be experienced by the patient until this has been dealt with. I use the word 'general' here to distinguish between what is the more usual highly specific demon with a particular job function to cause a particular condition such as arthritis, cancer, paralysis etc. It should not be assumed from this comment that the cause of a medical condition is always directly attributable to the presence of a particular demon, but one should always be aware that this is a possibility.

Following the incident at Simon's house, the effect on the villagers was dramatic. First the story of what had happened at Capernaum was getting around, and then the news that Simon's mother was up and perfectly well, after Jesus had prayed with her, attracted many sick people to the home. By the time Jesus had finished his meal there were crowds outside the house wanting to see him.

From miles around the sick had come, or had been brought, and the scripture describes Jesus as healing a lot of people from diseases and casting demons out of many of them. The demons recognised Jesus. His profile was easily recognised by the spiritual powers who were in fear and trembling at the consequence of his presence.

As they came out, some of them screamed *"You are the Son of God"* - as if he had no right to be present in what was to them Satan's kingdom. But this declaration, though the truth (the demons did not attempt to lie about who Jesus really was) was both premature and from a source that Jesus was not prepared to acknowledge as a means of declaring his Messiahship. So, at this time, Jesus ordered the demons not to speak out such things, but he didn't stop them screaming. It seems that for some demons the scream is the means of exit, and to have stopped the screams, therefore, would have inhibited deliverance and prevented some people from being healed.

The events at Capernaum had an effect similar to dropping a lighted match into a can of petrol! Suddenly the people were clamouring both to hear him speak and to receive ministry from him, *"so he preached in their synagogues throughout the country"* (Luke 4:44 GNB). It seems as though popular demand had, for the time being, over-ridden the antagonism of the Pharisees and doors were opened to him wherever he went.

And so it is today. When ministers of the Gospel effectively minister healing and deliverance there is no shortage of people in need who will listen to the preaching and teaching. Good teaching is a very powerful foundation on which to build a ministry of evangelism, healing and deliverance. Without teaching the people do not have a vision of what God can do for them and what may be required of them. And *"where there is no vision the people are unrestrained"* (Proverbs 29:18 NASB). I have been regularly astonished at the way good teaching has exposed the demonic strongholds in the lives of individuals and churches, making ministry in the power of the Holy Spirit not only possible but dramatically effective.

The ministry of healing and deliverance, in the context of evangelism, is an incredibly powerful means of bringing people under the sound of the Gospel in such a way that the convicting power of the Holy Spirit is given free access to their hearts. Evangelists please note!

Jesus Encounters a Dumb Man
(Matthew 9:32)

Matthew's account of the reason why this dumb man could not speak is simple and graphic - because he had a demon! We are not told whether the demon was affecting the tongue, the voice box or the speech centre in the brain (we have encountered all these, and other, forms of demonic dumbness). But we are told that the direct consequence of the demon's presence was very specific, and that as soon as the demon was driven out by Jesus the man started talking.

The senses are particularly vulnerable to demonic attack and appear to be easily controlled by demons. On many occasions we have seen people undergoing deliverance become dumb for a while as the demon is driven from its place of residence and tries to create maximum havoc on the way out! But this is a different phenomenon from a person being demonically dumb through, for example, the speech centre in the brain being controlled by a resident demon.

Demons on the way out can have a restricting effect on the throat, the voice box, the tongue, the lips or even on the muscles of the jaw, making not only speech, but opening the mouth quite impossible. All of these are exit defense tactics in order to try and hang on to their place in the body. Clearly resident demons can also control any of these organs, or the speech centre in the brain, to induce dumbness.

Not all dumbness is demonic. There are many dumb people with genuine physical defects which make it impossible for them to speak. But I believe a significant proportion of those whose speech systems are apparently in good working order, but who are nevertheless dumb, are as they are because of the presence of a controlling demon with a very specific job function.

I believe also that some such cases are the consequences of a curse on the generation line of the victim, such as might result from an ancestor having his tongue cut out as a punishment, or having participated in such an obscene act on someone else in a Satanic or witchcraft ritual. Several times I have seen a person become totally dumb when they were being delivered of the guiding demonic spirit of a sacrificed victim (usually a baby) whose tongue had been cut out as part of a ritual sacrifice. See the next section for further comment by way of a case study on this aspect of demonisation.

The Blind and Dumb Demoniac
(Matthew 12:22-32)

This incident is the touchstone for a longer discussion about the authority Jesus has to drive out demons. Comment on this is made in chapter nine. All three synoptic Gospels include the discussion, but only Matthew tells us of the blind and dumb demoniac whose healing started the discussion off!

One of the dangers of studying individual cases in the Gospels is the temptation to think that once you have understood one case of, for example, blindness, you have understood them all! This is manifestly not the case, for not all cases of blindness have the same root cause. Some are caused by physical damage or injury, others by disease or, as in this case in Matthew's Gospel, by the presence of a demon.

If you look at the ways Jesus healed blind people you will see several different ways in which he treated them - ranging from putting mud on their eyes to ordering out a demon! He appeared to vary the ministry according to the root cause of the blindness.

Some people may question how it is possible for a demon to take away the capacity to see of an otherwise normally sighted person. It is easier to understand once one has appreciated that the action of a demon can be highly specific to a particular organ, and even to different functions of a particular organ, producing symptoms which are perceived at a physical level but which are caused by the presence of a demon. There are no simple answers, but I have seen people healed and restored when a demon has left.

Jane had received some ministry previously in her progress towards wholeness. Suddenly she came under severe attack, and before our very eyes she was struck blind, totally blind. *"Once I could see, now I am blind"* was her cry, reversing the words of the man who had been healed by Jesus.

For thirty-six hours she was totally unable to see anything, and for much of that time she was also totally deaf and dumb as well. She lost the use of all her primary senses. Mercifully taste and touch were unaffected. It was a very frightening experience for her, and those of us with responsibility for her care learnt to trust the Lord in a new way as we saw him lead us through the nightmare-like crisis.

Conversation with her was impossible. At times she could communicate with us by writing the spidery scrawl of a newly blinded person on yards of paper, but then the demon would even take over her hands and praying was all we could do. At some times she got partial hearing back and on those occasions she could communicate with us by 'one squeeze of her hand for yes and two squeezes for no' when answering specific questions we put to her.

It was a testing time, but the Lord showed us that the spirit attacking Jane had once been the guiding spirit of a child that had been sacrificed to Satan in a Satanic ritual (see Deuteronomy 18:10). Before the sacrifice the child was silenced by cutting out the tongue, deafened by piercing the ears and blinded in a similar way.

It seems that the guiding demonic spirit of a person generally assumes the characteristics of the person at the time of death, so that when the spirit attacked Jane, it brought with it conditions of deafness, dumbness and blindness commensurate with the child when it was sacrificed. I do not put these details in this book to shock or frighten anyone, but to be wholly realistic about the horrors and deceptions of Satan. He is a foul enemy.

But more importantly than that I want to stress the wonder of the cross, for it is through the shed blood of Jesus and by the power of his name that as believers we have the authority to bring healing and deliverance to those who have been afflicted by the evil one and overcome all the works of the enemy (Luke 10:18-19) including demonically induced blindness. We must not be ignorant of Satan's devices.

For Jane, her healing and deliverance began with forgiveness of those who had perpetrated such a horrific act against another human being. For Nehemiah 'repenting on behalf of the ancestors' was a vital step towards the power of God coming upon him for his great work in rebuilding the walls of Jerusalem (Nehemiah 1:6-7).

This act of forgiveness unlocked the stronghold the demon had upon her. We were then able to place the demon, and its assemblage of lesser spirits that were under its control, under our delegated authority as believers in the Lord Jesus Christ. As, one by one, we cast these spirits out, Jane's senses gradually returned, until, finally, when the controlling demon left, her eye-sight was restored to normality.

It was an awesome faith-building experience as the Lord gave us, one by one, the keys to her deliverance and healing. For the normally sighted thirty six hours of blindness is a very, very long time indeed. And for those of us who were praying and hanging on in faith, by much less than the finger nails, it was an eternity. We learnt that one finger nail with God is a sheet anchor into the security of his love. Retrospectively I can thank God for the experience and see his hand at work in the crisis. We learnt so many lessons in those never to be forgotten thirty-six hours.

Having seen someone blinded by a demon and then healed through deliverance, I have no problem with believing Matthew's comment as to why this man in the story was blind. Sceptics may say that Matthew was without modern medical knowledge and cannot have known the real reason for the man's blindness - hence he just explained it away by attributing it to a demon. Such sceptics need to start listening more carefully to what

Jesus actually said and did - they will find that Jesus knew rather more about the subject than they do!

The Epileptic Boy
(Matthew 17:14-21, Mark 9:14-29, Luke 9:37-43)

The account by Mark is the fullest of the three descriptions of the healing of this boy. But each account contains significant extra details, and when all the symptoms that the boy had are culled from the three accounts and put together it is clear that the boy suffered from grand mal epilepsy. (See Deliver Us From Evil by John Richards for a full assessment of the symptoms)

Jesus, with Peter, James and John had just shared the incredible experience of talking with Moses and Elijah on the mount of Transfiguration. While they were away the other disciples were clearly carrying on the teaching and healing ministry and, as so often happens in life, when the key person is away a crisis occurs!

Jesus was the key person. The crisis was an epileptic boy that they could not heal. Jesus was greeted on his return from the mountain by the anguished father of the boy, who clearly was under the impression that the disciples should have been able to heal him. His distress was great, for their prayers had failed and it seemed as though his last chance of having his son back, healed, had gone. He complained to Jesus that his disciples had been unable to help.

At this, Jesus does not speak to either the boy or his father, but addresses the disciples directly and expresses something of his frustration with them when he says, *"How unbelieving you people are! How long must I stay with you? How long do I have to put up with you? Bring the boy to me!"* (Mark 9:19 GNB). The disciples must have been dismayed at their Master's words, but I think we must understand that it was out of compassion for the boy and his father that Jesus expressed his frustration with the disciples. Later, when the disciples asked Jesus why they couldn't get the demon out of the boy, Jesus told them, *"It was because you haven't enough faith"* (Matthew 17:20) and *"Only prayer (and fasting in some translations) can drive this kind out"* (Mark 9:29 GNB).

It is important to note that Jesus never accused the sick boy or his father of not having enough faith. It was the ministers of healing (the disciples) who were under scrutiny. Sometimes sick people are wrongly accused of not having enough faith. The responsibility for ministering healing lies firstly with the minister, not with the sick person. If, as a result of Holy Spirit discernment, the sick person is told something he has to do, but he refuses to do it (remember Naaman who, initially, refused to dip himself in the Jordan), or there is a mountain of scepticism and unbelief that the person will not repent of, the onus has then been transferred to the sick person.

Secondly Jesus drew attention to the need for prayer and possibly fasting. Most of the early manuscripts from which our modern translations are made include the words 'and fasting'. It is only some of what are believed to be the earliest manuscripts that exclude these two words. Jesus certainly expected people to fast for the right reasons (in spite of what he said about the disciples not fasting whilst the bridegroom - Jesus - is present). In Matthew 6:16 he did not say to the disciples *"if you fast . ."* but *"when you fast . . ",* implying that they would and should fast from time to time.

We have found on numerous occasions that special seasons of prayer (and sometimes fasting) have been strategic in preparing both the ministry team and the counsellee for deliverance. This is an important scripture that needs to be understood by critics of the deliverance ministry who claim that the ministry must be wrong because *"Jesus cast demons out with a word and you're taking weeks!!"* They forget that, like the disciples, we are not Jesus, of whom every demon in hell was desperately afraid!

They forget, too, that Jesus told the disciples that some deliverances would be hard for them without prayer and fasting. Whilst the reference is only brief, it is nevertheless highly significant, for it introduces the concept of 'degrees of difficulty' in delivering the severely demonised. This is certainly commensurate with our, and many other people's, experience.

The actual deliverance of the boy is also very significant. Firstly Jesus does not disagree with the father's diagnosis of the boy's condition, that it is caused by a demon. The father reports that *"whenever the spirit attacks him it throws him to the ground, and he foams at the mouth, grits his teeth, and becomes stiff all over"* (Mark 9:18). I recognise that epilepsy is not necessarily demonic in origin. But in this case, it clearly was.

The disciples brought the boy to Jesus and as they were bringing him the demon recognised Jesus, tried the only defence system it knew and threw the boy down in another fit *"so that he fell on the ground and rolled around, foaming at the mouth."*

Jesus did not immediately move in to heal the boy but asked the father a very important question, a question that we have often found to be very important as part of the pre-ministry counselling - as with the lady who had had sinusitis for twenty-five years - *"How long has he been like this?"* The father answered *"ever since he was a child"*. We are not told what information Jesus deduced from this answer, and probably there was a longer conversation on this issue with the father.

There was one lady we ministered to, who was healed of epilepsy, who had been like this for seventeen years. In her case she responded to a specific word of knowledge which exposed pre-marital sexual sin precisely seventeen years earlier and the entrance of a spirit which, in her case, had brought along epilepsy on its coat-tails. The length of time was an important part of the pre-ministry investigation. Carefully recording information such as this can be highly strategic when it comes to the actual ministry.

Finally, Jesus makes another comment on faith when the boy's father cries out in anguish *"help us if you possibly can!"* Jesus tells the father, *"anything is possible if you have faith"*. The father pitifully replies, *"I do have faith, but not enough"*. Note that Jesus does not condemn the man for not having enough faith, but immediately commences ministry to the boy. Jesus only ever said that we need faith the size of a grain of mustard seed, with which we can move mountains (Matthew 17:20-21). Sometimes I hear people talking about healing and deliverance as if it needed faith as big as a mountain to move a mustard seed!

Not only was the boy an epileptic, but the Gospel tells us that he was also dumb. When delivering him Jesus addresses the 'deaf and dumb spirit' and orders it to come out and never return to him again. In this instance the name of the demon that brought the symptoms of epilepsy was 'deaf and dumb spirit'. In the case of the woman described above it was a spirit of fornication. The response of the demon here is also interesting. Far from meekly leaving without a fuss, it immediately screamed and then threw the poor boy down again and into one more bad fit, before coming out!

At this point the boy looked limp and dead. Again this is not unusual either after a major deliverance or an epileptic fit. So I can fully understand the crowds reaction, thinking the boy had died during ministry. The contrast between the writhing demonised boy, and the corpse-like figure a few seconds later, would have been so severe as to induce thoughts of death in the onlookers. Jesus simply took the boy by the hand and helped him to his feet and gave him back to his father.

What a victory that was. Verse 25 of Mark's account says that the crowd were closing in on Jesus before the boy had been delivered. Possibly they were beginning to get angry that Jesus wasn't going to heal the boy, and if he couldn't heal him, they were asking themselves 'was Jesus really everything he claimed to be?'

We do not know; but what we do know is that there was no further problem from the crowd when they saw the boy completely healed before their very eyes!

Jesus never seemed to be concerned about even dramatic manifestations when someone was going through deliverance. But some critics of deliverance ministry have been heard to say, *"you should never allow demons to manifest, they should always go out quietly"*. On paper that sounds nice, but it is wholly unscriptural and, from our experience, totally impractical! With many of the heavily demonised people we have had to deal with it has been quite impossible to stop some of the manifestations that do occur during deliverance.

Whilst I would love, for the sake of the counsellee and our ministry teams, everything to happen nice and quietly (decently and in order!), I take great encouragement from the fact that with Jesus it was usually messy and noisy with lots of screams and manifestations! We should not expect the modern-day ministry of deliverance to be any different in this respect from the ministry of Jesus.

Over the years we have had many 'observers', both from the UK and overseas who have come alongside us to see the ministry of healing and deliverance in action. Some have come as sceptics, but those who have stayed with us and actually seen what God has been doing in peoples' lives, have left rejoicing at the healing power of Jesus. Hard evidence of changed lives cannot easily be refuted.

The Women and Mary Magdalene
(Luke 8:1-3)

At the beginning of Luke 8 there is the briefest of references to a very important aspect of deliverance ministry. The chapter begins with the extension of Jesus's travelling ministry when he went around with

the twelve through towns and villages preaching the Good
News.

Luke tells us that as well as the disciples there was a
group of women who used their own resources
(presumably money and time) to provide for the needs of
Jesus and the disciples. Sunday school teachers,(and
even some preachers!) can give the impression that, far
from being a man, Jesus was some un-earthly kind of
being who never needed food cooking for him or his
washing done! Luke is a careful observer of small details
and some of the 'throw away lines' in his Gospel contain
very revealing cameos of life with Jesus.

The women in question are described here as *"Mary
Magdalene (out of whom seven demons had been cast
out), Joanna, whose husband Chuza was an officer in
Herod's court; Susanna and many other women"*.
Obviously it wasn't just one, or at the most two women
who were involved, but quite an entourage!

There is one factor, however, which completely unites
this unlikely band of females (ranging from officers'
wives to prostitutes!) into a body of dedicated supporters of
Jesus. They had all *"been healed of evil spirits and
diseases"* (Luke 8:2 GNB). Nowhere in the scriptures do
we have any such similar reference to a body of men being
united together because of the common experience of
having been delivered and healed.

The text here is quite specific and very significant, for it
describes deliverance from evil spirits as 'being healed'.
All the translations (from the King James to the Good
News) translate this phrase in a similar way. There is
another passage which indicates something similar to
this.

In Luke 7:21, Jesus is specifically described at a
particular time as curing *"many people of their
sicknesses, diseases and evil spirits"*. Again indicating
that healing (curing) can include what we now describe
as deliverance. Further confirmation of this is found in

the following verse when the healings referred to in verse
21 are used by Jesus in verse 22 as evidence to a
messenger from John the Baptist (who was then in
prison) of his Messiahship.

Jesus says, *"tell John what you have seen and heard: the
blind see, the lame can walk, those who suffer from skin
diseases are made clean, the deaf can hear, the dead are
raised to life, and the Good News is preached to the poor.
How happy are those who have no doubts about me".*
Significantly Jesus describes all these healings, and
never mentions an evil spirit once! Yet in the previous
verse Luke (the careful recorder) tells us that some of the
healings Jesus described were effected through
deliverance from evil spirits!

We have, therefore, to be very aware that other references
in the Gospels, where people are simply described as
having been healed, may also have been descriptions of
both healing and deliverance ministry. Conversely, today,
we must be alert to the possibility that those who come for
healing may be sick because there is an evil spirit present
that needs to be cast out - even if there is no immediate
evidence that the person is demonised or very obvious
manifestation of a demon during prayer. With
experience, those ministering deliverance will learn to
discern the presence of the demonic, even when there is
no obvious manifestation.

Returning now to the women who accompanied Jesus,
and their common experience of deliverance (the uniting
factor which held them together in grateful service of the
Lord). It is generally believed that one of these women,
Mary Magdalene, had been a prostitute and, therefore,
had a history of sexual activity. She is described as having
had seven demons cast out of her.

In the next volume, when discussing demonic entry
points, there is an extensive section on inroads through
sexual activity. Sexual sin always affects the spirit and
opens up a potential gateway for demonisation. Where
there has been sexual sin, therefore, of any nature,

deliverance is usually an important part of the healing process.

This is especially so in the case of women who have been taken advantage of by men, whether or not the sexual participation was voluntary (as it presumably was in Mary Magdalene's case, although no-one knows why it was she got involved in prostitution in the first place) or involuntary (in the case of those who have been forcibly abused, either as children or as adults).

What I can say is that we have extensive experience of ministering to the sexually abused and those who have been wrongfully taken advantage of in sexual relationships, and we have found that deliverance has been a major key in bringing them through to complete wholeness. Sexual abuse brings with it a whole chain of problems, but if there has been demonisation, no amount of other care and treatment will bring complete healing without deliverance also being part of the ministry that is given.

By including this discussion here I am not trying to imply that Joanna, Susanna and all the other women had had sexual affairs, but it does seem to be clearly stated that they needed deliverance. Our experience of the past four years has been that as many as one in two of the women who have come to us for help have been sexually abused at some time during their life. Most have also been demonised as a result, and it is not unreasonable to suspect, therefore, that probably half of this group of women, who had taken their needs to Jesus, had problems which originated in this area.

Sexual abuse is talked about in detail in the Old Testament - it is not just a twentieth century phenomenon - for example, read Judges 19. It is one of Satan's most successful methods of effecting demonic interference and was probably as rife in Jesus's day as it is now.

Another reason which makes me think that many of these women might have been sexual abuse victims lies

in their willingness, after deliverance and healing, to
spend their lives in serving Jesus. For Jesus was probably
one of the first men they had ever met whom they found
they could trust one hundred per cent. They had no
reason to fear the possibility of any abuse from him.

His sexuality was totally subject to the control of the Spirit
of God and there was, therefore, not a hint of a sexual
innuendo in his conversation, or any salacious look from
his eye, or any wrongful touch from his hands. Women
who have been abused know exactly what lies behind the
looks, words and touches of those with sexual problems.
Their spirits sense the wrong spirit that underlies the
various contacts that men can try to make.

In ministering to women we have seen time and time
again how grateful they are to God for what he has done
for them. They have known that deep down there was
something inside them that had been controlling their
lives, and it was only the power of the name of Jesus that
has set them free. Their gratitude has known no bounds
and their willingness to be totally obedient to the voice of
the Holy Spirit has challenged me on many occasions as
they have responded to the love of Jesus.

This whole discussion does highlight the need for sexual
purity in the hearts of those men who minister to women.
It is important that men should be involved in ministry to
the abused - but not alone, women should always be
present - for it is part of their healing to be able to receive
help from the opposite sex.

Men, especially, should be on their guard against the
enemy taking advantage of a counselling situation to
introduce lust into the proceedings. Some of the most hurt
women I have ever met are those who eventually
summoned up the courage to share their sexual story
with a man, but were then taken advantage of by their
counsellor. The sexual and spiritual consequences of this
are devastating.

I thank God that Jesus ministered to women, that they could trust both him and the disciples, and that God is still willing to deliver those who have been demonised through their own sexual sin or that of others against them. This is a big topic and in this book we can only touch on some key aspects of the subject, but at this point I must underline that any who wish to help the sexually abused in Christian ministry must also be comfortable with deliverance. It is an essential part of the ministry!

The Storm on the Lake
(Matthew 8:23-27, Mark 4:35-41, Luke 8:22-25)

All three Gospel writers include this significant story. Mark tells us that it happened on the same day that the crowd by the lakeside was so big that Jesus had to get into a boat and use it as a platform from which to teach the people (Mark 4:1). It had been a tiring day, thousands of people pressing in on him, and now Jesus needed a rest. *"Let's go to the other side of the lake,"* he said. So Jesus stayed in the boat, the disciples got in, off they went and Jesus, exhausted from the day's ministry, fell asleep on a pillow in the back of the vessel.

The enemy often chooses moments when we are apparently off guard to launch his most dangerous attacks. Jesus was no exception to this frequently used tactic of demonic combat. The ministry of Jesus was beginning to have an effect in the region. His teaching was unseating demonic strongholds, and one wonders if the powers of the air had understood Jesus's intentions in going to the other side of the lake (to set free the Gadarene demoniac) and moved in to do everything possible to prevent that boat from reaching the other side. If the disciples had been aware of what Jesus intended to do at the other side of the lake, they might not have been too keen on going there either!

Suddenly, half way across the lake a violent storm blew up from nowhere. The disciples were experienced fishermen. They were able to read the weather and would not have set out across the lake if they had seen such a storm brewing. This storm apparently came from nowhere and was totally unexpected. When it hit them they were caught so off guard that immediately water began pouring into the boat and they were in danger of sinking. A freak storm nearly devastated the boat.

These experienced fishermen were afraid. But there was Jesus, a carpenter with little experience of the sea, fast asleep in the back of the boat as if they were paddling a dinghy for relaxation on the flat calm of a village pond! The disciples knew he was tired after the day's ministry, but things were desperate. So they woke him and in their fear and desperation spoke with words which could only have sounded like a rebuke from the crew, *"Don't you care that we are about to die?!"* (Mark 4:38 GNB).

Jesus then did one of the most remarkable things in the whole of his ministry. He stood up in the middle of the boat, which must have been crashing from side to side in the gale, and spoke a command into the face of the wind. One could have forgiven the disciples if they had thought he was mad. For who, in their right mind, would think of shouting at the wind and the waves. It was as mad as sitting on the shore of the Atlantic Ocean and telling the tide not to come in, as King Canute is reputed to have done!

The frustration which the disciples showed in their rebuke to Jesus was probably about to boil over into anger and rage. What they wanted was help from Jesus, not this. Pulling on the ropes, baling out the water, anything else would do, but not, surely not this, shouting at the wind!

"Be quiet," he commanded the wind. *"Be still,"* he commanded the sea. And immediately the wind died down and there was a great calm. This time the rebuke was from Jesus to the disciples. I can see the shocked amazement in their faces as ropes, now limp in the calm, slipped from their hands, as baling buckets dropped to the

deck, now eminently redundant. Words were almost unnecessary, but Jesus nevertheless questioned them, *"Why were you so frightened? Have you still no faith?"*

It is easy to have understanding with hindsight. My sympathies are entirely with the emotions of the disciples. They were human beings, they were rightfully afraid. They did not have that perfect insight into what was happening in the heavenlies. Just because Jesus was asleep physically does not mean that his spirit was switched off and insensitive to what was going on, but they were not to know that.

Jesus was at peace because he had already won the battles with Satan in the wilderness and he knew that whatever the demons tried to throw at him, they would not, and could not, take his life from him before he chose to lay it down. And his time had not yet come. And that was the end of the matter as far as Jesus was concerned. While he was asleep the angels were in charge.

It's easy to say such things retrospectively and from our perspective, but the disciples had not seen Jesus exercise authority over the elements before. Now, if they had found a sick and demonised man in the middle of the lake, floating on an improvised raft, that would have been no problem. Jesus can heal the sick and we've got him in the boat! Their faith would not have needed stretching a millimetre to have coped with that situation. They were used to Jesus commanding demons to leave people!

But standing up in the middle of the lake and commanding the wind and the waves was a very different matter. After all, they weren't quite used to the idea that demons were not always in people. It was a major new learning curve for the disciples. A faith stretching experience of enormous magnitude. An essential lesson which they would remember and pass on to other Christians with enthusiasm, as they told of how they learnt about the powers of the air, and the victory that Jesus had over them.

No doubt Paul, in his Mediterranean exploits, remembered the stories well. He had learnt that whatever happened, provided he remained in that position of complete obedience to the will of God as revealed to him through the Holy Spirit, the enemy could not take his life from him before the appointed time.

Whilst the wind and the waves are not normally controlled by demons, there is little doubt that on this occasion, the disciples ran into a demonic storm whipped up by the enemy. And what Jesus was speaking to, when he commanded the wind and the waves was not the elements themselves, but the spirit that was behind the elements. There is little difference between this and addressing the sickness in a demonised person. Whilst one might speak to the sickness, one is really speaking to the spirit that is behind the sickness.

On one occasion, on a calm and sunny day, we were delivering a semi-derelict chapel of the resident demonic powers that drew occultists to the site for their witchcraft rituals. We all sensed that the powers were being broken, when, suddenly, a storm came up from nowhere and we were at the centre of an almighty gale with huge raindrops being lashed against us by gale-force winds. We carried on praising God for the victory, spoke against the powers behind the storm, and it died down again as quickly as it had come up.

The demonic powers were throwing in their last trick to distract us from the work God had given us to do that afternoon. And in the case of the demonic powers that resided over Galilee, perhaps the storm that raged on that day was the last weapon they had in their armoury to try and prevent Jesus from landing at Gerasa and doing the special work he was going there to do.

The Gadarene Demoniac
(Matthew 8:28-34, Mark 5:1-20, Luke 8:26-39)

Gerasa, Gadara and Gergesa are all variations of the same name. So whether people talk about the Gadarene demoniac, the Gerasene demoniac or any other similar sounding demoniac, they are talking about the same person and the same incident. They are recalling the day when Jesus was willing to confront the local madman, who was totally out of control and had enormous supernatural strength and of whom everyone else was petrified. Not the sort of guy to have around if you want a nice quiet life!

The only significant difference between the three different accounts is that Matthew describes two men, whereas Mark and Luke say there was only one. Possibly Matthew remembers the man as having been so savage that he seemed to have the strength of two! But what is far more likely is that the burial caves in this area were often frequented by demoniacs and Matthew is linking two separate deliverances into one composite account. In all other respects the stories are similar with various extra details provided by each writer. In commenting on this incident I will draw on information from each of the accounts.

The Significance of the Graveyards

All three writers tell us that the area of Gerasa where this violent man was to be found was a burial ground, giving an aura of terror to an already sinister place. Why should anyone want to live amongst the dead?

We have ministered to quite a number of people with witchcraft or satanic practices in either their own background or that of their ancestors, and one of their presenting symptoms has been a strong compulsion to visit graveyards, lie on the tombs at night, or, most compellingly, lie on the grave of a freshly buried corpse. In the demonic realm what appears to be happening on these visitations is that demons from those who have died are attempting to transfer to new homes and the demons already inside a living person are trying to attract new demonic powers to enhance their power and further demonise their host.

What is certainly the case in the story is that the man was highly demonised and that his demons had been successful in attracting a huge army of evil spirits, many of which will have come from the dead who had been buried in the tombs. The more demonised a person is the greater the control by demonic powers and the supernatural strength that can be displayed through the victim's body.

Supernatural Strength

The effect of this man on the local community was severe. Matthew tells us that the local road had become a no-go area such was his fierceness. Mark and Luke describe the chains that had been used to attempt to contain his violence and protect the community from his menaces. But nobody had been able to get chains on him strong enough to hold him down. Many times people had tried, but always in vain, for whatever chains they had been able to get on had always been smashed. He was simply too strong for anyone to control.

People who manifest this particular demonic characteristic are not permanently in a state of exercising supernatural strength. The strength manifests itself to protect the demonic kingdom within the person, or to give prowess to the host who uses the demons to give him power and influence, or, we have found, during the actual process of deliverance (rather like when Jesus delivered the epileptic boy, the demon's characteristic of epilepsy was manifested during deliverance).

We once ministered to a man who came for counselling because he had marriage problems. Two years of good pastoral care from his minister had not helped. When we started to pray for him demons came to the surface and it was soon obvious why he had marriage problems! His wife was having to contend, not with her husband, who genuinely wanted to be a good husband and father, but with her husband's demons which had enormous strength and power.

In his job on a building site he would impress his workmates with feats of supernatural strength in the lunch-hours, carrying unbelievably large numbers of bricks. He had no idea that he had been using demonic power to do these things. Deliverance not only changed him but healed the marriage problems and three years later the relationship is doing fine. (It is not unusual in marital situations for people to try and counsel into the relationship when the bottom line is that one, or both, of the partners needs deliverance. Only then can the couple begin to relate as husband and wife instead of Husband's demons versus Wife's demons!!'

Martial arts are listed in our counselling check list as a demonic entry point for the above reason. Whilst healthy physical fitness and muscle training is part of such sports, there is a demonic dimension to them which changes their nature from a sport to a demonically empowered activity.

When we watch such sports what we are observing is a contest between one contestant's demons linked with his body against the body and demons of the other contestant. It is never portrayed as such in the publicity for these sports, but once having had to deliver people of the demons that have come in through participation you have a very different perspective on things!

Cutting and Screaming

Mark adds another significant detail in his account of the story of the Gerasene demoniac. He tells us that the man wandered through the tombs day and night screaming and cutting himself with stones - presumably sharp flints or other such sharp edges with which it was possible to draw blood.

In the story of Elijah's confrontation with the 450 prophets of Baal, Elijah watches on while the prophets call on their God to bring fire down on their sacrifice. Nothing happened, *"so the prophets prayed louder and cut themselves with knives and daggers, according to their ritual, until blood flowed. They kept on ranting and raving . . ."* (1 Kings 18:28-29 GNB). We see here that cutting themselves until blood flowed was part of the traditions of Baal worship.

Baal worship is a form of demon worship and a severe occultic practice. Exodus 20:5 tells us that one of the consequences of idolatry is that the sins of the fathers are visited on the children. And that can mean the demons which enter a person through occultic sin can travel down the family line affecting future generations. One person who came to us for help regularly cut herself to *"satisfy the pressing demands of her demons for blood"*.

It seems possible, therefore, that the Gadarene demoniac could have been a descendant of Baal worshippers and that his madness was partly a result of demons that had come upon him because of the sins of his ancestors. As a result he was now forced, against his will, to fulfil the rituals of a form of worship which was probably foreign to him.

We have ministered to many people who try and cut themselves with glass, razor blades or other sharp instruments. Rarely is this an attempt to commit suicide by cutting the wrists but is designed to create pain and draw blood. For some, this has become a means of masking intense emotional pain that cannot easily be fought - the physical pain caused by cutting themselves is a focus for pain which distracts from the real source of hurt inside.

Others, however, have been descendants of those who have been known to be involved in occultic worship of demons and the demon controlling the desire to draw blood has been specifically associated with occultic practice. There may not be many Baal worshippers around today, but there are many Freemasons, and not many people realise that the name of the masonic God, Jahbulon, is an amalgam of the names of three gods, the middle one of which represents Baal!

Nakedness

Luke adds another significant detail in his account. *"For a long time this man had gone without clothes"* (Luke 8:27). People who are mentally deranged very often lose all sense of personal modesty. It is not unusual for patients in mental hospitals to wander around naked for preference, giving the staff endless problems when visitors arrive!

It is interesting to observe that many of the rituals of witchcraft and Satanism are carried out in the nude, and many of them include sexual acts and perversions as part of the initiation ceremonies and ongoing practices of the covens. Nudity, under demonic direction, becomes part of the way of life.

It is not surprising, therefore, to find on occasions that those whose ancestors have been involved in such occultic practices, are afflicted by spirits that make the person want to remove their clothes, for that is a prelude to intensified demonic activity. It seems possible, therefore, that both the Gerasene demoniac, and many people who are 'mentally ill' and suffer in this way, could be generational victims of demonisation through occultic sin.

Certainly we have experienced the situation where the person we have been ministering to has had to fight for their sanity in this respect, against demonic powers within that were doing everything they could to make them remove their clothes. The ministry team has also had to help preserve the modesty of counsellees who were so demonised that they had become temporarily out of control in this respect.

The whole subject of nudity has much wider implications, however, than the nakedness of witchcraft rituals. In the past twenty years the world has become progressively less self-conscious, and nakedness on beaches, films, television and in print has progressed at an astonishing speed.

In order to understand something of why Satan and his demons encourage nudity, and are behind the world-wide explosion in pornography, we need to return to Genesis 2 and 3, which we last looked at in Chapter 5 on the fall of man. Prior to the fall the flesh-life which God had given to man was totally sanctified and holy. There was no need for any shame or embarrassment, either between man and woman in their nakedness, or in the presence of anyone else (Genesis 2:25). In the Genesis account that third person was the Lord himself.

The moment that mankind gave entrance to Satan the potential was there for demons to corrupt the flesh and spoil what God had planned for mankind in sexual relationships. Sex was intended by God to be primarily a spiritual act of total unity which is completed by men and women, who are committed to each other in a covenant relationship, through the mind, the emotions and the will and finally through bodily sexual intercourse. The Hebrew word for sexual intercourse used in Genesis is the same word as is used for 'knowing' God, confirming the intense spirituality that God intended for sexual bonding.

Embarrassment at being naked does not stem from how you feel about your own body, but from not wanting others to see the genital areas. Embarrassment at genital nakedness was a direct consequence of the fall, and doing something about it was Adam and Eve's first action after becoming sinners! Not that they were or should ever be embarrassed in front of each other as husband and wife, but because they were expecting a visitor from whom they naively tried to hide their nakedness - as if one can hide anything from God!

But in their spirits they knew that things could never be the same again and that from now on it was wrong for others to see their nakedness. The key to this lies in the understanding of sex being spiritual first and bodily second, or even third. For it is through the spirit that Satan and his demons have direct access to the flesh, and Satan has always wanted to pervert and destroy everything that God created.

Before the fall there would be no danger in anyone seeing our sexual nakedness, but after the fall Satan's perversion of the flesh introduced the potential for lust. To lust is directly contrary to the very nature of God (who is love) who created us in his own image. Hence a primary reaction to the fall was, inevitably, an immediate move to be protected from Satan's corruption.

Covering up the nakedness was, therefore, a rightful response from Adam and Eve, which was confirmed by the Lord himself, when (Genesis 3:21) he *"made clothes out of animal skins for Adam and his wife"*. What had happened was this. Man had become like God in his spiritual understanding and now had *"knowledge of what is good and what is bad"*.

That knowledge was the one aspect of God's understanding which had been withheld from his creation, man. I believe that God wanted to protect man from what had happened in the heavenly realm, when Satan rebelled and was expelled from heaven. However, God had chosen to give man freewill. He did not want to create a race of automatons who were unable to do anything else than what he wanted, like supernatural gnomes who could be wound up at the beginning of time to always perform perfectly according to an eternal clockwork programme!

But the Lord nevertheless wanted to warn his creation of the danger that lurked in the heavenlies without removing his freewill - hence the story of the tree of knowledge of good and evil, where man had a choice and could use his freewill not to eat of the tree and, therefore, choose eternal protection from all that Satan would throw at him. *"But,"* God said, *"eat of the tree and you will surely die!"* The death God meant was not immediate physical death, but death to the spiritual relationship with the living God that was, until then, marked by purity, innocence and holiness.

Man could now differentiate between love and lust. Within man was God's nature - love. But now, Satan's character was also being implanted upon mankind and the capacity for lust became part of man's fallen nature. It is only within marriage that looking on each other's sexuality for the expression of love (giving, not taking) is allowed. Which of us could say, with a clear conscience, that we could look on the sexuality of a member of the opposite sex who we find attractive and be totally free from the possibility of lust? Covering up the nakedness was God's immediate response to the fall. It must have saddened him enormously to have to do this, but the greater aim of protecting mankind from the demonisation that comes through the expression of lust had to prevail.

Hence the comment made by Jesus on adultery in the Sermon on the Mount, *"whoever looks at a woman to lust for her has already committed adultery with her in his heart"* (Matthew 5:28 NKJV). Jesus is saying here, in another way, that sex is primarily spiritual, and that as far as God is concerned spiritual adultery is as much a sin as physical adultery.

The effects on the other party will inevitably be greater if the physical act of adultery is committed, but from a sin point of view spiritual (heart) adultery is as much an offence against God as the act of sex itself. For adultery of this nature is the outworking of lust, and is joining in with Satan's rebellion against God. (Similar comments would apply to homosexual lust where men are lusting after men and women after women, and by saying that I am not giving sanction by default to the rightness of allegedly loving homosexual relationships. These can never be right before God).

When we begin to understand the spiritual nature of sin we begin to get a far deeper appreciation of the wonder of redemption and of the forgiveness that God made freely available for all who believe. None of us could stand before God were it not that for the redeemed their sin is covered by the blood of Jesus. Praise God indeed!

This whole discussion may have seemed a long diversion in our study of the Gadarene demoniac, but it is vital to an understanding of a major aspect of demonisation. Satan and his demons encourage nakedness and pornography, because it encourages lust which (like all sin) is a form of rebellion against God. Encouragement of lust strikes at the deep spiritual significance that God intended for sexual relationships and debases both men and women, irrespective of whether they are the one who looks or the one who is looked at.

It is not surprising, therefore, that so many rituals of witchcraft and Satanism are done in the nude or that in these days, when there is such a world-wide rise in occult activity, we are in an era of unprecedented nakedness presented to the world in ways that, so often, cannot be avoided. Christians need to be constantly in prayer for their children, that their minds may be protected from the sexual onslaught of the world.

Sadly, many married men (and some women) are made especially vulnerable to pornography by the unwillingness or inability of their partner to express themselves sexually in an uninhibited way, but that's another story which will have to wait for fuller discussion at another time and in another place!

The Actual Confrontation with Jesus

The moment Jesus landed at Gerasa the demoniac's demons were aware of his presence. They knew who

Jesus was and that he was the only person who had ever walked the face of this earth who had the power and authority to challenge their strong hold on this wild man of the caves. Immediately they saw Jesus, therefore, they recognised the power of the Holy Spirit working through him and reacted strongly to his presence, as they will when faced with Christians who recognise the demonic and are ministering in deliverance.

It has been our regular experience that the demons often know when the person is going to a place where Spirit-filled Christians will be able to discern the presence of the demonic. We have heard many amazing stories of how demons have sought to prevent people getting to Ellel Grange. And right on the doorstep they have dared to reveal their presence and have cried out from a person things like 'Don't go in there, it's dangerous', 'Get away from here, now', and on quite a number of occasions we have had to carry people into the building because their demons had so physically controlled them that it was quite impossible for them to have entered unaided!

Most of our ministry team have had things said or shouted at them during ministry. Words such as 'I hate you', addressed at a person on whom there is a special anointing of the Holy Spirit, are not unusual. Conversely, however, if the person ministering to an individual does not recognise the need for deliverance and has no discernment, therefore, of the demonic, the demons will lie low and remain hidden and unchallenged, knowing that they need not fear eviction. Such counselling is not a threat to them, for they know that whatever happens during the ministry time they will be able to regroup and continue their attacks on the person after the 'ministry' is over!

If we are moving in ministry at a level that does not accept the possible presence of the demonic, or from a ministry model that will only deal with the demonic if it manifests, then most of the demonic strongholds in peoples' lives will remain hidden and ministry will, inevitably, be superficial. When ministering to people in churches, at healing services or on our training courses it is not unusual for people who are, ordinarily, very nice people to suddenly want to strangle me, spit at me, swear at me, pull faces at me or demonstrate some other violent response! This is only because I have recognised the demonic that is operating in the person's life and started to deal with it. The person usually gets quite a shock to find themselves behaving like this, for they themselves have only asked for ministry because they felt they could trust me!

The demons in the Gerasene demoniac immediately took the battle to Jesus and made the man cry out *"Jesus, Son of the most high God, what do you want with me!"* The question is similar to that which demons had asked on other occasions, and almost identical to what the demon said in the synagogue at Capernaum at the beginning of Jesus's ministry. The demons knew that there was to be an appointed time for Jesus to deal with them, but they certainly didn't want that moment to come!

At this point Jesus must have said, *"Come out of the man"*, for both Mark and Luke record that the conversation with the demon was only continued because the demon at this point had remained entrenched and refused to go. The demon's response to the command to leave was a cry for clemency, *"I beg you, don't punish me."* Mark quaintly adds that the demon even said, *"For God's sake, don't punish us."*

The fact that the demon was still there, after Jesus had commanded it to leave, must be a source of much encouragement to those who have experienced difficulty during deliverance ministry! So Jesus changed his method of approach to the situation and asked the demon a question, *"What is your name?"*

If you know someone's name you are in a far stronger position to exercise authority or power over them. All schoolteachers know the difficulty of exercising discipline if they keep on forgetting the names of their pupils! In this case Jesus appeared to be addressing the ring-leader of the demons, for in answer to the question, it responded *"Legion - for we are many."*

In answering the question, it gave away the fact that there was not just one demon there, but a whole army of them. A Roman legion contained up to 6000 men and the implication, therefore, is that up to 6000 demons were occupying the man. It is not surprising, therefore, that he was so strong and so much out of control.

On a number of occasions we have encountered similar cases, when demons that have been challenged as to their identity have also responded with the name Legion. Indeed, there have, in severe cases been several 'Legion demons', each with their own private army of evil spirits under their control.

Whenever one talks about this particular deliverance, some people ask the inevitable question? How could 6000 spirits possibly live inside the body of one human being? The problem with understanding such seeming impossibilities is that we try and imagine demons in spatial three dimensional terms, often with images in our minds from some of the speculative drawings of demons that most people have seen. It is, perhaps, a little more helpful to think of demons, not so much as huge ugly creatures, as undoubtedly some of them are, but more as germs, the size of which is infinitesimal, but the effect of which can be life-threatening.

Germs are only a real threat to us if we are attacked by a variety which our bodies are not protected against, or if we do not practise sensible health and hygiene precautions in our normal living. It's a bit like that with the demonic. If we live in obedience to the Holy Spirit (practise good spiritual hygiene!), and we are on our guard against the unexpected attack from outside sources, then we need not fear being demonised. But if our spiritual hygiene is poor, and in our lives there is an open wound caused by sin, then who is to say just how

many demons are likely to gain access to us through that
entry point?

Just as there could be countless germs in a festering
physical wound, so there could be extensive demonisation
through a festering spiritual wound. Ungodly activities in
pre-conversion days can also be a source of ongoing
problems if the demonic consequences of these things
have not been dealt with through deliverance on coming
to Christ.

However many demons were present in the man, they
knew that eventually they would have to leave him,
because they were facing Jesus himself. Mark tells us
that they pleaded with Jesus not to be sent out of the area.
The significance of this question probably related to the
ruling spirit who was in charge of the area, and to whom
the demons inside the man were ultimately answerable.
If the demons had been sent out of that particular area
they would have found themselves under the control of a
different ruling spirit and there may have been
inter-demonic war and even demonic punishment as a
result.

We have heard demons squealing in terror, not at the fact
that we were casting them out, but at the punishment
they were getting from higher demons for giving away
vital information about how they had entered in the first
place! As a general rule demons hate each other and are
only united in any way because they are equally afraid of
their ultimate master, Satan. They will also fight each
other for self-gain and elevation to a higher position. On
one occasion, a demon whimpered pitifully before we cast
it out, complaining about how cruel we were to cast it out
just after it had won promotion in the ranks!

The anxiety the demons expressed in the Gospel account,
about not being sent from their particular area, also gives
an important clue to a very common problem,
homesickness. Not all homesickness has a demonic
origin, but there are many occasions when someone is so

unnaturally uncomfortable away from home that it is obvious something quite deep is happening in their life.

It is generally put down to being something emotional, but we know in some cases it is because the person has demons who are answerable to the local ruling spirit and which are very uncomfortable once they go outside the territory of their own demonic control. The demon then makes the person feel uncomfortable, so that they become convinced that they want to go home. Whereas it is the demon who wants to get off the territory of an alien ruling spirit and get back to safer ground! There are good emotional reasons as well why people do often want to go back to a place of personal security, but in cases that seem irresolvable and quite irrational, demonic involvement is probably the real answer.

Luke tells us that the demons also pleaded with Jesus not to send them to the abyss. The abyss is believed to be the place of torment and punishment for fallen angels and demons, who are currently imprisoned in the depths of the earth awaiting their final curtain call on the world's stage.

Jude tells of some fallen angels who *"did not stay within the limits of their proper authority, but abandoned their own dwelling place: they are bound with eternal chains in the darkness below, where God is keeping them for that great Day on which they will be condemned"* (Jude 6 GNB). And Peter tells us that *"God did not spare the angels who sinned, but threw them into hell, where they are kept chained in darkness, waiting for the day of judgement"* (2 Peter 2:4 GNB). For the time being, roaming about the earth under Satan's command was clearly preferable to being sent to the abyss, and the demons were in fear lest Jesus would send them there.

Luke then tells us that Legion put in one more plea to Jesus, which, this time, Jesus acceded to. *"Send us to the pigs, let us go into them."* The story of what happened is well-known. Jesus agreed to this being their destination and the demons, already having been ordered to leave, immediately fled from the man and went into the whole herd of 2000 pigs. The effect on the pigs was traumatic. Such was the shock of an average of three demons per pig landing in the herd that they turned tail, ran towards the sea, fell over a cliff, and were drowned. It is not recorded where the demons went to after that.

After years of thought, and discussion with many people, I have only ever come up with one remotely satisfactory answer as to why Jesus risked bad relationships with the local farming community by destroying their herd of pigs. It was because of his love and compassion for the man. When one deaf and dumb spirit came out of the epileptic boy the effect on the boy was devastating as a major manifestation took place. Then, much against its will, the demon was dislodged from its hiding place.

The effect on the man of 6000 demons leaving in a similarly reluctant fashion, at the same time, would probably have been such that he would not have survived the ordeal. The demons, however, had chosen to go willingly into the pigs, and if they would leave without a fuss, then the man would be spared the terrible ordeal of the demons tearing his flesh as they went. On some occasions we have seen actual physical injuries (including tearing of the skin and bleeding) to people caused by demons as they left. I don't think we should take this story as a spiritual precedent, however, authorising us to cast demons into animals as a general rule of deliverance!

Whatever the real reason, it was Jesus who agreed to them going, so they went and the man was free. *"People . . . found the man from whom the demons had gone out sitting at the feet of Jesus, clothed and in his right mind . . . the man had been cured."* (Luke 8:35-36 GNB). An amazing miracle had taken place and the man, not unnaturally, was so grateful to Jesus that he wanted to go with him. But Jesus sent him away, saying, *"Go back home and tell what God has done for you."* (Luke 8:39 GNB).

Opposition to Deliverance Ministry

Sadly, the reaction of the local people, even after they had seen the man whole, was not one of rejoicing, but one of fear. The man had been so well known for the terrible powers that controlled him, that their uninformed response to Jesus was probably that they thought he must have even more powerful demons! In which case they did not want him anywhere near them, thank you very much! So Jesus went away, putting into practice what he was later to teach the seventy-two, that whenever they went into a town and were not welcomed, they were to wipe the dust of that place from off their feet and move on. (Luke 10:8-12).

Unfortunately there are many people today in our churches who do not want anything to do with the deliverance ministry. Because the ministry is not something they have been familiar with in their own lives and ministries they reject both it, and the people who are ministering deliverance. They sometimes, even, condemn good ministries with accusations of using an ungodly power.

I remember praying for one person who had a deep need of healing from spirits of infirmity that affected him and, as a result, everyone around him. Superficially he did want to get better (from the symptoms), but the presence of the Holy Spirit upon him was stirring up the enemy, and he immediately said, in a voice which sounded like his, but which was definitely not him speaking, *"Don't ever pray for me like that again!"* The enemy had been confronted and used all that man's religious tradition to put an end to the idea of any praying that would really expose and unseat the demonic strongholds which controlled his health.

Graham Powell, who has had many years experience of the deliverance ministry, says the following in his book Christian Set Yourself Free: *"There is another price which has to be paid by many who set others free. It is the cost of being faced with discredit and all sorts of accusations. Attacks often come through fellow believers who are blinded to the subtle workings of the enemy and feel they are doing God a service by speaking against such things. In dealing with demons, we are exposing and tearing down Satan's inroads into lives. This is the last thing Satan wants. No wonder he gets upset. Casting out demons is sure to be a controversial issue. Satan will see to that."*

I hesitated about whether to mention the price of being involved in deliverance ministry in this book. I do not want to see anyone turning away from doing the works of Jesus that he has commissioned us to do. But then I thought about Jesus himself, who so needed people around him who could be totally trusted, but still warned that to follow him would be like taking up a cross of their own - and the cross only meant one thing - crucifixion. For us, crucifixion is unlikely to mean being literally nailed to a wooden cross, but the crucifixion of self, one's own ego, reputation, career and even ministry and having to endure pain, insults, betrayal and false accusation.

Jesus said to those people, *"If one of you is planning to build a tower he sits down first and works out what it will cost, to see if he has enough money to finish the job. If he doesn't, he will not be able to finish the tower after laying the foundation; and all who see what happened will laugh at him. 'This man began to build, but can't finish the job!' they will say."* (Luke 14:28-30 GNB). We need to be aware about the cost of following Jesus in all its aspects, so that when there is opposition we will, at least, understand and know where it's coming from. In our experience it is usually those with a strong religious reputation to protect, or an already 'successful' ministry that does not incorporate deliverance, that are most easily used by the enemy to oppose the ministry of deliverance.

They need to remember that it was in the context of deliverance ministry that Jesus said to religious people, *"Anyone who is not for me is really against me; anyone who does not help me gather is really scattering."* (Matthew 12:30 GNB). I have often heard that verse quoted, out of context, to support a particular line of religious action, but rarely have I heard it used in its proper context of supporting spiritual warfare against the powers of darkness and encouraging people to help Jesus gather in the harvest, by fulfilling his commission to deliver people of demons!

Talking to Demons

Another major issue which the ministry to the Gerasene demoniac introduces is that of talking to demons. It is the only deliverance ministry recorded in the Gospels in which Jesus engaged in any sort of conversation with the demons inside a person. In other ministries the demons certainly cried out, but it seems as though Jesus's immediate response of *"Come out!"* was normally sufficient to set the person free. In this instance it was not enough!

The Gerasene demoniac is the most severely demonised person which the Gospel records describe as having been delivered by Jesus. It is in the Gospels for a purpose, and one of those purposes is to demonstrate to us that there were occasions when even Jesus found things to be hard. The passage we have already looked at about the epileptic boy is equally encouraging in this respect, for Jesus introduced here the concept of degrees of difficulty in deliverance ministry when he said to the disciples, *"This kind comes out only with prayer (and fasting)"*, implying that more than just ordinary praying is necessary on some occasions (Mark 9:14-29).

The significance of Jesus talking to the demons on this occasion seems to lie in the need for the demons to understand the authority Jesus had over them. Having been challenged to speak their name, and having then done so, they recognised that Jesus was someone whose commands had to be obeyed.

The conversation Jesus had with the demons was solely so that the man could be set free, and that is the only valid reason for talking with them. Anything more than this is using the demons to find out information which is unrelated to the task of delivering people from the powers of darkness. This is close to mediumship and is expressly forbidden in the scriptures. (Deuteronomy 18:10-15).

We have often found with very severely demonised people, that brief conversation with the demons to find their names, has been a necessary stage in undermining their authority in the person's life. Another question we have found to be just as powerful in this respect is *"How did you get in?"*. When the demon realises it has to answer this question, and reveal the way it gained a foothold in the person's life, a significant hold over the person has been broken.

As with Legion in the Gerasene demoniac the demons themselves will often come out with statements and comments - sometimes as a means of playing for time, in the hope that we will give up and leave the demon in residence.

Often demons have looked at those ministering and said such banal things as *"Aren't you tired, why don't you stop and have a rest!"* All such comments need to be rebuked accordingly and the ministry pressed home, for when they start saying things like that it is clear they have lost most of the ground on which they are standing.

Those, also, who criticise this aspect of deliverance ministry and say *"You should never talk to demons, they always tell lies"* are themselves being dishonest with the Gospel accounts. There is no record of a demon ever speaking a lie in the New Testament. Both in the Gospels and the Acts of the Apostles they are recorded as always telling truth. Jesus never rebuked a demon for dishonesty! That doesn't mean to say that demons are not basically deceitful creatures, they are. Their job function is to whisper Satan's lies into our hearts and lead us into sin, which is simply rebellion against God.

But when demons were face to face with Jesus, in a confrontational situation, they knew that Jesus would know what was truth and what was deceit. A similar thing happens when demons are challenged in the Name of Jesus by believers who are exercising a rightful authority in deliverance ministry. The demons will try to lie, but such lies are readily discernible by those ministering, and time and again we have reprimanded them and made them speak *"the truth that Jesus Christ of Nazareth who came in the flesh would confirm as being the truth"*.

That is a 'formula' which is very powerful when confronting the enemy. No demon could ever come in the flesh, and such a phrase totally and uniquely identifies the one in whose name we have such authority, and distinguishes him from any demon (of which there are many) who has adopted the name Jesus so as to deceive people into thinking they are worshipping the Son of God.

There are many who call themselves 'Christian', who are not truly born again, do not know Jesus, and have come under the curse of religion which is devoid of a personal relationship with the Lord Jesus and are now worshipping a demon! No wonder Timothy had to warn that *"some people will abandon the faith in later times and will obey lying spirits and follow the teachings of demons"* (1 Timothy 4:1 GNB).

The Heavily Demonised

This story of Jesus, specifically going to the other side of the lake and ministering healing to the Gerasene demoniac, offers hope to the heavily demonised and those who have the responsibility for caring for them. Ministering to such people is not easy, for the demonic web has often been wound very tightly indeed around the spirit, soul and body of the individual.

What we have found, however, is that when one systematically applies the truths of God's word to the lives of such broken people then a way into the demonic jungle can be found. It often takes great love and patience to win the person's confidence before any ministry is possible, but it is worth the effort.

It can be like having a huge ball of tatty bits of string which are all knotted together in a hopeless mess. But look for the ends, see where they are fastened and piece by piece you will see the ball untangled. There will be a fight, the demons will put up strong resistance to being dislodged from their home, but keep persevering and the victory will come!

We have also found many people who have suffered for many years have never understood that their problems could have a demonic root. Explaining to them that there is a possibility they are demonised offers them a ray of hope, whereas formerly there was no hope. Deep inside our spirits we know when truth, that is relevant to our lives, has been spoken, and the same is true of those who are told for the first time that it looks as though Satan has managed to find a way of controlling them from within via evil spirits.

For many that is the best news they have ever heard, for they have known they have been battling with powers that are beyond their control and that they are not mad. But others have not believed them. Far from making them feel how evil they must be, knowing the truth enables them to get rightfully angry in their own spirits at what Satan has done and start fighting with you against the powers of darkness. Facing such truth is the beginning of freedom.

But just one word of caution - deliverance ministry should never be considered as a replacement for a clean walk with the Lord, obedience to him and dealing with the flesh. Demons should never be used as an excuse for sinful behaviour, and neither should sinful behaviour which will result in demonisation be entered into, on the assumption that you can always get delivered later! That is putting God to the test wrongfully - the sin that Satan tried to push Jesus into during his temptations in the wilderness.

I believe this particular deliverance ministry of Jesus has, therefore, great significance to the church. Jesus was showing the disciples that they must seek out the lost, the hopeless and the less socially acceptable cases, even if it means going a long way out of your way to 'save' one apparently hopeless person.

The consequences of seeing just one such person healed, and then testifying to the saving, healing, and delivering power of God, are so great that Satan will do everything in his power to obstruct such ministries - even stir up the most vicious storm on Galilee that the disciples had ever encountered!

So be on your guard against the enemy's counter attacks - both from the outside and from the inside. It has been my own experience that Satan knows my own personal weaknesses very well indeed, and it is not unusual to experience severe attacks in these areas either just before or just after major ministries that are particularly strategic to the Kingdom of God.

It was not for nothing that Peter warned us of the enemy by saying he is *"like a roaring lion looking for someone to devour"* (1 Peter 5:8 NIV). He had experienced the viciousness of Satan's attack on his weak spots the night before Jesus died. Be encouraged, Jesus did not reject him, he reaffirmed Simon Peter as a man anointed of God for work in his Kingdom!

The Syro-Phoenician Woman's Daughter
(Matthew 15:21-28. Mark 7:24-30)

This particular deliverance ministry has four special features which are not expressed through any of the other healings through deliverance that Jesus did.

Firstly it is what we would call today a proxy-deliverance, where the mother of the girl came to Jesus pleading for help for her demonised child who was left at home. Secondly it is a ministry to someone who was, at that time, beyond the limits of Jesus's ministry of deliverance. Jesus's initial calling was to the House of Israel, but this woman and her daughter were not Jews and initially Jesus told her that he could do nothing for her.

Thirdly Jesus uses this particular ministry to illustrate that deliverance is a 'bread ministry' (bread meaning staple diet) for the people of God. And fourthly he demonstrates through this story that persistence in asking, which is a product of faith, will be rewarded.

Proxy-Deliverance

We are often asked if we can pray for deliverance for someone who is not present at the time of praying. By way of encouragement I refer them to this story when Jesus did just that. But I do not make a general point of saying that this is a normal ministry to be applied in all situations. For there is a unique feature to the story that does not apply to every situation and which would seem to restrict its general application.

The ministry requested was to the daughter of the woman who was, presumably, still a child and under the rightful cover of her parents. What we have found in practical experience is that where someone is under the cover of the person requesting prayer this can be an effective and rightful ministry. But when children grow to maturity, and become adults in their own right, they move outside the spiritual cover of their parenting and they have to make decisions for themselves about whether or not they are coming to Jesus for healing and deliverance.

This woman's child was under her parental cover. And the Gospel records that when, at the end of the interview, Jesus agreed to pray for her daughter, that she was healed at that very moment. We know of similar instances where there has been an instant change in a child's condition when we have prayed deliverance for that child through the parents.

We have found this ministry to be particularly effective when we are dealing with generational deliverance, where demons have come down the family line and have passed through the parents to the child. This is generally effected via a demonic control that is still in the parents, so that we have sometimes ministered deliverance to both the parents and the child at the same time!

When deliverance has taken place in the parent, we have ordered the demon to take with it the demons it has placed in the children as well, with considerable effect. Whilst we have never had any problems with the child during such ministry, we would caution, however, that there should usually be someone with, or near, the child, whilst ministry is taking place elsewhere.

We have sometimes been asked to pray in this way for someone who is not under the cover of the person who is asking us to pray. Whilst I am always happy to pray for someone's healing, it is only on rare occasions that I have administered proxy-deliverance in this way for someone who has not been the child (or the wife, who is under the cover of her husband) of the person seeking help.

The occasions when I have been at peace over doing this have only been when the individual has received a special burden from the Lord for the demonised person and is willing to stand proxy in this way, knowing the personal cost of battling against the enemy. This sort of ministry only seems to be effective when there is a strong and Godly soul-tie between the people concerned.

Ministering Deliverance Outside Israel

For Jesus his first calling was to come as the Messiah for the Jews, the people on whom God's hand had been since the beginning of time. His secondary, but critical, calling was not only to die for the sins of the Jewish people but for the sins of the whole world, so that Gentiles could be grafted into the vine and inherit all the blessings that God had promised his own special people. It was only after his death and resurrection that that time would come with the dramatic events of Pentecost.

So when this Canaanite woman from across the border presses her needs amongst the crowds, she is, at first, ignored by Jesus. But she persists and becomes quite noisy in her pleading. The disciples have clearly had enough and ask Jesus to send her away. Then Jesus explains why he cannot minister to her needs, but she still persists in her request for help for her daughter who is at home in a terrible condition, sick because she has a demon.

We need to compare this story carefully with the occasion when the Roman Officer pressed his claims for healing on behalf of his servant (Matthew 8:5-13 and Luke 7:1-10). It was a not dissimilar situation, but on this occasion Jesus makes no mention of his only being called *"to the lost sheep of the house of Israel"* but immediately accepted the request from the officer, channelled through some Jewish elders, to go to the Roman soldier's house and heal the servant.

At the end of both this and the incident with the Syro-Phoenician woman, Jesus says similar words to both her and the Roman Officer, commending them for their great faith. Clearly Jesus was impressed that people who had no historical Jewish ancestry or religious tradition should have such faith that they would ask Jesus to heal, believing that he had the power to do so. But Jesus's initial reaction to the two situations is radically different - to the lady it was No, but to the gentleman, Yes!

Now I do not believe there was anything sexist in Jesus's two responses. He, perhaps more than anyone else of his day, was willing to give women their rightful place in society and family life. So why the radically different responses? Is it possible that the difference lay in the type of ministry that was required? And that Jesus was quite happy to heal the sick of whatever race but dealing with demonic powers in non-Jews (non-believers) was not something he would normally do unless the person was willing to submit to the authority of the God of Israel?

This would be wholly consistent with what Jesus said on another occasion about the danger of casting a demon out of a person and leaving the house clean and tidy, but vulnerable to re-invasion. There is no danger of such vulnerability if the Holy Spirit fills the space and it was only after the resurrection and Pentecost that it became generally possible for Gentiles to be filled with the Holy Spirit.

So why then did Jesus minister deliverance to this woman's daughter after all? I believe the key lies in her response to Jesus's statement as to why initially he could not minister to her. Jesus had said, *"It isn't right to take the children's food and throw it to the dogs."* The woman then replied, *"That's true, sir, but even the dogs eat the left overs from their master's table."*

The word 'dogs' was clearly used to refer to people who were not Jews, such as this woman. But this woman was clearly not just any old dog! She was a woman who, even though not a Jew, was willing to imply by her statement that the God of the Jews was her master! It was this statement that brought forth Jesus's commendation, *"You are a woman of great faith!"*

Even though she was not a naturally born Jew, she was, nevertheless, a Jew by faith! So her daughter would, rightfully, come under the protection of the God of the Jews, and there would be no danger to her through the aftermath of deliverance ministry. She was a New Testament equivalent of Uriah, the Hittite man who swore total loyalty to the God of Israel (2 Samuel 11:11), or of Ruth, the Moabitess who showed such deep devotion to the God of Israel that she eventually married a Jew and became part of Jesus's ancestral line (Ruth 4:13-22).

Jesus recognised that this woman's heart was right before God, even if her birth certificate would tell someone, who was tied to the letter of the law, something different. But Jesus was no Pharisee - for him the spirit of the law was of greater significance than the letter! So he healed her daughter and Mark tells us that she *"went home, and found her child lying on the bed; and the demon had indeed gone out of her."* (Mark 7:30 GNB).

Bread for the Jews

Bread is a staple diet. Not something that is only consumed on special occasions like smoked salmon! Jesus described the ministry that the woman's daughter needed as *"the children's bread"*. By this I believe he was implying that deliverance ministry is a basic essential of the spiritual diet for the children of God! And Jesus also said that it is not *"right"* to give this particular ministry to the *"dogs"*, the non-Jews for the reasons outlined in the previous discussion.

The key point for emphasis here is that throughout the active ministry of Jesus since he was baptised in the River Jordan, he had been in confrontation with the powers of darkness. Deliverance ministry had been an integral part of the prophecy of Isaiah and Jesus had not ceased to set people free, day in and day out, from the works of the enemy. Jesus had made it part of the staple diet that he gave to the crowds who came to hear him.

The life and ministry of Jesus must, above all others, be the example that the Church should follow in seeking to be obedient to the Great Commission. Any other example will leave the church wanting. One has to conclude, therefore, that if any sector of the church is failing to follow Jesus in casting out demons then that sector will suffer.

The real situation throughout the world is that only small sectors of the church do take this part of the Commission seriously. It is not surprising, therefore, that so much of the church is moribund or bound by social or ardently religious traditions. Until the church returns to its original calling and starts serving to its people the bread that Jesus served, we will have a body (of Christ) which is suffering from severe malnutrition and which will be walked all over by demons!

As a Christian people we must come to terms with the sort of church we want. If we choose to give the people the bread that Jesus offered, it will be a body that is willing, whatever the cost, to be obedient to the word and works of Jesus. If we opt for an alternative diet we are in danger of running on the spiritual spot, generating lots of heat, but definitely no light, and going nowhere! Bread is for the children - the people of God!

The Blessings of Persistence

There are numerous places where Jesus commends persistence in prayer when asking God for things (eg Luke 11:5-8). At the same time we are commended for holding a position of trust and faith, believing that God will supply our needs through his heavenly riches (Philippians 4:19). The reality of the Christian walk is that there should be a divine balance between persistence in asking and quiet confidence in believing.

The two positions are not mutually exclusive. It's interesting to note that Abraham, who is generally portrayed as the father of faith, had to be reminded on at least nine different occasions about God's promise that he would have a son by Sarah and be the father of nations. It seems that even he had difficulty in believing!

This woman certainly persisted and Jesus commended her. The important point to note in asking God for things

is that when we know that what we are asking for is rightfully ours by faith, then we also have the faith to be persistent. If, however, what we are asking for is manifestly not part of God's perfect will for us, then to continue asking him becomes presumption and sin.

So the key question is *"Have you heard from God?"* If so ask away and he will rejoice to honour your faith, even if you are asking for something which, humanly speaking, is so way out that it can only be God who put it into your mind! I know this from the personal experience of having seen God bring the whole ministry of Ellel Grange into being out of nothing, and against much sceptical opposition. God had said it in the first place so I could both hold the faith position and trust, and keep on asking God to fulfil what he had promised. Other Christians who had been so negative towards the vision could not divert me, because I knew what God had said to me, and they didn't. But I was sorely tested!

There are many people we have counselled who have been struggling with demonic problems for quite some time. But deliverance is 'bread for the children', so they are right to keep on asking God to set them free. In many cases deliverance only happens when the person has confessed some sin, or forgiven somebody, or received deep emotional healing or whatever the Holy Spirit has shown has been a blockage to the deliverance has been removed.

Sometimes we have seen, retrospectively, that for God to have set people free of all the demonic strongholds at once would not have been healthy in the long term. For there would have been left many unhealed weaknesses in the person's life that were unresolved and further (and possibly more severe) demonisation would have been the inevitable result. As the Lord brought deliverance, step by step, he also brought healing, so that yet more deliverance could take place.

God, in his mercy, only brings us to deliverance when we are in a position both to receive the deliverance and hold the new position in victory. If, for example, somebody has been crying out for deliverance from a spirit of lust, and yet the individual hasn't come to terms with avoiding situations when the lust can be fed (such as looking at pornographic magazines or watching erotic films) then God will not be able to deliver that person.

James was right to say *"resist the devil, and he will flee from you"* (James 4:7). For if, by our behaviour, we tell the demon that we want to hang on to the conduct that both gave the demon entrance and feeds its desires, then it will be able to sit pretty knowing that it has been given a right to stay!

The persistant cry of those seeking deliverance must not be for deliverance alone, but also for the Holy Spirit to reveal anything in their life which is preventing deliverance from taking place. For example, we have discovered time and time again, when dealing with demonised people, that the initial healing needed is not deliverance, but healing of the emotions. When those things have been dealt with deliverance has often been a relatively simple and very effective ministry.

The Woman with the Spirit of Infirmity
(Luke 13:10-17)

This, the last of the individual deliverance ministries described in the Gospels is, nevertheless, one of the most important. Only Luke the doctor who carefully described important cases, includes this ministry in his Gospel record. Clearly the story of the woman whose spine was bent double and who was healed by deliverance captured the imagination of his medical mind.

This is another of the many healings that Jesus did on the sabbath following a time of teaching. The leaders of the synagogue looked on healing the woman as 'work' for Jesus, and were angry at the way Jesus was so cavalier with what they thought was the law of God, but which, in practice, was the legalism of man's religious mind. I do not think the woman who was healed was complaining!

The Entry Point

There are a number of significant points about this healing, but the most important is that of all the deliverances Jesus did, this is the only one which indicates that there is a definite entry point at which evil spirits can come in. Luke's account begins with describing the woman who had had an evil spirit for eighteen years and who, as a result, had a spine that was so bent that she could not straighten up at all - a severe case of curvature of the spine.

Luke only knew this important piece of information because of the dialogue Jesus had with the leader of the synagogue about the healing which had taken place on the sabbath day. Jesus said to the man, *"You hypocrites! Any one of you would untie his ox or his donkey from the stall and take it out to give it water on the sabbath. Now here is this descendant of Abraham, whom Satan has kept bound up for eighteen years; should she not be released on the sabbath?"* (Luke 13:15-16 GNB).

What we are not told in the narrative is what happened eighteen years previously to give the demon the right of entry into the woman, but possible likely causes are the death of a relative from whom the spirit of infirmity transferred, sexual abuse or sexual sin. All three of these are very possible roots by which the demon entered, but whatever it was, Jesus was very specific about the timing. The entrance by the demon could be pinned down to a definite event at a specific moment in the woman's life.

We have ministered to many hundreds of people who have been suffering from spirits of infirmity that have come to them from a relative who died at about the time the symptoms commenced. Spirits of infirmity are generally quite specific to a particular condition and will induce the symptoms of that condition in the next generation, or whoever is unfortunate enough to get the demon. It seems that this is the most common method of transference of a spirit of infirmity from one person to another. Usually the transference is between people who already have a soul-tie together.

Talking in these terms can have the effect of making some people afraid of 'catching demons' from their parents, aunts or uncles when they die. This whole subject will be discussed in considerable detail later, but at this point I would want to assure all readers that if they are walking cleanly before God in obedience to him and wearing their spiritual armour against the attacks of the enemy, then they have little reason to be alarmed.

In the Old Testament there was a specific ritual for being cleansed after coming into contact with the dead, indicating that it was a potentially dangerous time for those left alive (Numbers 19). Under the new covenant we come under the protection and cleansing of the blood of Jesus, but it has to be applied to be effective.

Believers Can be Demonised!

Whether or not believers can be demonised has been a contentious subject for too long - but it is only contentious in the minds of those who have never done any deliverance ministry and never seen the amazing healing that God can bring to the lives of Christians when they are set free from evil spirits.

In the story Jesus refers specifically to this woman as being a Daughter of Abraham. That was a very specific phrase, indicating that this woman wasn't just a member of the Jewish race, but was a person for whom her relationship with God really mattered - i.e. she was a believer! This is a very important aspect of this story, for Jesus draws special attention to this woman who, as a believer, is nevertheless demonised.

We have ministered deliverance to many hundreds of people who had come from churches that did not believe in deliverance ministry and certainly would not countenance the thought that a Christian could possibly be demonised. As a result people have been condemned to endure symptoms that never responded to prayers for healing or medication, just because the theological perspective of their church's leadership was tunnel-visioned.

I say this, not in any way to be critical of, or condemn, those who still think this way, for I have been there too! It would, however, be totally contrary to all that I now believe from the scriptures, and have seen demonstrated in practice, not to say here, unequivocally, that Christian believers can be, and often are, demonised. God has given the deliverance ministry to the church so that the Body of Christ can be set free of the demonic strongholds that are tying it down.

Chapter 12 provides a more detailed look at this topic and addresses the problem that some have in believing that an evil spirit can be present in a person at one and the same time as the Holy Spirit.

The Healing of the Back

The actual ministry to the woman was in two stages. First he freed her from the infirmity by saying *"Woman you are free from your illness!"*. At that point the demon which was causing her particular illness was despatched from her body. But she was still bent double. Now Jesus dealt with the physical symptoms of the deformity by laying his hands on her and healing her. Immediately she was then healed and straightened herself up, praising God.

Sometimes with this type of healing one has to remember that after deliverance the person may well need prayer for healing as well, but this is not always the case. There are times when both deliverance and healing seem to be simultaneous (as with the Syro-Phoenician woman's daughter), but others when there can be quite a time gap between the deliverance and the healing. There are no rules to be followed - instead we have to be obedient in ministry to what the Holy Spirit is saying. We must learn to listen to him!

Over the past five years we have seen many people healed of long-standing infirmities through deliverance and healing ministries. With many such cases it is important to establish the entry point, especially if there is any sin attached to the route through which the demon entered. For in these cases confession and repentance is a vital step towards wholeness.

The next volume will deal in detail with the many different possible entry points that we have encountered in ministry and give practical guidelines on how to undermine the rights of the demonic to be there and then cast out the spirit.

Other References to Deliverance Ministry in the Gospels

In addition to the specific healings through deliverance referred to above, which comprise over a third of the healing ministries that are actually described in the Gospel accounts, there are numerous references to times when Jesus was healing people in large numbers, and deliverance ministry is referred to as part of what was happening at the time.

Matthew 4:24 (GNB). *"The news about him spread through the whole country of Syria, so that people brought to him all those who were sick, suffering from all kinds of diseases and disorders: people with demons and epileptics, and paralytics - and Jesus healed them all."*

Mark 1:32-34 (GNB) and Luke 4:40-41 (Similar references). *"After the sun had set and evening had come, people brought to Jesus all the sick and those who had demons. All the people of the town gathered in front of the house. Jesus healed many who were sick with all kinds of diseases and drove out many demons."*

Mark 1:39 (GNB). *"So he travelled all over Galilee, preaching in the synagogues and driving out demons."*

Mark 3:11 (GNB) *"And whenever the people who had evil spirits in them saw him, they would fall down before him and scream, 'You are the Son of God'."*

Mark 6:12-13 (GNB) *"So they went out and preached that people should turn away from their sins. They drove out many demons and rubbed olive-oil on many sick people and healed them."*

Luke 6:17-18 (GNB) *"A large crowd of people was there from all over Judaea and from Jerusalem and from the coastal cities of Tyre and Sidon; they had come to hear him and to be healed of their diseases. Those who were troubled by evil spirits also came and were healed."*

Luke 7:21 (GNB) *"At that very time Jesus cured many people of their sicknesses, diseases, and evil spirits, and gave sight to many blind people."*

In Conclusion

This has been a long chapter! Working through the Gospel accounts of deliverance ministry will, inevitably, have introduced many new concepts to some readers. I would not want anyone, however, to feel in any way condemned if they feel now that they should have seen these things before.

God is restoring this ministry to the Church in this day for a purpose and I rejoice with all those, young or old, who are now beginning to step out in faith and venture into scripturally sound, but hitherto possibly unknown, territory in the power of the Holy Spirit.

No-one who is prepared to examine the Gospel accounts with an honest intellect can but be impressed by the extent of the deliverance ministry of Jesus, but equally they will recognise the power that God has given us to follow in his footsteps. We are not alone - he has promised to be with us in our obedience to the Great Commission until the end of time (Matthew 28:20).

Whenever Jesus was faced with sick people he ministered to them according to the root cause of their condition and not just according to the presenting symptom. Where the root cause was a sickness or disease he healed the person. Where the root cause was a demon he cast it out. Where there was both demonisation and sickness he delivered and healed. The ministry was simple, direct and effective in complete fulfilment of the prophecy of Isaiah 61:1 which he had applied to himself at the outset of his ministry in Nazareth.

Chapter 9

Encounters with the Demonic in the Acts of the Apostles

When Pentecost dawned, not one of those waiting in the upper room had any expectation of what was going to happen next! Jesus had gone back to heaven, and they were being obedient to his command to stay in Jerusalem and wait for the gift that the Father had promised (Acts 1:4-5).

Some of them had been present when Jesus was baptised in the Holy Spirit as he came up out of the river Jordan. Were they, too, going to hear voices from heaven and see doves descend? No-one knew. Jesus had said something about them speaking in strange tongues (Mark 16:17) and that hadn't happened yet. What sign would they see or experience? How would they know it had happened?

They need not have been anxious, for *"when the day of Pentecost came . . . suddenly there was a noise from the sky which sounded like a strong wind blowing, and it filled the whole house where they were sitting. Then they saw what looked like tongues of fire which spread out and touched each person there. They were all filled with the Holy Spirit and began to talk in other languages, as the Spirit enabled them to speak"* (Acts 2:1-4 GNB).

There was no doubting that it had happened. The effect was immediate and dynamic, resulting in an amazed crowd questioning what it was all about. Then Peter, under the anointing of the Holy Spirit, preached to the crowds and three thousand believed and were baptised. The reaction to all this in the demonic realms must have been one of sheer horror. Jesus had gone, but replacing him was an army of men and women, behaving just like

Jesus. These disciples were let loose in Jerusalem and *"many miracles and wonders were being done through the apostles, and . . every day the Lord added to the group those who were being saved"* (Acts 2:43-47 GNB).

Whenever there is a great move forward under the anointing of the Holy Spirit, watch out for Satan's backlash. Once more it came through the religious authorities who had so hated Jesus. They quickly had Peter and John up before the Council for healing a lame man. On that occasion, however, the Council's hands were tied, such was the popular support for what had happened. So Peter and John escaped with a warning and were told very strongly that under no condition must they speak or teach again in the Name of Jesus (Acts 4:18).

All this time the powers of darkness were being pushed back. *"And crowds of people were coming in from the towns around Jerusalem, bringing those who were ill or who had evil spirits in them; and they were all healed"* (Acts 5:16 GNB). Christianity was spreading fast, as preaching, healing and deliverance were quickly established as the normal pattern for ministry in the early church. They were being obedient to the commission and were teaching a body of believers to be disciples.

Ananias and Sapphira
(Acts 4:36 - 5:11)

In spite of the white hot nature of the early church's enthusiasm for the Gospel, there were some problems. If Satan cannot stop a work of God from the outside, he will try to operate from the inside, like a modern day fifth columnist, using any weakness, or demonic presence, in the membership.

The group of believers provided for each others needs out of the generous giving of those who were being converted. Capital, in the form of property was being converted into eternal gold as people sold fields and houses, so that the work could continue unabated, and the leaders could distribute the money that was realised, according to need. Barnabas was one of those who sold a field and handed over the money.

No doubt Barnabas was commended and thanked for his generosity. Satan was watching and, no doubt, used a demon to fire an arrow of jealousy at a couple who would also have enjoyed such approval. They, too, had a field. So Ananias and Sapphira sold their field, but the motive was wrong. They didn't really want to give all that money away, but neither did they want to be seen as being mean - no-one would know just how much they got for the field. So they agreed together to keep some of the money back.

Sin had been conceived in their hearts and put into practice. I believe at that point a demon will have entered in, so that when Ananias brought the gift to the Apostles, Peter, operating in the full discernment of the Holy Spirit, not only saw the gift in Ananias's hands, but also discerned the deception and saw the demon (described by Luke as Satan). Peter's question was right to the point, *"Ananias, why did you let Satan take control of you and make you lie to the Holy Spirit by keeping part of the money you received for the property?"* (Acts 5:3 GNB).

Ananias's sin was not that he had kept back some of the money, but that he had let people think he had given it all. It was a sin, Peter said, not against men, but against God. On hearing this awesome truth, Ananias dropped down dead. When Sapphira came in, she was given a chance by Peter to repent and speak the truth, but she repeated Ananias's story, and she also dropped down dead.

I don't believe that Peter had any idea what the consequences would be of facing Ananias (Acts 5:3) and Sapphira (Acts 5:9) with their sin, but later in his epistle he wrote, *"Be alert, be on the watch! Your enemy, the Devil, roams round like a roaring lion, looking for someone to devour"* (1 Peter 5:8 GNB). I don't think the memory of what happened on that day was ever very far from Peter's mind, and I can well imagine he used the illustration on many occasions in his teaching and preaching.

The sin, as described by Peter, was *"putting the Lord's Spirit to the test"*. It was Jesus's temptation in the wilderness all over again. Jesus recognised it and responded to it firmly, but Ananias fell for the temptation, believed he could get away with the sin of testing God in this way and the early church learnt a devastating lesson in spiritual honesty.

There are few Christians who can read this story without coming under the fear of God. For they know in their hearts that time and time again they have tested God with their continued sinfulness. Somewhere, deep down, a voice has said, God won't really mind if you sin, he'll always forgive you. So just one more time they try and get away with it, until the demon behind the sin is in control and they are trapped into a lifestyle of sin from which there seems to be no escape. And whatsoever a man sows, that shall he also reap.

The scripture is clear and unequivocal, and whether the consequences are immediate and exemplary as they were with Ananias and Sapphira, or longer-term, as they were with Samson, David and many others, I do not believe we can flaunt the word of God that he speaks into our hearts with impunity. Yes, God is a God of mercy, and my own belief is that because of the blood of Jesus, which was shed that we might be set free from the power, guilt and consequences of sin, Ananias and Sapphira will enter heaven, but will be deprived of all the treasures that they could have built up through obedience to God in their Christian lives. (See Paul's teaching on the things that can be built on the foundation of Jesus Christ in 1 Corinthians 3:10-15)

It is not for us to question how God acts. And whilst summary death may seem to be harsh justice, He is sovereign and sees all things and there are times when things happen like this even today. I personally have been through an experience when a man, who was not a

Christian, was attacking me personally to such an extent that my life was under threat and my business was in danger of going bankrupt. After many weeks of aggression, he finally warned me that in ten days I would not exist. He had given me ten days to live. During those ten days I became very conscious of the presence and power of God. On the tenth day I had a telephone call telling me that he had dropped dead that morning. God had dealt with the aggressor in a final and uncompromising way.

I do not include that story in this book to try and demonstrate that this is the way God always acts to protect his people, or include the story of Ananias and Sapphira to demonstrate that this is how he always acts in judgement. But we must not be surprised when remarkable things do happen under the anointing of the Spirit of God. I believe there is more happening in the supernatural in events like this than we may at first realise. Even angels are recorded in the scripture as having been despatched by God to punish by death as well as to minister to the saints! (Eg Acts 12:23).

With Philip in Samaria
(Acts 8:5 - 8:40)

In the face of all his opponents Stephen preached the longest single sermon recorded in the scriptures. At its end, the members of the Council were so incensed that they ground their teeth in anger, rushed at him and stoned him to death. But the scripture records that Stephen was full of the Holy Spirit, marking the contrast between the Spirit in Stephen and the evil spirits that were motivating the authorities against this fearless Christian martyr.

Chapter 8 of the Acts of the Apostles begins with the poignant statement, *"And Saul approved of his murder."* That act signalled the beginning of cruel judgement upon the Christian community, who were mercilessly persecuted. Saul tried to destroy the church; going from house to house, he dragged out the believers, both men and women, and threw them into jail. Those who escaped fled the region, but the life of Christ that was hidden within each one, could not be destroyed and when Philip, for example, reached Samaria, he immediately began to preach the Gospel.

Luke records that there was great joy in the city, for people listened intently to what Philip said, they saw him performing miracles and witnessed *"evil spirits coming out of many people with a loud cry, and many paralysed and lame people healed"* (Acts 8:7). Deliverance ministry did not get left behind in Jerusalem, but was part of the Gospel experience wherever it was preached.

There then followed a fascinating and significant encounter, from which we can learn much, between Philip and Simon, a powerful Samaritan sorcerer, who professed conversion to Christ. Scripture tells us that Simon was known in the area as 'the great power of god' and claimed to be someone great.

In making such a claim Simon was almost certainly declaring that he had within him a guiding demonic spirit of someone who had been great and famous, which was deceiving people into thinking that Simon's power came from God himself. Simon had learnt how to tap into both the knowledge of this demon, and the powers that the demon could exercise, for his own gain.

When ministering deliverance it is a relatively common experience to come up against a guiding spirit from someone who has been long dead. People who believe in re-incarnation will describe, sometimes under hypnosis, their alleged 'past lives'. What they are describing, however, is not their past lives, but the lives of the people in whom the demons had previously lived, giving the impression that the person had lived previously.

Belief in re-incarnation is always a demonic deception of the most simple kind, but those who are hooked into this philosophy of religion are completely blinded to the truth of what is happening. It is only the light of Christ, and subsequent deliverance that can set them free from the bondage they are in. Belief in re-incarnation is also one of the deceptions which can underlie a vegetarian philosophy of life. Vegetarianism is an integral part of many Eastern religions.

We do not know whose demons Simon was now hosting, but we do know he used them to gain considerable stature (and no doubt money) in his Samaritan community. When Philip ministered in Samaria, Simon was among the hearers. He was astonished at what God was doing through Philip and recognised that there was a power here that was totally superior to his. So he professed belief in Jesus, was baptised and *"stayed close to Philip, and was astounded when he saw the great wonders and miracles that were being performed"* (Acts 8:13 GNB).

News of the Samaritan mission got back to Jerusalem, and Peter and John were sent down to investigate. When they got there they found that the converts had been baptised in the name of Jesus, but had not received the Holy Spirit (Acts 8:14-17). For these converts there was a definite time-lag between conversion and being filled with the Holy Spirit - probably several weeks or even months.

Whether the gap was one day or one year is largely irrelevant. But what is significant is that this incident introduces the concept, which some fight so hard against, of being filled with the Holy Spirit at a time subsequent to conversion. We have ministered to hundreds of people who have been Christians for many years but, as Peter and John found in Samaria, have not been filled with the Holy Spirit.

It was this experience, of watching people being filled with the Holy Spirit when Peter and John laid hands on them, that finally blew Simon's mind! He had never seen anything like this before. He had been used to dealing in the spirit world, but the impartation of the very power of God to others was a concept that was totally beyond his experience or imagination. He wanted that power for himself. *"So he offered money to Peter and John, and said, 'Give this power to me too, so that anyone I place my hands on will receive the Holy Spirit'."* (Acts 8:18-19 GNB).

There is no indication in the scripture that Simon had not been genuinely converted when he first believed, but what appears to be obvious from Luke's account, is that he had not been delivered of all the evil spirits that had been in him prior to his conversion.

He is typical of hundreds of people we have had to deal with who have been involved in occult practices prior to becoming Christians. The demons remained and over the years produced a sad demonic harvest of sickness, rebellion and resistance to the work of the Holy Spirit. How important it is that when people become Christians they should also be set free of the demons that were controlling them when they first came to Christ. If they don't they are likely to build up for themselves (and others!) major ongoing problems in later life.

For Simon there was an immediate consequence. Clearly he had not repented of all his occultic past and saw here another power from which he could certainly earn even greater reputation and possibly more money as well. Peter's response was graphic. *"May you and your money go to hell, for thinking that you can buy God's gift with money! You have no part or share in our work because your heart is not right in God's sight. Repent, then, of this evil plan of yours, and pray to the Lord that he will forgive you for thinking such a thing as this. For I see that you are full of bitter envy and are a prisoner of sin."* (Acts 8:20-23 GNB).

Peter's words indicate that he recognised there was demonic power operating in Simon's life, in particular a spirit of envy, but he wisely did not minister deliverance, but told Simon to repent. Repentance is one of the most important foundation stones for healing and deliverance. There would have been no point in Peter ministering deliverance unless Simon was truly repentant and I believe time was necessary in his case to prove his repentance.

We have learnt this lesson in ministry the hard way by trying to cast demons out of people who were unrepentant in their hearts about the sin which gave the demons a right of entry. I realise now that such deliverance should not be attempted, if the demons have come in through known sin, unless there has been genuine repentance and turning from the sin.

For some, ministry has been ineffective because repentance has not been real. They, and often those who minister as well, have wrongfully concluded that nothing demonic was present in the first place, and compounded the problem by giving the demons absolute right to control the person, without fearing detection and consequential eviction, because they have been proven 'not to be there'!

Unfortunately, on the other side of the coin, there are some who minister deliverance who have gone so over-board on repentance that their ministry has become unbalanced. They say, for example, that if a demon is not coming out easily then it is always because the person is unrepentant over something. That is certainly not always the case. There are plenty of other reasons why demons do not come out easily and whilst lack of repentance is a common enough one, those who minister must be more discerning than make sweeping statements which, if untrue, put the person into terrible condemnation.

We hear no more of what happened to Simon, but his story is an important and salutary warning to people not to want the power of the Holy Spirit for the wrong reasons. I personally struggle with the contrasting ways in which God dealt with Ananias and Sapphira and with Simon. It seems as though their sins were just as great, so why the summary justice meted out to one and the opportunity to repent to the other?

Healing Through Deliverance

There is no obvious answer, but I believe we would have a purer and more powerful church if we were less concerned about the details of the problem and more concerned to see that the church is freed from both the deception that overcame Ananias and Sapphira, and from wrongful motives such as the envy and greed of Simon. Maybe these two were highlighted for particular attention as a warning to the generations to come, including the present one!

The Magician Elymas

(Acts 13:4-12)

After Philip's Samarian exploits, followed by his dramatic excursion to Gaza, where he was instrumental in the conversion of the Ethiopian eunuch, Luke moves on in his journal to the even more dramatic event on the road to Damascus.

Saul kept up *"his violent threats of murder against the followers of the Lord"* (Acts 9:1 GNB), but on the way to Damascus to persecute Christians there, the Lord himself met him, he was struck down, blinded and then led by the hand into Damascus where another Ananias ministered to him and Saul was healed (and delivered?), filled with the Holy Spirit and then baptised. The most dramatic turn round there has ever been in the history of the church.

By the time we reach Acts 13 Saul himself has been persecuted for preaching the Gospel and has had to flee for his life for a time to Tarsus (Acts 9:30).

He is now at Antioch, and clearly integrated with the body of believers there, when the Holy Spirit sets him apart, with Barnabas, for missionary service and they set sail for Cyprus. In Cyprus the Governor, Sergius Paulus, wanted to hear the word of God, as preached by Paul and Barnabas. But Sergius Paulus had a friend, Bar-Jesus, a Jew who claimed to be a prophet, but who was, in fact the local magician and who went under the Greek name,

Elymas. The demons that controlled Elymas went immediately to work and created opposition to the preaching of the Gospel. Elymas tried to turn Sergius Paulus away from the faith.

Those who are, or who have been, involved in the occult have within them demons who cannot stand the truth of Jesus. They do not mind religion, or even Christian activity that does not confront the work of Satan or threaten his kingdom. But in the face of Holy Spirit anointed ministries they will inevitably be exposed. There have been many people who have visited Ellel Grange who had not thought that their problems could possibly be demonic in origin - in spite of their problems not having yielded to prayer, discipline or, even, healing ministry. But as they have been faced with spiritual reality, and their previous understandings have been healthily questioned, the demonic has been forced into the open and deliverance and healing have become possible.

A recent television programme focused on deliverance ministry at Ellel Grange. In the correspondence that followed there was very little opposition to the idea of deliverance, but several people took me to task for proclaiming that Jesus was the way, the truth and the life and no-one could go to the Father except through him! Such truth (exclusivity, opponents of Christianity say) is a threat to demons, because it is only in His name that they can be evicted from their strongholds in peoples' lives.

The truth that Saul preached was a major threat to Elymas - especially if Sergius Paulus the Governor were to be converted. Aggressive action was required! But Elymas had reckoned without the discernment that Saul now had. For Saul was *"filled with the Holy Spirit and looked straight at the magician and said, 'You son of the Devil! You are the enemy of everything that is good. You are full of all kinds of evil tricks and you always keep trying to turn the Lord's truths into lies! The Lord's hand will come upon you now; you will be blind and will not see the light of day for a time.'"* (Acts 13:9-11 GNB).

In deliverance ministry I often look the person directly in the eyes - just as Saul did with Elymas. It seems as though that through the eyes one can make direct contact with the demon in a very positive way. Saul did not make any attempt to deliver Elymas, but exercised authority over the demon and a judgement of temporary blindness on Elymas for his sin. *"At once Elymas felt a dark mist cover his eyes, and he walked about trying to find someone to lead him by the hand"* (Acts 13:12 GNB). The judgement exercised by Saul was identical with his own Damascus Road experience of temporary blindness.

The fact that Saul did not attempt to deliver Elymas is further important evidence from the history of the early church that deliverance ministry is normally only for those who have turned to Jesus. Unless the Holy Spirit can 'fill the house' there is no way that the person can be protected from further, and probably more severe, demonisation.

We are not told whether or not Elymas was converted as a result, but we are told that the Governor was *"greatly amazed at the teaching about the Lord."* So often when the enemy attacks in this sort of way the Lord is able to turn what the enemy intended for harm into advantage for the Gospel. Paul was able to say from profound experience, *"All things work together for good to those who love God"* (Romans 8:28 NKJV)!

But we are required to continue to trust God in the middle of trying circumstances and not be deflected from what the Holy Spirit has put in our hearts. If we choose to be deflected, and divert from the path God intended, we will miss out on some amazing blessings as God turns circumstances upside down. Continued obedience in the midst of opposition produces some of the most amazing fruits, as the next incident we are looking at in Saul's life will illustrate. It was, incidentally, in Cyprus that Saul lost his original name, from then on he was known as Paul.

Snakes at Philippi!
(Acts 16:16-24)

Christians normally assume that obedience to the Holy Spirit is going to lead to a period of great blessing. They are right, but when they fondly imagine that the great blessing they are anticipating will not disturb the peace and serenity of their immediate circumstances, or lead them into any form of hot water, they are looking for something that is not based on the reality of the scripture or the terms of spiritual warfare that are implicit within the scripture.

Obedience for Moses led to forty years of torment at the head of a rebellious people who would not follow where God was leading. For Jesus it led from the excitement of popularity at the beginning of his ministry to the agony of the cross at the end. In 2 Corinthians 11:23-29 Paul lists just some of the many hardships he endured in his ministry, including many times in prison, one of which happened on his first visit to Philippi.

His journey to Philippi, however, began by waiting on the Lord for guidance as to where he should next preach the Gospel. The Holy Spirit would not let him go to a variety of places, but when he had a vision of a man from Macedonia crying out for help, he knew it was of God and Paul and Silas left immediately for Neapolis, from where he went inland to *"Philippi, a city of the first district of Macedonia"* (Acts 16:6-12).

There they met up with a group of Jews at their riverside place of prayer, one of whom, Lydia, a dealer in purple cloth, was converted. She, and the people of her house were baptised and so the embryo church at Philippi began to take root. When a body of believers was established it seemed to be Paul's policy to stay with them as long as was necessary to see them established in the faith and going on with God. So Paul and Silas stayed with Lydia and continued the ministry that God had started as a result of their obedience in leaving Asia behind and bringing the Gospel into Europe for the first time.

The ruling spirits in the area were not unaware of what had happened! Their territory was being invaded by a person who was a real threat to the strongholds they had built up in the lives of local people. For the third time in the Acts of the Apostles we see a local occultist being used by Satan. First there was Simon at Samaria, then Elymas in Cyprus and now, in Philippi, a slave girl, who made money for her owners by using an evil spirit within her to predict the future.

Such people Satan can easily use - the spiritual battle for control of their lives has already been won. One should not be surprised, therefore, to find people, even inside local churches, who have an occult background, or whose parents were involved in the occult, being those who consistently oppose the work of the Holy Spirit. Satan will always use those who already have such demonic strongholds to oppose the work of God.

The demon in the girl recognised the Holy Spirit inside Paul, and shouted out to people that *"These men are the servants of the Most High God, who proclaim to us the way of salvation"* (Acts 16:17 NKJV). As it was with Jesus, so it was with Paul. The demons proclaimed the truth about who Jesus was, and here they were proclaiming the truth about whom Paul served. But they were not doing it in a way that encouraged the work of the Gospel. For it was hardly helpful to Paul to have someone who was so well-known as an occultist, and who was still practising in the occult, commending his ministry! One can do without such commendation. This girl was well-known at Philippi for who she was and what she did. For her to be commending the ministry of Paul would automatically have labelled Paul's ministry as being occultic!

Paul had an extended time of ministry in Philippi, and was clearly building a body of believers and discipling them. But every day this woman would be around shouting and interrupting the ministry. What is very significant is that Paul must have recognised the demonic source of her railings the first time he met her, but he chose to do nothing about her interruptions. He gave her plenty of time to respond to the preaching and seek Jesus for herself.

I believe he will have known that the potential danger to her of being delivered, before she had made Jesus Lord, was considerable. Paul will have known what Jesus said about the possibility of seven devils worse than the first coming back in. He did not want to make a mistake. So he waited, no doubt hopeful that she might respond to the preaching, and certainly waiting on the Holy Spirit for direction.

It was only after many days (Acts 16:18) that Paul decided that enough was enough. She was clearly not going to respond to the Gospel without being delivered, and such were the interruptions to his ministry that he couldn't allow it to continue, for her actions would be preventing others from entering the Kingdom of God. So he acted, decisively and effectively. He confronted the demon, cast it out and that very moment she was set free. We have no knowledge from the scriptures as to whether or not she responded to the Gospel subsequently, for events at Philippi moved very quickly from that moment on!

Firstly, her owners realised that Paul had deprived them of their means of making money through her occult powers. Secondly they summarily seized Paul and Silas, took them to the authorities and accused them of teaching against their local customs. Local *"justice"* was immediate and harsh. Paul and Silas were given a severe beating and thrown into jail. The jailor threw them into the inner cell and fastened their feet between heavy blocks of wood. But God, who knows the end from the beginning of stories like this one, was not the slightest bit alarmed by what was happening to these two men, and neither, it seemed, were Paul and Silas, who were still singing hymns of praise to God at midnight!

The result was devastating! A major earthquake, the conversion of the jailor and all his family, and the introduction, therefore, of the Gospel to a Roman officer and his family who, in their lifetime of service in the Roman army, would subsequently take the Gospel all over the Empire! Once again, Satan's tactics in attacking and attempting to destroy the ministries of God's people had overstepped the mark, and there was even greater glory to God as a result. The following day they were released from prison and returned to Lydia's house before going on their way to the next town!

The key lesson from this particular encounter with the demonic is that it is not wise to minister deliverance to those who have not come to Christ, unless you have a very specific anointing from the Lord to do so, as Paul must have done on that particular day. The Lord had greater plans than Paul and Silas were aware of, but it was their obedience which subsequently released the power of God into the prison.

We should not assume, however, that because, on this occasion, the Lord used Paul and Silas's visit to prison in an extraordinary way, he will bless our ministry in similar ways if we step outside what is normally good ministry practice, without having a specific anointing.

There may be times when God tells us to 'break the rules', but such occasions will be exceptions. For example, this is the only incident in the whole of the New Testament when deliverance is ministered to someone who is not either coming to Jesus personally for help, or through hearing and responding to the word of God.

We must not move out of faith, into presumption, by operating in a way that implies God will always cover our mistakes, even when we know we are making them! He will cover our mistakes, when they are genuine mistakes made in good faith. It is only things which 'are not of faith' that are sin (Romans 14:23). But when we know something is not right and we do it anyway, that is certainly not 'of faith' and it is, therefore, sin.

Presumptive action will not bring down the blessing of
God - no matter how good an idea our proposed actions
may seem to be!

Another view of this whole passage is that Paul and Silas
did make a mistake, and learnt from this experience that
they shouldn't be ministering deliverance to people who
are not willing to make Jesus Lord. And that the
punishment Paul and Silas received, and all that
happened subsequently, was not as God had originally
purposed events for them in Philippi. But because they
had acted in faith, God still blessed them and eventually,
through the agency of a mighty miracle, used even their
mistake to his glory. We certainly don't find Paul, or
anyone else, ministering in this way again!

Another lesson found in this story, is that most
translations of the scriptures refer in Acts 16:16 to the
woman as having a spirit of divination, or fortune telling.
The Greek word actually used here literally means the
'spirit of a python', this being the descriptive word for a
spirit of divination. But it is wholly consistent with the
teaching of Jesus in Luke 10:19 when Jesus tells the
disciples that he has given them authority *"over snakes,
scorpions and all the power of the enemy"*.

Jesus clearly expected people to come up against demons
that would manifest as snakes. On many occasions we
have seen people slither across the floor in snake-like
movements as demons have manifested and come out of
them. Such demons have often been associated with
occult practice. The Acts 16 ministry of Paul is direct
confirmation of what Jesus taught.

At Ephesus and The Sons of Sceva
(Acts 19)

Paul's ministry was one of extended travel and stops of
varying length along the way to preach the Gospel and
make disciples. His stays varied enormously from a few
days to as long as three years here in Ephesus (Acts 20:31)

where, he says in a final speech to the elders of the church there, it was *"with many tears, day and night, I taught every one of you for three years."*

Ephesus was undoubtedly the most-important city in the whole of Asia Minor. It was a thriving commercial and religious centre with a population exceeding a third of a million. But it was also one of the greatest world centres of occult practice, being the guardian of the temple of Diana in which was an image, probably made from a meteorite, of Diana that allegedly came down from 'heaven'.

The name Diana is the Roman equivalent of the Greek Goddess Artemis, both names being descriptive of the same demonic deity. In Greek and Roman mythology the goddess is associated with both the moon and with hunting. The scriptural allusion to Artemis or Diana as being a goddess who is worshipped all over the world is probably accurate, as images of her are known from many cultures widely dispersed from Ephesian society. There have been several times during ministry when we have come up against 'spirits of Diana' whose character and origin is consistent with mythological descriptions of her nature and powers.

So, in choosing to spend three years in this city Paul was deliberately setting out to minister the truth of Jesus into a major population centre that was based right in the heartland of Satan's earthly occultic kingdom! It is not surprising, therefore, that at Ephesus he also encountered some major opposition to his ministry.

He taught at first in the synagogue, and some became believers, but there was such opposition from those that did not believe, that the daily teaching times had to move to the hall of Tyrannus where, for a period of two years, Paul taught and ministered (Acts 19:8-10).

Though Paul was the most educated of the apostles, his ministry was not just academic. It was very much modelled on the ministry of Jesus where welcoming, teaching and healing were the foundation stones of his work. As a result *"God was performing unusual miracles through Paul and even handkerchiefs and aprons that he had used were taken to those who were ill, and their diseases were driven away and the evil spirits would go out of them"* (Acts 19:11-12).

Clearly Paul both healed and delivered people as an integral part of his work, and this aspect of his ministry was even extended to those who could not be present at the meetings via handkerchiefs from Paul that were taken to the sick. Paul would minister deliverance in the name of the Lord Jesus and see the evil spirits leave as he commanded them to go, words that others thought they could adopt as a formula for doing similar work (Acts 19:13).

We have learnt, however, that one must never teach Christian healing and deliverance as a technique that can be followed by anyone and which is bound to achieve the same results as someone else! For ministry in the power of the Holy Spirit depends on God using an anointed channel to minister directly into a person's life using the gifts of the Holy Spirit. A person who is not filled with the Holy Spirit is a channel that is not anointed for ministry and people will very quickly find out, sometimes to their very considerable cost, that Jesus cannot be manipulated into doing what they want him to do!

Sceva was a Jewish High Priest whose seven sons were Jewish exorcists who travelled round the area attempting to drive evil spirits out of people (Acts 19:13-14). But the effectiveness of these exorcists was severely limited and when they watched Paul at work they were very impressed with the power and authority he displayed. When they saw people being healed and delivered in the name of Jesus they took careful note of just what Paul said and did. They then went away with a 'magic formula' thinking they had learnt exactly what to do!

They attempted to deliver a man and addressed his evil spirits *"in the name of Jesus, whom Paul preaches"* (Acts 19:13 GNB). But far from finding that this formula worked they were immediately challenged themselves by the demons who responded, *"I know Jesus and I know about Paul; but you - who are you?!"* (v.15)

The demons are spiritual beings and they can see in the supernatural. They can see whether or not the Holy Spirit is in a person, and they know that if they recognise the presence of the Holy Spirit in the deliverance minister they are up against Jesus himself, and they have to bow the knee to whoever is commanding them out.

But the demons in this man saw nothing of the Holy Spirit, or Jesus, in the sons of Sceva and they responded appropriately prompting the man to such violence that he overpowered all seven sons of Sceva, tore off their clothes and left them to run for their lives, stark naked and wounded!! I doubt if they ever tried to exorcise someone in the name of Jesus again. They found out the hard way that to have the authority of Jesus one must also be in the service of Jesus and be part of his Kingdom.

The final outcome of this episode redounded to the Lord's glory, for the people of Ephesus realised that the power and authority in which Paul ministered came from Jesus himself, and they recognised that demons were real and dangerous. It is probable from the text that the man in question was involved in the worship of Diana and the people realised that the man was in such a violent mess because of his occult activity. For they were all filled with such fear, that the believers, who at any time in their lives had themselves been involved with Diana worship (or other occult activity), went scurrying home to collect every possible piece of evidence of their earlier involvement.

A small mountain of occult literature was accumulated and burnt in public (Acts 19:19) - books to a total value of fifty thousand silver coins! That is repentance. It is not repentance to renounce occult activity, but hang on to the artifacts or literature associated with the activity. That is a sin equivalent to the sin of Achan, when he hung on to gold and silver spoils which God had ordered to be destroyed (Joshua 7).

For Israel this sin resulted in their failure to capture Ai (after the brilliant success at Jericho) and the personal consequence for Achan and his family was death. Repentance of occult activity not only involves a turning from the activity in the future but a destruction of items from the past - items which are cursed, and which will continue to bring a curse on the family line if preserved. Some such items of jewellery even become family heirlooms and are worn round the neck cursing future generations.

The implications of this passage, for example, for ex-freemasons is obvious. Repentance must involve both renunciation of all the vows and practices of freemasonry and destruction of all the artifacts which are such an essential part of masonic ritual. Some find this hard, but until it is done they will never be free of the curse of freemasonry upon them or their family line. We have found on numerous occasions that masonic artifacts have been preserved as 'memorials' of father, or a favourite uncle, but they have brought with them a devastating curse, especially on the families of born again Christians who renounce freemasonry as being of the enemy.

Ephesus, the world seat of occult worship, had never seen a bonfire like it. It was a powerful witness to the people of the city. After ministering to the young man I referred to in Chapter 6, who had become severely demonised through listening to heavy metal music, I watched him bring out his records and cassettes and smash them with a hammer. The heavy metal tapes, carrying with them messages of violence and sexual perversion (as well as, in some cases, Satanic backtracking), had opened him up to powerful demonisation.

After deliverance his repentance was vividly demonstrated as he destroyed all such cassettes and records. Keeping them would have left him vulnerable to their continuing influence. The fruit of his ministry was demonstrated by his complete change of lifestyle after deliverance. Immediately after deliverance he was baptised and is now completing his training as an evangelist at a Bible College!

Similar action is required by those who have been hooked on pornography. No-one will be free of the demons that compel people to look at pictures and films, vicariously experiencing paper and plastic sex, unless they repent by destroying every piece of pornographic material in their possession. Then they have to make determined efforts to avoid all situations which will make them vulnerable in the future. James' advice to resist the devil so that he will flee from you still holds good today, and much deliverance takes place through practical repentance.

So many people in the city were responding to what Paul was teaching by destroying their occult objects, and not continuing to buy more, that the finances of the purveyors of occult goods were being affected and silver workers employed by Demetrius were in danger of being made redundant! The ruling spirit of Diana over the city was at work and soon there was a major uproar in favour of Demetrius and against Paul and his workers. When people's pockets are adversely affected by the preaching of the Gospel you can be sure that antagonistic action will be a consequence!

It is worth quoting here the whole of Demetrius's speech to his fellow Ephesians: *"Men, you know that our prosperity comes from this work. Now, you can see and hear for yourselves what this fellow Paul is doing. He says that man-made gods are not gods at all, and he has succeeded in convincing many people, both here in Ephesus and in nearly the whole province of Asia. There is the danger, then, that this business of ours will get a bad name. Not only that, but there is also the danger that the temple of the great goddess Diana will come to mean nothing and that her greatness will be destroyed - the goddess worshipped by everyone in Asia and in all the world!"* (Acts 19:25-27 GNB).

It doesn't take much imagination to guess who Demetrius's speech writer was! The ruling spirit of Diana was behind the whole charade, and as its influence gripped the people the now huge crowd became *"furious and started shouting 'Great is Diana of Ephesus!'"* Two of Paul's co-workers were grabbed by the hostile crowd and rushed to the theatre - the great auditorium which is known to have seated up to fifty thousand people.

It took the town clerk, Alexander, who happened to be a Jew, two hours to get through the continued chanting of *"Great is Diana of Ephesus"* and bring some sense into the meeting, implying that they would be guilty if the event turned into a riot, and with that the meeting was over and the danger had passed. But it must have been a very frightening experience for Paul and his co-workers. They had come face to face with the very angry ruling spirit of the city who stirred up hatred against them, using the loss of commercial profit as the motivating factor for starting the disturbance.

This whole episode is ample evidence, as if in this modern day we needed such, that the occult is powerful and dangerous and that there can be no compromise for the people of God between the things of Satan and a wholehearted commitment to Jesus Christ. I would urge all those reading this book to ask the Lord to show them anything in their home which is of the occult and which should be totally destroyed. The sacrifice may sound great, especially with potentially valuable heirlooms and antiques, but the price of being disobedient could be incalculable.

There are many people to whom we have ministered for whom this has been the key to their healing and deliverance, as well as to the release of the whole family line. Cursed objects carry with them a hidden potency, releasing demonic power into the home and family.

Keeping such objects hidden, such as in the attic, does not diminish their potential for harm.

Freemasonry objects, special rings, jewelry, missionary souvenirs of witchcraft origins, holiday mementos that can carry with them the curse of false religions etc should all be treated in the same dispassionate way. I believe that leaders in the Body of Christ have a major responsibility to teach their congregations in these areas so that they will not be deceived by the wiles of the enemy.

In Conclusion

I have heard people say that there is too much emphasis in some ministries on dealing with the occult. They look at the Gospels and say that they find nothing there in the ministry of Jesus which even suggests that there had been any occult involvement in the lives of those Jesus either healed or delivered. That is a very good reason why we should not base our theology on just one section of scripture!

For when we look at the Acts of the Apostles what we discover is that incident after incident is related to the occult and the demonisation that has arisen as a result of occult involvement. It seems as though in the Gospels we find out a lot about casting out demons, and that in the Acts we learn a lot about occultic entry points and the power that lies behind the occult in opposing the work of God.

We cannot afford to ignore the important lessons contained in the Acts. If we do so our ministries will be minimised in their effectiveness and we will be guilty of not being able to offer many thousands of people the help they so desperately need and which Jesus made provision for in equipping the church to set the captives free.

Chapter 10

The Teachings of Jesus on Aspects of Deliverance

Whilst the amount of direct teaching in the Gospels on healing or deliverance may seem relatively thin, there is rather more than one might imagine, and more on deliverance than healing. Each reference, however, is quite profound in its consequence and implications for personal ministry.

It is easy to miss these passages of scripture and demote them in significance when compared with the other direct teaching of Jesus on more popular subjects! I have learnt from experience that if we pick and choose the passages of scripture which we like and understand, to the exclusion of others which we might have to wrestle with a little, our Christian growth becomes stunted and unbalanced and the effectiveness of our ministry suffers severely.

Much of the church, for example, dismisses the whole of Jesus's deliverance ministry, and teaching about it, as irrelevant to this day and age, because they no longer 'believe in demons'. They assume that Jesus only talked about demons because he 'was a man of his time' and was limited in his knowledge and understanding of things medical! He would not have used such terminology, they surmise, if he had been educated in psychiatry and been ministering in the latter years of the twentieth century instead of first century Palestine!

Evelyn Frost, whose research into the healing and deliverance ministries of the early Church Fathers is much to be commended, unfortunately set this theological approach in concrete when she introduced the section on demonology in her book, *Christian Healing*, with these words, *"The practice of exorcism by Christ was associated with the current belief in the existence of demons. The searchlight of science has been cast upon these shadowy forms conjured up in the darkness of ignorance, and the ghosts have disappeared."* Unfortunately such erroneous printed words, from such an authority, have had enormous influence on minds that wanted to believe them, or, possibly, on minds that were already demonically influenced by unbelief!

Another sector of the church totally accepts the integrity of the scriptures, and believes that Jesus was indeed delivering people from demons, but because they also think that believing Christians cannot be demonised, they again dismiss the deliverance ministry of Jesus as being largely irrelevant to the twentieth century church. The result, again, is a distorted and unbalanced theology which brings much criticism to the deliverance ministry because the root cause of peoples' problems is never dealt with. This leaves Christians struggling with ineffectiveness and condemnation because they cannot overcome their problems. The demonic dimension is dismissed.

The above theological viewpoints together account for the opinion of most of the church that is not involved in deliverance ministry. They are generally ignorant of the way deception controls their thinking and behaviour, and are, therefore, vulnerable to the demonic. One of the most important maxims of war is 'Know Your Enemy', a maxim that has often been disregarded in many of our churches today.

The enemy rejoices when he is assumed not to exist, or attitudes towards him are so naive that people believe he can't possibly have any influence on their lives or churches. Ignorance of the enemy and his tactics has been the cause of losing many battles!

In this chapter we face up to some of the weighty issues that are raised by the teachings of Jesus in specific passages which are directly relevant to the whole subject of deliverance.

The Beelzebul Syndrome
(Matthew 12:22-30, Mark 3:20-27 and Luke 11:14-23)

It seems that whenever Jesus exercised his authority over the powers of darkness there was controversy. Things haven't changed! Wherever there is an effective deliverance ministry taking place there will be opposition and controversy - often dressed up as very good intentions - from concerned Christians who do not want to see the ministry 'go off the rails'. This is one of Satan's primary techniques for breaking up any effective work of God which is a serious threat to demonic strongholds.

The controversies will rage, sometimes with great intensity and a depth of feeling that will surprise, and even shock, you. They will cover a huge range of issues, from the underlying theology of deliverance to whether or not one should cast out a demon without the Bishop's permission (a serious question, especially for Anglicans, who are under the authority of their Bishop. Whilst policy does vary from diocese to diocese, in most of the United Kingdom dioceses either the Bishop or his appointed adviser are supposed to be consulted before any ministry of deliverance takes place).

Satan does not mind what the point of the controversy is, for as long as there is controversy those who are ministering deliverance will have to spend some (or possibly all) of their time and energies justifying their ministry instead of actually doing it. And that, in itself, is a major victory for Satan - for the work has had to cease, and Christians (demonically influenced no doubt) have done his work for him!

The words of Jesus to the Pharisees are a salutary warning to those in leadership who are in a position to teach and apply the truth about healing and deliverance, but stubbornly refuse to be obedient to the word of God:

"How terrible for you teachers of the Law! You have kept the key that opens the door to the house of knowledge; you yourselves will not go in, and you stop those who are trying to go in!" (Luke 11:52 GNB).

I call this raising of controversy, against those who commit themselves to evangelism, healing and deliverance, the Beelzebul Syndrome, because when the church hierarchy of Jesus's day, the Pharisees, heard that he had restored the eyesight and speech of a blind and dumb man through deliverance, they raised a controversy to try and discredit the ministry of Jesus.

The controversy they raised was the authority by which the demon had been cast out. To the question being asked by the crowds, *"Could this be the Son of David,"* they replied by saying that *"He drives out demons only because Beelzebul, the ruler of the demons, gives him power to do so."* (Matthew 12:24 GNB). The bottom line, therefore, of their argument is that Jesus cannot be the Messiah because he is of the devil.

Those who oppose deliverance ministry within the church today are not suggesting that Jesus is 'of the devil', but I have heard accusations of using occult power against those who would cast demons out today. I believe that of those who do oppose deliverance ministries, most do so because they themselves want no part in them! Firstly they may not have seen such ministry and do not appreciate, therefore, the power Jesus gives his present day disciples. Secondly they may be apprehensive about the implications of getting involved. However, like the Pharisees, they may also be jealous of those who do minister effectively in territory that they fear to enter.

Mark tells us that the controversy was not restricted to the religious leaders either. It had spilled over into Jesus's family situation. When he went into a home for a meal, presumably on the day the blind and dumb man had been healed, there were so many needy people following him that he didn't have time to eat. So his family also got involved and tried to restrain him from the work he was doing because people were saying, *"he must have gone mad"*. A message was sent into the house (Mark 3:32-35) to tell him that his mother and brothers were outside and wanted him.

But Jesus discerned precisely what was happening, how they were being used to try and stop the work of healing and deliverance that he had been called to do. So *"Jesus answered, 'Who is my mother? Who are my brothers?' He looked at the people sitting round him and said 'Look! Here are my mother and my brothers! Whoever does what God wants him to do is my brother, my sister, my mother'"* (Mark 3:35).

In saying this Jesus was not saying that families don't matter, but he was placing a higher priority on obedience to God than subjection of a God-given ministry to the wishes of his family. And in the context of the scripture the higher priority was, in that instance, on the ministry of healing and deliverance. By implication, therefore, the people who are ministering in this way to those in need are truly mother, brother and sister to Jesus!

At that point the words in Jeremiah must have been very much in Jesus' mind, for the Lord said to that most persecuted of prophets, *"Even your brothers, members of your own family have betrayed you"* (Jeremiah 12:6 GNB). On another occasion, when Jesus was warning followers of the cost of discipleship, he said, *"a man's worst enemies will be the members of his own family"* (Matthew 10:36 GNB).

There must have been many times when the controversies that raged about Jesus caused him deep hurt and emotional distress, but none more so than the accusation of using the devil's power to cast out demons. The Pharisees had not been with him in the wilderness during those forty days of battling with Satan, neither did they have the discernment of spirits to sense the demonic powers that were motivating them or see the demons that were in such fear of Jesus.

But Jesus did have the discernment, not only to understand what was happening in the demonic realms, but also to discern what the Pharisees were thinking (Matthew 12:25). In another passage (John 2:25) we are told that *"no-one needed to tell Jesus about themselves, because he himself knew what was in their hearts"*. And what Jesus saw prompted one of the most salutary warnings to religious leaders he ever gave.

Jesus immediately countered the thoughts and words of his accusers with an argument of calculated simplicity. He called Satan's territory a kingdom, accurately describing the rule that he has as 'god of this world' (2 Corinthians 4:4) and in control of the fallen angels and demonic powers. But, said Jesus, if I was casting out demons by Beelzebul that would mean different factions within his kingdom would be fighting each other, and there would be no way Satan's kingdom could last very long if there was such a state of anarchy amongst the ranks of evil (Luke 11:17-18).

Looking behind the conversation into eternity, Jesus, with his Father, had been watching Satan's kingdom exercising power and control in the world for thousands of years. They had seen that it was well-organised and there was no danger of it collapsing into a chaotic mess through palace revolutions! If that really was the nature of Satan's kingdom there would have been no need for Jesus to have come to earth in the first place - the cross would have been unnecessary and mankind would not, any longer, have been the victim of Satan's control, because his kingdom would have disintegrated long ago.

The very fact that Jesus was walking this earth was conclusive evidence that Satan's kingdom was not divided against itself! But this was not evidence that the minds of his listeners, and especially the Pharisees, could be expected to grasp and understand. They needed a more down to earth illustration. So Jesus turned to the Jewish exorcists with whom the Pharisees clearly worked. These were men who sought to free people from evil spirits using religious ritual.

Jesus did not indicate that they could not cast out evil spirits, but affirmed their work and used the fact that they were able to cast out demons by telling the Pharisees that if he cast out evil spirits, and they thought he was using the power of Beelzebul, then they had to apply similar thinking to their own men who did similar work! Which meant, ultimately, that if Jesus was of Satan (Beelzebul), so were the Pharisees.

Once again Jesus had turned the Pharisees arguments (of which there were many, Luke 11:53-54) around and used them to defend himself against attack. The scenario here was not unlike the time when the Pharisees brought the woman 'taken in adultery' to Jesus. In a similar way Jesus used their stone-throwing questions to make nonsense of his accusers! *"He who is without sin among you, let him be the first to throw a stone at her"* (John 8:7 NASB) he said to them. No-one dared take up the challenge.

Jesus concluded the discussion by affirming that *"it is not Beelzebul, but God's Spirit, who gives me the power to drive out demons"* (Matthew 12:28 GNB). It was only after the Holy Spirit came down upon Jesus, following his baptism, that he started to minister with power in deliverance. From then on he began to challenge and overthrow Satan's demonic rule in peoples' lives.

The Beelzebul Syndrome has not gone away. Some pharisaical Christians, are still seeking to undermine genuine works of God, by raising controversy about deliverance ministry. This diverts attention from their own misunderstandings and failure to live out this aspect of the Gospel. If they were actually doing the works that Jesus had commissioned them to do, it is unlikely they would have the time to monitor the orthodoxy of others! There would be such a path beaten to their door by those in need that, like Jesus, they would have little time over for eating and drinking!

Conversely, however, I would not want anyone reading this book to assume I am saying that orthodox Christian belief no longer matters, and that providing we are doing the works of Jesus (healing the sick and casting out demons) we can believe and do what we like. That is as much a heresy as condemning people for doing the works of Jesus. Whilst Jesus was undoubtedly charismatic in his exercise of the gifts of the Holy Spirit, he was also very, very orthodox in his beliefs, even affirming that he had not come to add or take away one little thing from the law! (Matthew 5:17).

The issue at stake, therefore, is not so much our orthodoxy as our obedience to that inner witness of the Holy Spirit which will confirm us in the ministry that God has given us to do. That witness has to be tested against scripture, the corporate witness of the fellowship of believers God has placed us in and those to whom we are accountable before God.

For some obedience will lead to a radical new direction, when compared with the work that others might be doing at the present time, but that does not mean to say it is not orthodox in terms of God's will and purpose for their life. Some find it quite tiresome when God does not restrict himself to the limitations of human tradition! But the scriptures are full of stories of men and women who have been prepared not to count the cost of doing what God has told them to do.

Jesus demonstrated this by being quite willing to pick grain and heal the sick on the Sabbath - notwithstanding the objections of the strict Sabbatarians who assumed that because of such gross disobedience he was no longer orthodox! And Simon Peter had something of a difficulty explaining to his Christian brethren in Jerusalem that this Gospel was not just for Jews! Chapters 10 and 11 of the Acts of the Apostles are a revelation in understanding that the orthodoxy of the Holy Spirit's direction was far more wonderful than the limited horizon presented by restricting the Gospel to Jews only!

The Jewish Exorcists

A commonly asked question about this passage relates to the Jewish exorcists. If they had not been filled with the Holy Spirit, how is it possible that they could cast any demons out? Such a question pre-supposes that the Holy Spirit was not at work at all before Pentecost, or before Jesus was baptised. As you read through the Old Testament you quickly realise that such an assumption is manifestly untrue. For the story of the Jewish people is that of men of God who responded to the leading of the Holy Spirit.

Under the old covenant there are blessings promised for obedience. I have no doubt that when people whose hearts were right before God sought him for deliverance, through people who were able to teach them wisely about what it meant to be obedient to God, then some of the power of the enemy would be broken.

But when Jesus started ministering deliverance he wasn't just preaching a form of religious discipline and obedience, through which the powers of the enemy were indirectly broken, he was speaking to the demons directly and giving orders which they actually obeyed. That was unheard of! It was this directness and authority that singled Jesus out from every other religious person who had ever previously tried to set a person free from the powers of darkness.

Can Demons Cast Out Demons?

Another issue out of the Beelzebul discussion that has to be tackled is: what does happen when people go to an occult healer and are apparently healed or set free from an evil spirit? If that really does happen, and there are plenty of 'testimonies' around to suggest it does, isn't that the equivalent of Beelzebul casting demons out? In this scripture, however, Jesus seems to imply to the Pharisees that such a thing cannot possibly happen, for if it did then

Satan's kingdom would quickly crumble, as it would be manifestly divided against itself!

To understand this apparent dilemma consider the following. Jesus actually set the man free from the demon and healed him of his blindness and dumbness. He was totally released from his bondage and clearly in a better state after the ministry than he was before. If it was Jesus who had healed him there is no possibility of there having been any religious deception entering into the ministry, for he was without sin and free from any deception. Jesus ministered to the whole person and there is no way that through Jesus symptoms would have been dealt with, but leaving the ultimate state of the person to be much worse than he was at the beginning.

When looking at occultically based healing and deliverance, however, it is always symptom oriented; and therein lies the potential for great deception. For scripture tells us that in the last days Satan himself will work supposed miracles that even the very elect may be deceived! (Matthew 24:24). Now if some of these miracles that Satan works are deliverances, which they apparently are, there has to be some deeper level of understanding, otherwise we have made Matthew in chapter 24 contradict what he wrote in chapter 12!

In Christian understanding the removal of symptoms and healing are not necessarily the same thing. Oh yes, they can appear to be the same thing, and certainly a person can be relieved of the condition that was afflicting them, but are they healed? If they are genuinely healed, then by comparison with the Gospel story, the total state of the person after being 'healed' will be better than it formerly was. Now, if someone is deceived into measuring wholeness and healing simply by observing symptoms, they will not be interested in looking at any other dimension that might be operating, and are in great danger.

For Satan is a master deceiver and his demons are both well-trained and under authority, so that if they are given an instruction from a higher authority they will naturally obey it, because the instruction will always be to Satan's ultimate advantage. So let's go to an occult healer for a moment, watch a person being 'delivered' of an evil spirit and see one of the things that can happen in the supernatural.

Jane (a totally imaginary person) has a physical symptom that is worrying her. It is a symptom that is caused by an evil spirit (though she is not aware of this) - in scriptural language, she is sick because she has a demon. We have met many, many people in such a condition. She goes to an occult healer, say a spiritualist medium. A successful medium is highly demonised and is under the almost total demonic control of very powerful demons.

Jane has lived a relatively innocent life. Other than this physical condition, there are no major problems or demonic strongholds in her life. She goes to church quite regularly and takes an active part in church life, but her church does not have a healing ministry, so she followed up an advertisement in the local paper about a 'church' that did. She ended up seeing the resident spiritual healer at the 'Christian' Spiritualist Church.

When Jane went into his room, the medium's demons looked at Jane, through the medium, and assessed the situation. They saw the spirit of infirmity, how worried Jane was and also how very vulnerable she was. The medium does not do anything that would upset or distress this first-time caller, but prays some very nice prayers and Jane gets healed of the symptoms. Jane is delighted, gradually loses interest in her own church, goes very occasionally to the spiritualist church, but now she's been healed that doesn't interest her very much either. She and her family settle down to a routine pagan existence.

What happened? First point is to remember that Satan's higher objectives will always over-ride lesser ones. Satan used the spirit of infirmity (which could have been passed down the family line when her mother died some six months earlier) to get Jane to go to the medium. Once there, some demonic interchanges took place, totally unheard by either the medium or Jane.

The medium's powerful controlling demon would probably give an instruction something like this, *"Spirit of infirmity in Jane, cease your actions for the time being, so that she can be healed; spirit of deception enter her mind and start your work of turning her away from God."* So instead of healing, further demonisation took place! There was a trade-off (loss of symptoms for more demonisation) which left Jane worse-off than she was before, even though she was pleased to be rid of the symptoms. But she wasn't aware that she was the loser in the deal.

She went away from the medium with more than she bargained for - the little spirit of infirmity, which her church should have dealt with as a matter of routine ministry, had done its job and opened the way for a spirit of deception which took her deep into spiritual bondage. Jane had given the spirit of deception a right to enter, through her sin of consulting a medium, and Satan's greater interests had been served, even though she had been 'healed', for the time being, of the symptoms.

The spirit of deception soon convinced Jane that going to church on a Sunday morning was disrupting her family life, and surely Jesus wouldn't want the stability of the family to be rocked, would he? Before long Jane and her family became occasional church attenders only - the traditional Easter and Christmas Christian! The spirit of deception is now well established and will lie totally dormant, though constantly on guard against any real spiritual life entering the family. The moment anything like that should happen the spirit will start to disrupt all sort of things in Jane and the family, until the threatened 'danger' is over!

The above story is not just a figment of imagination but pieced together from the way we have seen spirits work in hundreds of peoples lives. I remember one lady who went to a spiritualist healer in her early twenties. Like Jane she was healed of the presenting symptoms. But in exchange she received much more than she bargained for and for the rest of her life suffered from extensive undiagnosable pain. But every time she had an operation (and there were many) the surgeon could find nothing wrong. She was also spiritually deceived and one of those people who always had 'good ideas' that were, nevertheless, directly contrary to what the Holy Spirit was doing in the life of her church! In cases like this a spirit of curse usually enters placing the spirit of man in demonic bondage.

So, whilst in Jane's case, it appears that a demon (spirit of infirmity) was being cast out by a demon (the medium's controlling spirit), what actually happened was that the demonic hierarchy moved in with a changed plan for Jane's life. She was deceived into a spiritual bondage which would now be much more difficult to free her from in the future, should she ever come back to the Lord and seek deliverance.

Much of the world is seeking, and is content with, this sort of symptomatic healing. The church which abandons the ministry of Jesus in the supernatural realm of deliverance has no answers of its own. I believe we would be experiencing a lot more successful one-to-one evangelism if the Janes of this world received their healing through being delivered by the power of God! Her whole family, circle of friends and neighbours would have heard, and the glory for her healing would have gone to Jesus instead of a spiritualist healer.

I have known cases, too, where genuine deliverance of the presenting demon has indeed taken place through an occultist. But such deliverances have always been part of a demonic strategy in which the presence of one lesser spirit, having a particular characteristic has always been replaced with a spirit having a different, and more spiritually dangerous, consequence in the person's life.

First Bind the Strong Man
(Matthew 12:29, Mark 3:27 and Luke 11:21-22)

The controversy with the Pharisees about Beelzebul raises more issues than are included in the Beelzebul Syndrome discussion above. Matthew, Mark and Luke include, as part of the ongoing teaching arising from this incident, Jesus's directive about how to plunder a house. Fortunately this advice is found in the middle of a discussion on deliverance ministry, otherwise Jesus's intentions might have been misconstrued!

What Jesus says is that if you want to break into a strong man's house and plunder his possessions, first tie up the strong man. Then you will be free to take as much as you want of his possessions and, Luke adds, carry away the very weapons that the owner of the house was depending on for his defence!

This is, basically, very practical advice on the spiritual mechanics of major deliverance ministry. For there to be a strong man in occupation of a house, there has to be weaker men under his control. So Jesus is saying that the demonic kingdom operating inside a demonised person is one with a hierarchy of power and control; and if you want to deliver the person of all the lesser demons it makes a lot of sense to so invalidate the power of the strong man, that he is unable to defend his 'possessions' - the demon spirits who were defending him under his control.

I remember well the first night that the Lord showed us this scripture, early in the ministry of Ellel Grange. We were struggling to set someone free of a demon that was clearly manifesting in front of us, but it would not be dislodged and was obviously fairly secure in the hold it had on the person's life. We had done all that we knew in terms of undermining the power of the demon through forgiveness, repentance etc.

Sometimes the Holy Spirit leads you to ask questions in ministry which are strategic to the deliverance. Rather like when Jesus was led to challenge Legion as to his name. The question I asked of the demon was not its name, but 'Who is your master'. The silence which followed the question was indicative of the accuracy of the discernment, so I pressed on and eventually, very reluctantly, the demon told us the name of the higher demon in the kingdom to whom it had to answer. It was obvious that as it did it was being punished from within for giving away such important information.

We were then able to challenge the higher demon by name, whereupon it surfaced, and we addressed the strong man. I said to the demon 'I bind you in the Name of Jesus and by the power of his blood I forbid you to hold onto the demons under your control any longer'. I then went back to the demon that had originally challenged us and was able to deliver the person, not only of that demon, but of all the other demons (and there were many) that were also under the control of that particular strong man. We were then able to cast out the strong man because it had lost all the lesser demons (Luke's 'weapons the owner was depending on') and we then found it to be no longer a strong man, but just like any other demon!

There have been occasions when we have known it was right to be binding the strong man that was controlling a demonic kingdom, but we were unable to make any progress with the deliverance. On that occasion the Lord showed us that the strong man we were dealing with was not inside the person we were dealing with at all, but was a ruling spirit of the air which had direct control over the demons inside. On that occasion the Lord showed us how Satan has ruling spirits with specific job functions over nations and regions and that in some ministries we have to sever the demon inside the person from the ruling demon who is on the outside the person.

This was a revelation from the Holy Spirit which has enabled us to minister much more effectively to some categories of people; for example, those who have been victims of ritualistic sexual abuse. On occasions they have had to be set free from a ruling spirit of the air which acts like a slavemaster holding all such victims in a chain-like grip of Satanic power.

Another location for the strong man, that may be controlling a demon you are attempting to deliver, is inside another person! Usually this is only possible if there is a close 'soul-tie' (much more about soul-ties will be found in the next volume) between the two people involved, such as exists between family members, sexual partners, close friends etc. That soul-tie seems to act like a 'demonic tube' along which demons can move or through which power and control can be exercised.

It is this phenomenon which often accounts for the devastating manipulative control that some people have over others. Until the soul-ties are broken, which mercifully can be easily and quickly done through prayer, one is dealing with a demonic power that is totally beyond the control of the person you are seeking to help. We have found this particular ministry very profound when dealing with demonic power that has been exercised through previous sexual partners with whom, as the scripture says, (1 Corinthians 6:15-17), people have become one flesh. But when the soul-ties are broken release is often instant.

What we have found from experience is that Jesus's advice to bind the strong man is very practical and that this is often a necessary procedure in the course of deliverance ministry. But it is not a guarantee of instant success - it is just one of the ministry procedures that have to be remembered. There are many other reasons also why some deliverances are difficult and it is necessary to work through these - they are spelled out more clearly in the next volume.

To Gather or Not to Gather - That is the Question!
(Matthew 12:30 and Luke 11:23)

It is very tempting to look at scripture passages out of context, especially if it suits our particular theological perspective to do so! Often I have heard the words of Matthew 12:30 quoted to endorse the thrust of an evangelistic messages, *"Jesus said, 'Anyone who is not for me is really against me'"* (GNB). The threat of being considered to have been against Jesus on the final judgement day adding an effective bit of spiritual arm-twisting to the appeal to follow him!

Again, please do not misunderstand me. I do believe that if someone is not for Jesus, then they are indeed against him and that at the judgement day those that are truly for him will be those who enter into heaven by the narrow way that leads to life. But that is not the context in which the Gospel writers record these words as having been said.

They appear, almost identically, towards the end of the Matthew and Luke accounts of the Beelzebul controversy and discussions. They are omitted from Mark's account, but Mark includes a discussion (which has already been referred to) about those who are obedient to Jesus are really his mother, brother and sister - a passage which, in the context of the Beelzebul discussions has exactly the same significance.

So what is the relevance and context of this very important sentence from the lips of Jesus? The relevance is to the concluding discussions on deliverance which followed the attack by the Pharisees on Jesus for healing and delivering the blind and dumb man. Jesus explains how he casts out demons by the power of God's Spirit and that binding the strong man is part of a possible ministry procedure to undermine Satan's strongholds.

It is only then that he says, *"Anyone who is not for me . . ."* What Jesus appears to be saying is that anyone who is not for him in the deliverance ministry, which has been

the central part of the discussion so far, is against him!
The context is not to a general statement about following
Jesus (of which there are many such statements
elsewhere in the Gospels), but to a very specific aspect of
what it means to follow Jesus - support of and
involvement in the deliverance ministry.

At this point much of the church needs to be very
red-faced, both about their exegesis of this verse
historically and about their response to its implications
for their ministry! For what it appears that Jesus is
saying is this, in an amplified and contextualised
rendering of this scripture:

> *"Anyone who is not for me in the ministry of
> deliverance that God my Father has called me
> into, as part of the full Gospel of evangelism,
> healing and deliverance is really against me for
> they are, either directly, or indirectly opposing a
> vital part of my work which is given to me by the
> Holy Spirit and which proves that the Kingdom of
> God has come;"*

But that isn't the end of the matter. For the sentence has
not yet finished. There is not even a friendly full-stop to
hang on to as an excuse for avoiding the implications of
what Jesus says next!

Again in an amplified and contextualised version:

> *"Anyone who does not help me gather in the
> harvest (the flock) by setting people free from the
> powers of darkness, as I have set free this blind
> and dumb man today through deliverance, is not
> only failing to gather in the flock but is actually
> scattering it.*

The implication of these words is far deeper than the very
superficial way in which they are sometimes used in
evangelistic ministry or to try and make people support
what may well be a work of God, but which is totally
unrelated to the context of the scripture. Their
significance is awesome. In a nutshell Jesus is saying

that those who do not support deliverance ministries are opposing Christ and those leaders who do not practice deliverance ministry themselves are actually scattering the flock!

I have seen this operate on many occasions, where those who should be rejoicing in the victory of the cross stand against what is manifestly a work of the Holy Spirit, in setting people free from the powers of darkness. Those who will find this truth most unpalatable may well be those who pride themselves on having a Bible based ministry. However proud they may be of their Biblical tradition, if they are not supporting and exercising the ministry of deliverance they are opposing the Gospel.

Even more radical is the thought that people who are so deeply religious in their Christian commitment can even be scattering the flock. How could this be? What I have observed in this respect may be helpful to those who find it hard to understand.

A ministry which offers Christ as the answer to all life's problems is very attractive to those whose problems are many. They hear the Gospel preached effectively and faithfully, they respond to it and are converted. The church has done its job - allegedly - but leaves the poor convert (we'll call him Chris) to flounder in a new pool of life for which he is grossly unprepared. He needs help. Many at this stage not only need discipling in the basics of Christian truth - a job that is sometimes done quite well - but they also need personal ministry to help them overcome the problems arising from all that has invaded their being during their pagan years. That help has not been freely available within the majority of churches.

Twelve months later Chris is nowhere to be seen. Church hasn't been the answer after all and he returns to his friends in the world, who, at least, have time to talk to him about his other interests in life. God isn't totally dismissed, but he's definitely been put on the shelf as being somewhat irrelevant to Chris and his family. He is unlikely to try church again and will probably be discouraging and dismissive towards others who are in need and think that the Church might be able to help them.

So what went wrong? What happened to Chris? His church fellowship made one of the commonest mistakes in evangelism. They assumed that once he was 'in the fold' that God would take care of the rest and there was nothing more they can do! How wrong they were. When people come to Christ they usually carry with them quite a lot of excess baggage - some of which is the demons that entered in a variety of ways, including the the sins of an ungodly lifestyle and generational contamination. The time of conversion should be the beginning of ministry to Chris, not the end of it.

At that point Chris is more open than at any other time of his life to receive all the help he needs to become established as a dynamic member of the body of Christ. He may also need deliverance and unless he receives healing and deliverance ministry the demons he has, having had something of a spiritual shock through Chris's conversion, will regroup themselves and re-establish their strong-hold on Chris's flesh life and continue to plague him with all the old problems he had before he became a Christian.

Indeed, at that point the demons will intensify their efforts to show Chris just how many problems he's got! For Chris will then be forced to conclude (quite accurately!) that becoming a Christian hasn't made any difference after all. So Chris, at the end of the day, has tried Christianity, genuinely, but has found that it doesn't really work for him and he finishes up rejecting the church, compounding his sense of failure and condemnation and becoming a deterrent to others. What a sad story. The flock has been scattered and Jesus's warning to those who neither support nor do deliverance has been fulfilled.

Chris's story could be repeated many times over. Not all such people finish up leaving the church, however, for many stay within its walls, and continue to nurse their hurts and pains. Because they have so many unresolved problems, lying just below the surface, they will always be weak and perhaps even 'left to die' unless they are provided with the help that Jesus provided for us. Many who come through the doors of Ellel Grange wear masks of normality while underneath they are crumbling under the weight of hurts, condemnation and low self worth.

Inside the church they become a permanent drain on the leadership and the resources of the fellowship. Outside the church they are more of a put-off than an attraction to people in the world. Once again, failure to deliver the demons has resulted in the flock being scattered instead of being gathered.

Sin Against the Holy Spirit

The implications of this discussion would be hard enough without the teaching Jesus gave which immediately follows. For in Matthew 12:31 and 32 Jesus continues the discussion by implying that to scatter the flock in this way is linked with the sin against the Holy Spirit which 'shall never be forgiven'. One will be forgiven for all manner of sins against even the Son of God, but to sin against the Holy Spirit will not be forgiven.

There have been many treatises written about the 'unforgivable sin' and I do not intend to open up an in-depth discussion on this in the present work. Surely, however, it is a sufficiently salutary warning, for the church to take seriously the context in which Jesus spoke these words. The Pharisees had accused Jesus, implying that what was the work of the Holy Spirit in Jesus (on this occasion, deliverance ministry), was in fact the work of Satan. Let us be very cautious, therefore, about criticising a ministry on the grounds that it includes deliverance, lest we be found to be making the same mistake, sinning against the Holy Spirit, and opposing what God himself is doing to set people free.

That is not to say that those who do deliverance are, therefore, above criticism in any respect and do not have to be accountable for what else they may be saying and doing in the name of Jesus. We are all responsible before God for what we build on the foundation of Jesus Christ and Jesus himself warned that there will even be people who cast out demons who will not be found in the Kingdom of God (Matthew 7:22-23).

We must, however, examine ourselves on this issue, and allow the Holy Spirit to minister truth to our own hearts. For if we are not elevating the Lord Jesus Christ, by taking authority over the powers of darkness (demons) that would pollute the Body of Christ (cause sickness and distress etc), then we are in disobedience to one of the fundamental commands that Jesus gave to the disciples and the church. We are, indeed, then undermining one of the foundational purposes for which Jesus died (to defeat Satan and overcome all the powers of darkness) and, by implication, standing against those who do practise deliverance ministry. Jesus warned us not to judge others! (Matthew 7:1-2).

Seven Spirits More Evil Than the First
(Matthew 12:43-45 and Luke 11:24-26)

One of the commonest groups of questions asked of those involved in deliverance ministry is *"Where do the demons go when you cast them out?"* or *"Do you send them anywhere special?"* or *"How do you stop them going to someone else?"* Scripture is very silent on this whole issue!

There are only three comments within the Gospels which give us any clue whatsoever. The first is within Mark's account of the healing of the epileptic boy, where Jesus not only orders the demon to leave the boy, but also commands the demon never to *"go into him again"* (Mark 9:25). The second is within the discourses with the demons in the Gadarene demoniac where they pleaded with Jesus not to send them to the Abyss and Jesus finished up by despatching them, at the demons' request into the pigs.

The third, which is the primary reference for this section, is within the few verses contained in both Matthew and Luke which warn of the dangers of demonic re-entry, not just by the demon that has left but by an even worse colony of Satan's troops!

There seems, therefore, to be some conflict here with the first reference in Mark, for if Jesus commanded every demon that he cast out, never to return to the person concerned, then the potential for further demonisation of that person, from the same demon, could not arise! Clearly we need to unpack these two verses a little and illustrate them from experiences that will remove the superficial conflict that there undoubtedly is!

When Jesus gave instruction to the disciples to go and preach the Gospel, heal the sick and cast out demons he only gave them the bare bones of an order and no detailed instructions. He gave them power and authority to cast out demons, but did not tell them where to send them! (Luke 9:1-2). I am suspicious therefore of any teaching which contains precise guidelines in this respect for they would appear to be instructions which do not have the backing of scripture and the danger is that such instructions become part of a technique which can finish up in the flesh, as opposed to being used under the anointing of the Spirit of God. Not that scripture is specific on every issue that we have to determine in this whole area of healing and deliverance - it isn't, so we do have to apply both sanctified common sense and, on occasion, be willing to act under a specific anointing of the Spirit.

One cry which was expressed by demons to Jesus was *"Have you come for us before the appointed time?"* (Matthew 8:29 GNB). As soon as demons encountered Jesus they knew they were facing the one who, one day, at the appointed time, would cast them, with Satan, into the

lake of fire and execute the judgement that was reserved
for them. At that time they would be joined by those
angels which are already *"chained in the darkness below,
where God is keeping them for that great Day on which
they will be condemned"*. These are the angels in the
abyss who are under punishment already for *"not staying
within the limits of their proper authority"* (Jude 6 GNB).

Jesus never sent any demons to the abyss, although they
clearly recognised he had the power to do so. (Luke 8:31).
Nor did he assign them to the pit, outer darkness, the
eternal flames or any of a multitude of other places that I
have heard referred to by people in their enthusiasm to
get demons out! I don't think God will in any way judge
us for over-enthusiasm in dealing with the enemy, but I
do think it important that we try and operate within the
bounds of scriptural authority!

Those who would condemn the enthusiasts for their
graphic language in deliverance, but sit on the sidelines
and do nothing themselves, are in great danger and
should remember the caution that Jesus gave within the
parable of the sheep and the goats when illustrating the
final judgement. Jesus says there are those who were *"in
prison"* and *"you would not care for them"*, and so he says
to those who refused to help them *"Away from me, you
that are under God's curse! Away to the eternal fire
which has been prepared for the devil and his angels"*
(Matthew 25:41 GNB). When Jesus said he had come to
set the captives free he was not referring to those behind
literal prison bars, and we can't, therefore, dismiss this
passage as only referring to visiting real prisons, and not
having any relevance to deliverance ministry.

We also need to appreciate here something of the
dispensations of God's eternal timetable and realise that
we can only operate within the confines of these
dispensations (eras of time). Unfortunately wrong
dispensational theology has been used as a major weapon
by Satan, not only to stop deliverance ministry taking

place but also to prevent the operation of the Gifts of the Spirit in their entirety!

There is a school of dispensational thought which has had, and still has in some quarters, enormous impact and influence. It limits the operation of the gifts to the Apostolic period. It argues that Jesus operated in the gifts of the Spirit, and gave the apostles similar powers, so as to establish the credibility of Jesus as the Son of God. But once that had happened we moved into a new dispensation when faith was the only earthly gift we needed; when we die, we shall go to glory but in the meantime we live out our lives being obedient to what the scripture tells us to do in the natural, but we leave the supernatural well alone because we are no longer in the dispensation when that is allowed or required of us.

The dispensationalists have, therefore, given theological reasons for spiritualising the supernatural lessons from the New Testament and never having to do anything ourselves about putting them into practice. How Satan must have rejoiced to see his deceptions being so effective that a very powerful school of Christian theology was actually doing his work for him! For the net conclusion of this type of dispensational theology is that because practising the gifts is not allowed, anyone who is operating in them must be of the enemy, deceived, or, even, working within the occult! This seems to give them the right to whitewash their own powerlessness and condemn the rest of the body of Christ as operating in heresy or deception.

It seems to me that the main foundation for this theology is fear. For Jesus did say that in the last days Satan would perform all sorts of amazing tricks so that even the very elect may be deceived. Now if Satan can do such amazing things, and there is a possibility that people might be deceived, surely, they would argue, it is better for me not to risk any of these things than dabble in something that might be wrong?

Unfortunately they have overlooked the parable of the talents (Matthew 25:14-30). Here Jesus commends the servants who use their talents wisely, but the servant who, out of fear of making a mistake, and losing what he has, buries his talent in the ground and does nothing with it, is described by Jesus as being a *"useless servant"* and says *"throw him outside into the darkness; there he will cry and grind his teeth"* (Matthew 25:30 GNB). There is nothing in this parable to indicate that those who used their talents, but were unsuccessful, would be condemned. Condemnation is only handed out to the one who refused to use them at all!

The dispensations in which mankind has a part, and which are clearly expressed in scripture, are as follows:

1.   From the creation and immediate fall of man to the Incarnation of the Lord Jesus Christ.

2.   From the Incarnation to Pentecost.

3.   The Pentecostal Age, in which we are now living.

The next dispensation will begin with the second coming of our Lord Jesus Christ, but I do not propose to be drawn into eschatological, dispensational discussions in a book which is for the use of the saints in the present dispensation!

As far as deliverance is concerned, and the destination of demons after deliverance, it is important to realise that in the present dispensation the demons have not yet come to their appointed time, when they will join the angels already in chains, in the fire of God's judgement which is *"prepared for the Devil and his angels"* (Matthew 25:41). We do not therefore have any right, at the present time, to do other than Jesus did, and for the same reasons, which is simply to cast the demons out of the territory that they are currently occupying and forbid them to return.

Whereupon we hit a problem. If we have forbidden them to return, as Jesus apparently did, then why was it necessary to warn about the return of the demon, but this time with seven other demons worse than itself, so that the final state of the person is much worse than it was at the beginning?

Earlier in this book we stated that demons are legalists. They know their rights and will go wherever those rights have been legally granted. So what we have to look for is any way that after deliverance the demons can feel that they still have a legal right to return. There are two primary ways that this can come about.

Failure to Make Jesus Lord

The first reason relates to the Lordship of Jesus Christ and the need to be filled with the Holy Spirit. In spatial terms when a person is delivered of an evil spirit there is left a spiritual vacuum in the person. How will that spiritual vacuum be filled safely? The only spirit with which it is safe for us to be filled, and which we are urged in scripture to seek, is the Holy Spirit. Paul told us to be continuously being filled with the Holy Spirit (Ephesians 5:18). For if we are to be channels for the flow of the Holy Spirit, into the lives of others through ministry, then we will need continually to be refilled with the power of God.

Jesus was conscious, when the woman with the issue of blood touched him, that power had gone out of him (Luke 8:46). If that was Jesus's experience then we too must realise that what God gave us at our conversion, or when we were filled (baptised) with the Holy Spirit, is not sufficient for the rest of our days. We must continually draw upon the fountain which springs up within - the very water of life.

But there is no way we can be filled with the Holy Spirit unless Jesus is Lord of our lives. The Holy Spirit is a HOLY Spirit. The only way we, who are sinners, can be holy, is when our sin is covered by the blood of Jesus and we are wearing, therefore, a robe of righteousness, which is not earned through good religious practice, but is a free gift from God. It is only when Jesus is established as Lord of our lives that the Holy Spirit has free access to fill us with his spirit.

So, if an evil spirit is cast out of a person who has not asked for Jesus to be Lord of his life, then there is no way that the Holy Spirit can move in to fill the spiritual vacuum that now exists. It is for this reason that bringing the person to Jesus, that he may be born again of the Spirit of God is so essential and why it is only in very exceptional circumstances that I would actually minister deliverance to someone who has not already come into the Kingdom of God. For the danger is obvious.

Satan is no respecter of persons and as a backlash against ministry in the power of the Holy Spirit he will do everything he possibly can to undermine genuine deliverance ministries by attacking those who have been delivered. If the demons recognise that they have a legal right to return, because the Lordship of Jesus Christ has not been established in this area of the person's life, it would be wholly consistent with Satan's character to try and send seven more demons worse than the first; for if the final state of the person is worse than the first Satan would try and use this situation to discredit the only ministry that can actually oust demons from their strongholds in peoples' lives!

There have been a number of horror stories in recent years of things that have gone sadly wrong following deliverance ministry. It seems that most of these instances relate to deliverance ministry that has been inadvisedly carried out on people who had not, or were not willing to, become Christians and allow the Lordship of Jesus Christ to be established in their lives.

There is only one instance in the whole of the New Testament of someone being delivered who was not coming primarily to Jesus. The story of the woman with the spirit of divination in Acts 16 tells us that she railed against Paul for many days, her demons, nevertheless, crying out truth about Jesus. In the end Paul was not prepared to put up with the distraction any longer to his evangelistic ministry, so he took authority over the demon and delivered her.

But such was the backlash from her owners that Paul and Silas were thrown into Jail. Even for Paul the consequences were tough! We must be very cautious not to step out of the normal guidelines for ministry that God has given us, and if we do, we must be as sure as we can be that we have heard from God and that his anointing is upon our actions. Otherwise the consequences for the person, of becoming more severely demonised, and of unwelcome attacks upon the ministry, will be a major distraction from the work God really has called us to do.

So Jesus's warning about being further demonised following deliverance appears to be strong advice not to minister to people who are unwilling to come under his Lordship and who cannot, therefore, be filled with the Holy Spirit.

There is a second aspect to this warning, however, that needs to be looked at, which is picked up by Peter in his second letter. He talks about someone who has escaped from the corrupting forces of the world, which is a fairly graphic description of being delivered from evil spirits, and then again being caught and conquered by them.

Peter is severe in his condemnation of such people, saying that *"they are in a worse state at the end than they were at the beginning. It would have been much better for them never to have known the way of righteousness than to know it and then turn away from the sacred command that was given them. What happened to them shows that the proverbs are true: 'A dog goes back to what it has vomited' and 'A pig that has been washed goes back to roll in the mud'."* (2 Peter 2:20-22 GNB).

What Peter is warning us of is that we are always likely to be vulnerable in areas of our lives where there have been weaknesses. If we have already been delivered of evil spirits, we must be on our guard, therefore, to walk clean before God , especially in those areas from which we have been cleansed, otherwise we will be in danger of putting down the welcome mat to the enemy. He will then exercise the legal right, which we, through our sin, have given him, and reoccupy the territory that he formerly occupied, and bring back also even stronger demonic powers.

This particular passage of scripture highlights the difference between the world, the flesh and the devil, three categories of influence which some find hard to delineate. The world is that source of general influence, under Satan's overall control, and which offers temptations which are contrary to God's perfect will. The temptations offered by the world are attractive to the flesh for they seem to fulfil base desires which our fallen nature has, such as greed, lust, selfishness etc, etc. Our flesh life can also be consecrated wholly in the Lord's service and be, therefore, set apart for God, cleansed from the consequences of sin and whilst always vulnerable to the enemy, be set about by a hedge of protection.

It is when with our will we choose to allow the desires of the flesh to be fulfilled in ways that are contrary to the leading of the Holy Spirit that we are in danger of being demonised through the practice of sin. The world has then used the flesh as the means of getting a devil (demon) inside. From that point on the person is not only battling with temptations from the outside, but with a voice on the inside which is urging capitulation to the temptation, often by feeding the mind with apparently plausible reasons for giving in and sinning.

It would seem that a good description of a besetting sin is a sin which is being encouraged by the demonic from inside as well as temptation from outside. Without deliverance there will be a permanent battle raging which will keep the Christian under the control of the enemy. There are many Christians who struggle in this way, and because they have never been taught of the possibility of being freed from demonic power through deliverance they live out their lives in permanent bondage to Satan in specific areas of their lives.

We have ministered privately and confidentially to many Christian leaders who were desperate for help. Some had come to believe that they were not even Christians, such was the extent of the demonic hold on their mind and their flesh. Many suffered from deep sexual problems, and sinful desires, which they had never dared to confess and seek help for inside their own church because of the fear that being honest with their superiors would destroy their careers and, as a result, their families. They had lived in torment for years, thinking that no-one could help them, yet at the same time going through the motions of ministry, because in their heart they believed it to be true for others, even if it wasn't working very well for themselves.

Some have been deeply shocked at the extent of demonisation they have been labouring under, and the filth and violence that was manifested when the demonic finally had to surface. Many have gone back to their churches totally transformed people, with a holy hatred for the enemy and a Godly desire to start ministering freedom to their people. For some the legalistic bondage of dispensational teaching has gone out of the window as the liberating light of Jesus, as healer and deliverer, has come in.

No wonder Satan wants to keep the church ignorant of the need for deliverance ministry and do all he can to discredit, in the eyes of the rest of the church, those ministries that are moving powerfully in this area. He does not want to see a cleansed and powerful church. But take care, for as both Jesus and Peter warned, the enemy will not let up from his attacks and will, initially, try hard to regain lost ground through gaining a legal right over us.

Finally, before leaving this section, it is interesting to note that Jesus comments that when an evil spirit goes out of a man it chooses to go to the 'dry and waterless' places seeking a place to rest. Now why should a spirit choose to go to such arid regions? The only answer that makes theological sense is derived from the reference in Ephesians 5:26 to the washing of the church, by water, in order to present it to God pure and faultless, without spot or wrinkle.

Is this a reference to deliverance ministry? Not directly, but for the church to be cleansed and pure, any demons must of course be cast out. Water would appear to have a special significance, therefore, which will inevitably make the demons afraid. I do not personally come from a sacramental background, but I have learnt in this ministry not to dismiss any scripturally based practise which could be sacramentally used as part of healing or deliverance ministry.

On numerous occasions we have consecrated some water in the name of the Father, the Son and the Holy Spirit and then sprinkled the person, made the sign of the cross on the forehead or, even, in extreme cases used our swimming pool with considerable effect! The demons hate consecrated water. Often they will cry out *"Not that, it burns"* or words to that effect. So I can fully understand that if water has the potential for so much power over the demonic that when they leave a person they will certainly choose to go where water is scarce!

This may also give a new insight into the rite of baptism. Our swimming pool has often been used for baptism by immersion, and many people being baptised thus are delivered of evil spirits which are driven out of hiding by the sacramental way in which the baptism for deliverance is carried out. It is interesting that the Roman rite of baptism of a child has always included within it a deliverance prayer to set the child free from demonic powers that have come into it down the generation lines of the parents.

Arguments over the infant/adult baptism issue have created much heat in recent years. Few, if any, of the proponents of either practice have considered seriously the deliverance aspects of being cleansed through baptism. (In a different context I will look at Numbers Chapter 19, which talks extensively about the provisions under the law for being cleansed through the use of the water of purification.)

For children of Christian parents an infant ceremony of dedication and presentation of the child to God is wholly scriptural, as also would be the use of such a ceremony to minister deliverance to the child at the start of its life. (Our experience is that demons lift off children very easily. It is only as the child matures and gives the demons rights by its own sinful behaviour that generational demonisation becomes entrenched.)

The power of consecrated water may also, perhaps, give fresh insight into the otherwise puzzling healings that would take place at the pool of Bethesda, whenever the water was 'troubled' or 'stirred up', presumably by an angel (John 5:1-9). The first person into the pool would be healed. Was that because there was a special anointing of the water by the Holy Spirit, so that when someone went into the water immediately afterwards the spirits of infirmity, which afflicted the long-term sick, were driven out and the people were healed?

At a practical level we have certainly found the use of consecrated water (I prefer that phrase than the more commonly encountered Holy Water, which name carries with it an air of divine superstition) to be of significant value in deliverance ministry. This has been used in various ways according to how the Holy Spirit has led at the time. In recent years, Leanne Payne also has taught widely about the power of consecrated water to bring healing and deliverance.

Additionally, if the demons choose to go to dry and waterless places when they leave a person we have from time to time used that as a helpful phrase to accompany a command to leave a person - 'Go to the dry and waterless places' - on the grounds that if that is a place the demons would prefer to go to, they are more likely to leave quickly and quietly without hurting or harming the person. This is rather like Jesus allowing the demons to go into the pigs to protect the man from their power - only in that instance Jesus was able to turn the tables on the demons, because I doubt if any of them had bargained on the pigs sky diving into the sea of Galilee!

Your Father the Devil!
(John 8:31-47)

John's Gospel is notable for the relatively little attention John pays to either the healing or deliverance ministry of Jesus; but the in-depth teaching John does include, on many major issues, provides us with a unique insight into the life and teaching of Jesus. He tells us (in possible reference to other writings about Jesus), *"Jesus performed many other miracles which are not recorded in this book. But these have been written in order that you may believe that Jesus is the Messiah, the Son of God, and that through your faith in him you may have life"* (John 20:30-31 GNB).

John's purpose was, therefore, primarily evangelistic so that people may truly understand who Jesus is. Consequently much of the teaching John records is not found in the other Gospels. Some of this is contained in the somewhat puzzling encounter that he had with a group of believers - people who were not just Jewish believers in God, but people who, John tells us, actually believed in Jesus (v.31).

To these Jewish believers Jesus makes a statement which they find offensive. *"If you obey my teaching, you are really my disciples; you will know the truth and the truth will set you free"* (v.32). They could not take the idea that they, children of Abraham, who had never been anyone's slaves, needed freeing from anyone or anything. (They had clearly forgotten the years of exile when the people of God were carried off in slavery to Babylon!)

So Jesus explains, and outside of an understanding of the need for deliverance ministry it is hard to make much sense of what Jesus says to these believers. First, he says, *"Everyone who sins is a slave of sin . . . but if the Son sets you free, then you shall be free indeed"* (v.34-36). That particular verse of scripture is so often used by those antagonistic to deliverance ministry to demonstrate that Christians couldn't possibly need deliverance because the 'Son has set them free'. It is usually misquoted, out of context, for Jesus seems to use exactly the same scripture as part of his argument to demonstrate that these believers were subject to Satan and not free from his control!

Jesus goes on, *"I know you are Abraham's descendants. Yet you are trying to kill me, because you will not accept my teaching"* (v.37). Who was Jesus really speaking to here? This was a group of people who were believers in Jesus, yet he accuses them of not accepting his teaching. He acknowledges them as believers but at the same time tells them they are trying to kill him. Superficially it makes no sense at all.

Jesus continues, *"I talk about what my Father has shown me, but you do what your father has told you"* (v.38). (Most translations use a capital F for the first use of the word Father and the small f for the second word father.) Clearly John realises that Jesus is talking about two different fathers, and suddenly what Jesus is saying begins to make sense. He is talking about the allegiance shown to Satan (as father) by the people who are responding to the demonic that is trying to kill Jesus. But they do not realise that is what is happening, for they protest that their father (small f) is Abraham and that the only Father (capital F) they have ever had is God himself (v.39-41).

Jesus is slowly picking his way through the arguments as he faces these people up to the fact that in spite of being believers there is something in them that wants to kill him. Jesus knew that crowds are fickle and that before very long, people who had sworn allegiance to him during the good times would be baying for his blood and releasing Barabbas; it was only minutes later, after Jesus had declared to them that *"Before Abraham was born, I am"* (v.58), these very people *"picked up stones to throw at him"* (v.59).

So in verse 44 Jesus is much more specific about the nature of the father with the small f. He tells them straight, *"You are the children of your father, the Devil, and you want to follow your father's desires. From the very beginning he was a murderer . . ."* There it is, in unmistakeable language, these people, who are children of Abraham, who claim not to need freeing from anyone's slavery, are told by Jesus that there is something in them which naturally responds to Satan as father and whom they choose to obey.

Satan had always sought to destroy Jesus and here was another opportunity. Get these people to turn against him and they will carry out the wishes of Satan himself, because they will be responding to the ideas put into their minds by the demons within, who naturally respond to Satan as their father. Kill him!

Jesus, who had perfect insight into the thoughts and intentions of the hearts of those with whom he had to deal, saw it all happening before him. No wonder Jesus had said to these people you are in slavery and you need to be set free. No wonder Jesus said that it was only him who could set them free. For the one they were in bondage to was Satan himself (via demonic control) and it was only Jesus that could ever set anyone free from the power of the enemy.

This is an important passage of scripture when coming to terms with the extent of demonic power there is in the lives of many believers. In areas of their lives people often respond to the devil as their father, rather than to the Father of Abraham as their God. They would not describe it like that, but deep down in their lives, there may be rivers of poison which are flowing, and because of the influence of these rivers they are compelled to respond in their flesh to the voice of their father (Satan) whose demons have exercised so much power behind the scenes in their lives.

Those people often know who these powers are, for they daily wrestle with the issues in the mind and the spirit. But others are totally unaware of the extent to which Satan uses them to fulfil his purposes, and Jesus would say to them words that begin, *"Your father the devil ."* How we need to defend ourselves against the onslaught of demons and prepare our people for the freedom that only Jesus can bring. For truly, it is only the Son who can bring total freedom from the powers of darkness!

Another important point which arises from verse 36 is the two different tenses that Jesus uses when saying, *"If the Son sets you free (present tense), then you will be free (future)."* Jesus is clearly differentiating between two different aspects of the salvation which we can enter into through faith in him. The first, I believe, refers to the fact that when we enter into the Kingdom of God, by faith, then yes, the Son has set us free from the jaws of sin and death for eternity and our names are written in the Book of Life (Revelation 20:15). That, as it were, is the eternal dimension to our salvation. We will enter heaven and escape the punishment of hell.

There is, also, a temporal dimension to our salvation, however, which is worked out through the years of time between conversion and physical death, and which is not fully entered into at conversion but is still a future experience. Theologians would call this process one of sanctification. It is only through Jesus that we can be freed from all that would inhibit our relationship with God, but that process requires spiritual discipline and our willing cooperation.

No-one, whatever theological viewpoint they have adopted, would argue that the moment a person becomes a Christian they are totally sanctified, and will not have any more problems, either of health or welfare. Indeed, it

is not an uncommon experience for people to testify that at
conversion their problems increased! The argument is,
therefore, not so much about whether or not Christians
can have problems after conversion, but whether or not
those problems can have a demonic cause inside a
believer.

It is only when people become Christians, however, that it
is possible for them to be set free from any demonic
powers that may have been residing there before
conversion, for outside of Christ we have no power over
the enemy! Having ministered deliverance to many
thousands of people, it is a fact of hard experience, also,
that the demons do not automatically pack their bags and
leave when a person is converted.

Some find this fact hard to accept, but any who would
adopt, as a serious theological viewpoint, that a Christian
cannot be demonised, must also conclude that everyone
who is delivered of a demon, who claimed to have been a
Christian before deliverance, must have been in deception
and cannot have been a true believer. The problem with
mistaken theology is that it may sound alright in the
isolation of theological discussion, but when it is applied
to real situations the conclusions are often ludicrous. To
be considered sound, theology must hold true in the
market place of life as well as the debating chamber.

What Jesus taught and practised was very much in the
market place of life, and it worked for thousands of people
who were healed and delivered through belief in him. It is
interesting to observe that many of the people whom we
have been privileged to see set free, and healed, through
deliverance ministry have, formerly, been of the opinion
that Christians cannot be demonised; but having
exhausted every other possibility for their healing they
have reached the end of themselves and been willing to
give God a chance on his terms, and dispense with beliefs
that have limited God's ability to move in their lives.
Being on the receiving end of dynamic Holy Spirit

ministry has a habit of altering peoples' perception of the situation!

So when Jesus said " . . . *you will be free"*, I believe he was implying far more than is normally understood by those words. I certainly do not believe he was saying that the moment a person believes in him, that the believer immediately enters into total freedom from the presence of all the powers of darkness that have been operating there. The believer is, however, then in a position whereby freedom can be entered into and as the Holy Spirit sheds light then darkness can be dealt with.

The Great Commission
(Matthew 28:16-20)

Before Jesus went back to heaven he carefully summed up the commission he was leaving the church to begin and complete, before he comes again in great power and glory as King of Kings and Lord of Lords. On that great day he will be returning for a bride, his church - a bride that will be ready for him at his coming and which will have by then fulfilled the prophetic word that before he comes the Gospel must have been preached to all nations (Mark 13:10).

In the meantime we are the church at war against the powers of darkness and awaiting that great day. But we have been given orders to fulfil, and the parable of the wise and the foolish virgins should always be a salutary warning to the whole church to be ready for his coming - and that means being obedient to the last things the bridegroom told us to do, before going away to get ready for the wedding feast of the Lamb.

For if we are not doing the things that he told us to do at his coming we will be as the foolish virgins, rushing around to find oil (quickly trying to get some track record at fulfilling his orders and getting quite angry with those who will not now help them) but discovering it is too late, as they hear the Bridegroom's voice, in answer to their pleas to be let in, *"Certainly not! I don't know you."* Jesus concluded the story with this warning, *"Be on your guard, then, because you do not know the day or the hour"* (Matthew 25:12-13 GNB).

It is clearly imperative that we take seriously, therefore, what Jesus told us to do before he went back to heaven. These verses right at the end of Matthew's Gospel have become known as the Great Commission and have been accepted by all the mainstream Christian denominations as the foundation text, for evangelistic outreach and thrust, which has driven Christians of all traditions to the ends of the earth since the day they were first spoken.

Sadly, however, once a church has become established it tends to think of this commission as only being fulfilled by those with special missionary or evangelistic callings and that the rest of the church can gently while away time till either death or Jesus comes. That is heresy and sin, demonstrating gross misunderstanding of the life and ministry of Jesus.

So let us look very carefully at what Jesus actually said. It is divided into a statement, a command (with two subsections which are of particular significance to the thrust of this book) and a wonderful promise. We will look at each in turn.

The Statement Jesus Makes

"I have been given all authority in heaven and on earth." And what a statement that is. The disciples were standing on a hill outside Jerusalem not knowing what was going to happen next. They had been with Jesus for three years. They had followed him through thrill and crisis, yet Jesus was still a mystery to them for he was always surprising them with what he said and what he did next. He had already appeared to them several times since the resurrection and they wondered what was going to happen this time when they went to the appointed meeting place.

When he appeared their first reaction was to worship him. Then he drew near to them and began to share what were to be his final words. Their minds must have gone back to that amazing day some two years previously when he gathered them together rather like this. But then there were twelve. Only eleven were gathered on the hillside that day. He had begun then by giving them his power and authority, and telling them to go and do the same things that he'd been doing; preaching the gospel, healing the sick and casting out demons. It was new to them all. How could they do such things? But when they went and did what he had said, it worked. Amazing.

They had learnt a lot about obedience. Whenever he told them to do something they always had a choice. If they did what he said, there was always blessing, even if it seemed the most crazy thing in the world to do. None of them would forget how stupid they felt with five loaves and two fishes between twelve of them when he said, *"go and feed the crowd."* When they gathered the twelve baskets of crumbs afterwards they felt ashamed that they had ever doubted (Luke 9:10-17).

They had learnt to understand his every look. They'd seen the pain on his face when people turned away from him; seen the joy when little children believed and trusted him; sensed his excitement when people that had been bound with sickness for years were set free; shared his pleasure at some of the precious private times they had experienced together; felt the heartbreak of Judas's betrayal; seen his anguish as he had looked up at Calvary on his way to the cross; felt the pain as the nails were driven home; rejoiced with him when he came back from the dead. Never to be forgotten days, no-one could ever take away the memories of those three incredible years from these eleven men.

But what lay ahead now? Jesus kept on appearing and disappearing. They were confused, yet strangely excited. And here he was again talking about his power and authority. Last time he had spoken like this he had given them his power and authority over demons and diseases (Luke 9:1-2). Now he was talking about the authority he had in heaven and on earth. The last time he had talked to them about his authority he gave them a commission. He sent them out to preach the Kingdom of God and heal the sick and cast out demons. What was he going to say this time?

Whatever was to follow must be very important. They were standing in front of the one who had not only demonstrated his power and authority on earth but was now talking about his having all authority in heaven and on earth. They dare not ignore what he would say next. He had demonstrated that he did indeed have power and authority over death itself. Who could doubt any more one word that he might say?

The Commission

"Go, then, to all peoples everywhere and make them my disciples: baptize them in the name of the Father, the Son and the Holy Spirit, and teach them to obey everything I have commanded you" (Matthew 28:19-20); just one sentence, but a sentence that has empowered Christians for nearly 2000 years and has indeed changed the world.

Eleven people on a remote hillside of Palestine listened to a very simple and direct commission being given to them, but this time they did not have the bodily presence of Jesus to encourage and support them when things were tough! Luke, however, in his account of this incredible moment (Luke 24:49), tells us that Jesus also told them that the Holy Spirit, who had come upon him at his baptism was going to come on them. And only the disciples who had witnessed that first hand in the life of Jesus could have any idea about what that might mean.

What a task, to go, in the power of the Holy Spirit and make disciples for their Master. An impossible task it seems, but Jesus had said it, *and if he had said it . . !."Go, then. . ."* That little word, 'then', really mattered. It wasn't just a case of Go, and see how you get on, but Go, because I have all authority in heaven and on earth and you can, therefore, trust me to fulfil through you whatever I ask you to do.

There is no way that those eleven people could possibly go themselves to all peoples, everywhere. The key lay in them making disciples who would join them in the task. Not believers, but disciples. Jesus had seen that even believers (John 8:31-59) could be fickle and turn in a moment from being ardent followers to aggressive detractors. The eleven must gather round them more than believers, but people who are committed up to the neck and over the top in their following of Jesus, real disciples.

Aware that accumulating a body of believers may be relatively easy, but potentially dangerous to those first disciples if they were not well-grounded in their faith, Jesus wanted to give them some steps that must be taken so that believers could become disciples. There were two things that Jesus stressed as being of major significance - baptism and obedience.

1. Baptism.

If believers really want to join with other disciples in building the church, then there has to be a definite point at which they declare to the world that from that moment on they are committed to Jesus Christ. The first public step of Jesus's ministry was his baptism. It was a dividing point between the thirty years of preparation and the three years of public declaration of the things of God. I would not want to say that there are no other ways of declaring to the world one's commitment to Jesus Christ, but this is the way Jesus recommended the first disciples to go about things.

Baptism is always a dividing point - it represents a death and a resurrection. Death to all that life has been before conversion, and a resurrection out of the waters to a new life in Christ. It is a public declaration of discipleship, not just belief in Jesus. There are millions of people who 'believe' in Jesus, in the sense that they believe he was a good man, who died a cruel death, nearly two thousand years ago. But only a small fraction of those people have believed to the extent that they have unreservedly committed their lives to following Jesus, come what may.

The Ethiopian, whom Philip met on the roadside at Gaza, received the Gospel and immediately wanted to be baptised. So they stopped the chariot and Philip baptised him (Acts 8:38). The Philippian jailor demanded of Paul how he could be saved. Paul told him to *"believe in the Lord Jesus"*, but then, in the middle of the night the jailor and all his family were baptised at once (Acts 16:33). Belief was followed by the irrevocable action of baptism.

The first disciples had taught their new converts well and here they are, in the formative days of the early church, doing just what Jesus had told them to do, baptise them. Many of those who have come to Ellel Grange in deep need have not been baptised before. When they see what it really means to follow Jesus, many of them express the desire to be baptised immediately so that there should be no blockage to their ministry.

Such baptisms have sometimes been strategic in their ministry programme. In baptising some people in this way we have not tried to give the impression, that through the ministry of baptism, we are administering an initiation rite into any particular church. This is certainly not the case, for I do not believe that baptism was ever intended to be part of a denominational initiation, but an act of responsive obedience to the Lord Jesus Christ. If public baptism can conveniently be incorporated into a denominational service, then that can be helpful to both the individual and the church, but this requirement should never become a barrier to an individual's immediate response to what Jesus is asking of them, as they move from being a believer into the first steps of real discipleship.

For many of them the act of baptism has not only been an act of obedience, but it has also unseated much demonic power, and it has not been unusual for us to see a person go into spontaneous deliverance as they come out of the water. The demons cannot stand it when Christians, who know exactly what they are doing, unreservedly commit themselves to Jesus in this way.

We have also seen, on many occasions, how the demons have thrown up every possible defence they could think of to stop someone going through with baptism, even to the extent of trying to do the person physical harm so as the baptism cannot go ahead. And on a number of occasions we have had to have two members of the team on either side of the person as they went into the water to restrain the physical backlash of the demons.

We always consecrate the water before each baptism and I thank God for the testimonies there are to the cleansing, healing and deliverance that has come in many peoples' lives through this simple act of obedience. Why is it that we are so often surprised at what God does, when people are obedient to his word? After all, Paul did refer to the cleansing of the church through washing in water! (Ephesians 5:26).

It is impossible to raise this subject of baptism, however, without some sectors of the church holding up their arms in horror at the thought that some people, whom they believe to have been 'baptised' as infants, might possibly be re-baptised. For some this is a very hot potato indeed as it seems to run so contrary to all that their denominational church believes and practices.

I personally believe that an infant ceremony and an adult baptism are both important, but for very different reasons. The infant ceremony is an act of consecration of the child to God, in a Christian equivalent of the circumcision ceremony that marked the entry into the world of Jewish boys. It is also an important opportunity to take authority over any generational demonic powers that may have come down the family lines.

Where both the parents are Christians this is a very
special moment of committing themselves before God to
be the Godly cover for the child until he or she reaches
mature years when decisions can be made for
themselves. But I personally find it hard to reconcile the
New Testament practices of the early church with such
an infant ceremony and say that this is what the Bible
teaches baptism should be! Baptism always seems in the
scriptures to be an act that follows repentance from sin
and conversion. It marks people out as having committed
themselves to Jesus Christ by an act of their will.

I realise that for some this whole subject area is very
difficult territory indeed. This is a book on healing
through deliverance, however, and it would be
hypocritical of me were the book not to include mention of
what has been for some a very important aspect of
ministering healing to the demonised through baptism.
For I cannot pretend nothing happens when some people
are baptised. It does, and God blesses those baptismal
services amazingly. The whole team know that when
someone is being baptised there is often a major
manifestation of God's power and blessing in the region of
the swimming pool! Nothing can take that away from
those who are baptised as part of their ministry. We have
seen plenty of evidence as to why Jesus included baptism
as part of his guidelines for making disciples.

It is interesting to note that Matthew introduces a
Trinitarian formula for baptising people, whereas Luke
refers in the Acts of the Apostles to being baptised only in
the Name of Jesus. Some have tried to make theological
mileage out of the two different wordings. I consider this
to be futile. Personally, I normally use Matthew's
wording, for it is good to remind the person being baptised
that God really is their Father, that Jesus died for them
on the cross and rose again from the dead, and that the
Holy Spirit is the one who will daily fill you with his
wisdom, power and guidance.

On numerous occasions we have seen people baptised in the Holy Spirit as they have come out of the water. They have been so overcome by the power of God that they have floated on the water, enjoying the presence of God for some long time! Others have started to speak in tongues immediately afterwards. For others physical healing has been one of the blessings of baptism. God is a God of surprises, but those surprises are most often enjoyed when we are obedient to what God has told us to do.

For those who have been baptised as infants, and who wish, as an act of obedience to what the Holy Spirit has witnessed to them, to be baptised by immersion on personal profession of faith, we can, if so desired, use words which link their profession to a re-affirmation of any valid baptismal vows that were made on their behalf by their parents and God-parents.

2. Obedience

Obedience can only be considered as a theoretical subject when it is in isolation from the instructions that are to be obeyed. Jesus was not just a theoretician, or, in modern-day parlance an ivory tower theologian. He was essentially a practical man who had perfect knowledge of spiritual principles and the will of his Father, and a very practical understanding of how God's will should be put into practice.

In teaching the disciples how to make disciples, he first said baptise them, but then he told them to teach the new believers who were being discipled to obey 'everything I have commanded you'. Now that is a disarmingly simple instruction. It certainly must have made the first disciples think very hard about just what Jesus had commanded them to do. Perhaps that simple instruction was eventually instrumental in encouraging Peter, James, John and Matthew to put quill to papyrus and begin writing what later became parts of the New Testament.

When you think about it, there wasn't really any other instruction that Jesus could have given. If, in his three years with the twelve, he had taught them everything they needed to know, all that the disciples needed to be told was to tell others! And so the Great Commission to the churches, for all of time, is reduced to a simple matter of obedience to everything the first disciples were taught to do.

Luke's summary of the commission that Jesus gave the disciples is commendably brief. *"Jesus sent them out to preach the Kingdom of God and to heal the sick"* (Luke 9:2). In the previous verse Jesus had explained that he was giving them his power and authority to heal the sick, who may either be demonised or have a disease, or, possibly, both. The commission was reduced therefore to three things: Preach, Heal, Deliver.

Mark, in his version of the event (Mark 6:7-13), adds a few extra practical details such as the fact that Jesus did not send them out alone, but two by two - a very important detail indeed, and one that, if ignored, especially in deliverance ministry, can land people in a lot of hot water. He tells them not to take any baggage for their journeys and stay with those who welcome you; but quickly move on, with a quick shake of the dust off your feet, from places that will not listen to what you have to say.

Translating these guidelines into modern-day terms would seem to indicate that our conduct as evangelists and ministers of the Gospel must be commendably simple, and that we must not waste too much time or effort on fruitless ministries, when there are receptive people elsewhere who are keen to hear what we have to say.

The definition of a fruitless ministry must be left to the individual's discernment direct from the Holy Spirit. There have been many lonely and apparently unsuccessful ministries that have produced only a small handful of converts, but amongst that small handful have been key people whose ministries have shaken the world.

God alone is the judge of whether or not we have been obedient.

Finally, Matthew adds the instruction (that makes most preachers who want to expound this theme opt for Luke's version of the commission!) - raise the dead. Luke's version, which omits this embarrassing detail, is far more comfortable. But Matthew put it in, so Jesus must have said it.

Most preachers who do have the courage to teach from the Matthew version spiritualise this phrase and talk about raising the spiritually dead to vibrant spiritual life and health! Somehow, I don't think the one who did raise the dead meant us to re-interpret his down to earth instructions! Matthew also added a bit about healing 'dreaded skin-diseases', probably just in case these might get conveniently overlooked, through fear that they may be caught!

The bit about raising the dead is never an easy one to come to terms with. There were cemeteries in Jesus's day, but, mercifully, he never went near them and raised a congregation from yesterdays generations! (But note Matthew's comments that when the temple curtain was torn in two many of God's people were raised to life from the devastated graveyard - Matthew 27:52-53). Neither should we tempt God by testing him over something he is not doing. Thankfully, Ecclesiastes also tells us *"there is a time to die"* (Ecclesiastes 3:2) so we should not be anxious about everyone who dies, for the majority will have come to their time to die.

I believe that Jesus is only talking, therefore, about exceptional situations when death has come before that appointed time, and only then when God the Father gives a very, very specific anointing, through the Holy Spirit to those who are ministering. There are many well documented instances of people being raised from the dead in modern times. We do not have to depend on scriptural accounts for the only illustrations.

It is not a ministry that I have ever been asked (yet) to
carry out, although there have been times when I have
wondered, but I do know of reliable witnesses who have
been instrumental in seeing God bring life back into a
dead body. As with all healing ministries (and the
miracle of seeing the dead brought back to life is simply
healing a person who is very, very sick!) listening to God
and discerning what is in the heart of the Father must be
the key foundation stone for ministry.

The bottom line of all the above is that if the church today
is to fulfil the Great Commission it has to be involved in:

1.   Preaching the Kingdom of God.
2.   Healing the Sick. (including those with contagious
      diseases).
3.   Casting out demons.
4.   And, in very exceptional circumstances, raising
      the dead.

That is the scriptural measure of whether or not a
ministry is in line with God's word, and in fulfilment of
the instructions Jesus left with his disciples and passed
on to succeeding generations of Christians until we reach
the present time. In the context of this book, therefore,
deliverance ministry is absolutely central and should be
in the mainstream of Christian ministry. If it is not the
Body of Christ will suffer, the people will be deprived of
their bread and we will have to account to our Father one
day for why we chose not to do what Jesus had told us to
do.

The Promise Jesus Gives

"And I will be with you always, to the end of the age"

The promises of the scriptures are invariably conditional.
These words, the last of Matthew's Gospel are almost
always quoted in an unconditional sense and, therefore,
out of context. The condition applying to this promise is
that Jesus will be with all those who, as disciples, are

obedient to the Great Commission, right up until the very end of the age when Jesus returns again in great power and glory. (In John 14:15 Jesus had already said to the disciples *"If you love me, you will obey my commandments."* Then in verse 15 Jesus added that *"He would send another Helper, who will stay with you for ever."*)

The promise cannot be separated out from the rest of the commission and claimed universally to imply that because God is with us he will bless whatever we are doing in the name of the Church. Nothing could be further from the truth. For this promise is highly specific to the context of the rest of the Great Commission.

Every translation includes the conditional 'and' which connects the main part of the command with the promise. Understanding this is very salutary, for there must be very few of us who haven't been comforted by those beautiful words from time to time, and yet, did we have any right to receive such comfort from them if we were not actively involved in fulfilling the conditions? That is something for each one of us to resolve before God and, if necessary, come to repentance over and start again. It is a wonderful promise - would that the whole of the church could rightfully claim its blessing through obedience to the commands to preach, heal and deliver!

In Conclusion

There is far more teaching about deliverance ministry implicit in the Gospels than is normally, at first, appreciated. Clearly, Jesus considered it to be a primary ministry for the emergent church and there is no indication anywhere in the scriptures that at any time this ministry would be discontinued in favour of any other practice or that there would be any other dispensation (before Jesus comes again) in which it will not be required. The deliverance ministry is for now!

Chapter 11

Some Important Teachings on the Demonic in the Epistles

Some commentators have concluded that because they see little or no instructions on how to heal and deliver people from demons in the letters of Paul and others, that deliverance ministry was no longer part of the life of the church. Some conclude, wrongfully, that the gifts of the spirit, therefore, died out quickly after the death of Jesus and are not to be practised in the present dispensation.

Such a viewpoint is utterly naive and demonstrates gross ignorance of early church history, when deliverance of those who were coming out of a pagan world into the church of Jesus Christ was an essential pre-Baptism procedure. It seems that the normal procedure of bringing people into membership of the early church included what they described as exorcism.

A report of the Seventh Council of Carthage in AD276 by Crescens of Cirta stated that *"all heretics and schismatics who wish to come to the Catholic Church, shall not be allowed to enter without they have first been exorcised and baptised."* Vincent of Thibaris reports similarly from the same council that *"firstly by imposition of hands for exorcism, and secondly by baptism, they may then come to the promise of Christ."*

In her summary of the early church practices Evelyn Frost, in her book *"Christian Healing"*, states that "At the beginning of the Christian life stood Baptism, *preceded usually by exorcism* (my italics), when the old life as a member of the fallen race was superseded by the new life which partook of the resurrection of Christ."

Far from being a practice that the writers of the epistles had omitted, because of its irrelevance to the body of Christ, I believe that it was an integral part of the practice of the church. There was so much teaching on deliverance implicit in the ministry and stories of both Jesus and the earliest days of the church, that it was not necessary to include further teaching on the how and why of deliverance. (If it was a ministry that the church was not to carry out, for any reason, then surely there would have been strong warnings to this effect included within the epistles?)

There are no instructions in the epistles on how to preach the Gospel either, but I have not noticed anyone proposing that this (seemingly serious) omission should be used as a valid argument for not proclaiming the Kingdom of God! The command of Jesus to preach the Gospel was quite adequate for the early church, as was the command to heal the sick and cast out demons. There is some important teaching in the epistles about the demonic, however, although none of it is practical instructions about how to do it!

The Corinthian Discourse

(1 Corinthians 10)

The whole of 1 Corinthians 10 is about idolatry. In the law (Exodus 20) we are told not to have any idol in our lives, because the Lord our God tolerates no rivals. We are warned that idolatry brings with it a curse that the sins of the fathers will be visited on the children until the third and the fourth generations. We have seen in many hundreds of peoples' lives how that curse is passed on both socially, through the lifestyle of a family that is a consequence of an ungodly way of living, and demonically, through a spirit of curse which can transfer at conception, death, or at some stage in between, from the parents to the children (or grandchildren), bringing with it a spirit whose job function is to fulfil the terms of the curse in the lives of the children.

For example, we have had to free many children (both men and women) from spirits of freemasonry, when they themselves have never had any involvement, but have been descended from freemasons. I have seen how false religions in the generation line lead people to being controlled by ungodly spiritual power and even how religious spirits can be associated with Christian traditions which are out of the mainstream of Jesus-centred truth. These become controlling factors in the generation line, making descendants potential opponents of Holy Spirit centred Christian life and worship.

Idolatry, therefore, is a serious sin, with enormous potential consequences, which can lead to many ordinary Christians being in bondage to the demonic. In the early part of the chapter Paul illustrates his text from the sinful experiences of the people of Israel as they followed Moses out of Egypt. He cites sexual immorality, testing the Lord and complaining as scriptural examples of the fruit of idolatry in our lives (1 Corinthians 10:6-11). He tells us that these things are a warning to us, and concludes that part of his argument with the words, *"So then, keep away from the worship of idols"* (1 Corinthians 10:14 GNB).

In this passage Paul has opened up the whole subject of idolatry, as the practice of anything which takes the place of the living God in our lives. He then jumps, with devastating effect to our sharing in the body and blood of our Lord when we partake of the Lord's supper. He argues that what is sacrificed on pagan altars is offered to demons and not to God. By this he implies that if, in the living of our lives we get involved, for example, in things such as sexual immorality, testing the Lord wrongfully and complaining we are, as it were worshipping the demons behind these things. Then he says *"I do not want you to be partners with demons"*.

When people live their lives, without repentance, practising behaviour patterns such as the ones Paul mentions, he implies that they are in partnership with the demonic! A partnership is something which in law has a legal significance, binding the participants in the partnership together in a contract, which can only be broken by the further exercise of law with a document which dissolves the partnership.

Through the practice of sin people worship the demons that are behind the sin (idolatry) and Paul implies very strongly that we are then in partnership with demons! This means that where there is such sin in peoples' lives, a legal partnership has been entered into with the demons, and that for a person to be set free the partnership must be dissolved. But only the further practice of law can dissolve any legally entered into partnership, and as we have already said in Chapter 6, demons are very legalistic! If they have been given a legal right to enter through sin, then they will only leave once those rights have been legally removed.

There are two steps which have to be taken. Firstly there must be repentance from the sin which gave the demon a right of entry, and, secondly, the legal remedy must be applied. All the conditions of the law were fulfilled at the cross, and the full price was paid for all the sins of the world when Jesus, the Son of God, shed his blood for each one of us. The blood of Jesus is the full, and totally sufficient, legal remedy.

As with any remedy, however, it must be personally applied to the life of the individual for it to have any effect. At the very least this must mean that the Lordship of Jesus Christ has to be established, by an act of the will, in the area of life which had formerly been in partnership with demons. A new partnership must be established.

Paul links this whole argument to the Lord's Supper by going on to say that *"you cannot drink from the Lord's cup and also from the cup of demons; and you cannot eat from the Lord's table and also at the table of demons"* (1

Corinthians 10:21 GNB). He then continues the argument in the next chapter, with his teaching on the Lord's Supper, by giving us some guidelines as to how to prepare ourselves to receive the bread and the wine, and in so doing says some very strong things.

In the light of the teaching of the previous chapter, it is very obvious what Paul is trying to say with regard to being in partnership with demons and the possible consequences of not being right with God. *"It follows that if anyone eats the Lord's bread or drinks from his cup in a way that dishonours him, he is guilty of sin against the Lord's body and blood. So then everyone should examine himself first, and then eat the bread and drink from the cup. For if he does not recognise the meaning of the Lord's body when he eats the bread and drinks from the cup, he brings judgement on himself as he eats and drinks. That is why many of you are weak and ill, and several have died. If we would examine ourselves first, we would not come under God's judgement"* (1 Corinthians 11:27-31 GNB).

In this passage Paul is directly relating our physical health with our spiritual health. He talks about judgement coming upon us as a result of the sin of *"drinking from the Lord's cup and also from the cup of demons"* (1 Corinthians 10:21). It is clear from the Old Testament that God allowed demons to be used to visit his judgement on people.

Saul, for example, was troubled by an evil spirit from the Lord (1 Samuel 16:14). So we have to conclude that if our sin in becoming partners with demons can cause us to be sick, that some of that sickness can be demonic, and that deliverance will, therefore, be needed to bring healing. Paul makes it very clear that the sickness he is talking about can also be terminal, for he says some people in Corinth had died prematurely as a result.

Praise God that the converse of what Paul is saying is also true! If we come and take the bread and the wine in an attitude of repentance, seeking the Lord's face and asking him to expose any sin by the light of the Holy Spirit so that it can be dealt with before taking communion, then that can have the effect of bringing deliverance and healing into our lives.

Deliverance is increasingly seen, therefore, as a vital part of the ministry of the Gospel, without which people will be left in bondage to powers of darkness which have been legally defeated and should have been evicted. Unfortunately this has not, in recent centuries, been the normal practice of the church. As a result we now have a church which is in need of extensive deliverance, both because of the demonic that has been given a right through the sins of the present generation of members and the demonic which should have been dealt with in previous generations, but which has survived undetected down the family lines, affecting generations which were then unborn.

We have frequently held an informal communion service during the course of major deliverance ministry, especially when major sin (either of the person or in their generation line) has been exposed and repented of. In those circumstances we have seen on many occasions how the demons will do everything they possibly can to prevent the person actually receiving the consecrated bread and wine. They know that the anointing of the Holy Spirit on the sacrament will have a major effect on undermining the stronghold of the enemy. So the demons will try to force the jaw closed, make it impossible for the person to swallow, make the person spit out both the bread and the wine, or force the person to lie face down on the floor, make the wine taste or smell foul, in fact, anything to avoid the sacrament being received!

We have seen many people receive deep healing as a result of deliverance, following repentance from sin and making Jesus Lord of every area of their lives. So we, therefore, when dealing with a situation where sin has been uncovered, will frequently include a communion service as part of the ministry. We have sometimes also found that, after ministry is over, a brief communion service is a wonderful way of ministering Jesus to a person as they quietly celebrate the victory of the cross that has been completed in their life.

Gifts of the Spirit
(1 Corinthians 12,13 and 14)

These three chapters should be read and understood together. Chapter 13 is famous, whereas 12 and 14 are, in some circles, notorious, for the way they talk so blatantly about the use of the gifts of the spirit, which some sectors of the church so vigorously deny are for use today.

In reality, Paul's famous teaching on love is meant to be read as a description of the way the gifts of the spirit should be exercised in the life of the church. So often it is read out of context. Paul is not saying in this chapter that love is a substitute for the gifts of the Holy Spirit, but is stating, in unmistakeable words, that no matter what gifts of the Spirit we may have and demonstrate in our lives, unless we exercise them with love they will not count for anything in eternity.

Earlier in the letter (1 Corinthians 3:11-15) Paul expresses this even more graphically by saying that the fire of God's judgement will test our works and only what survives the fire will contribute to the reward that awaits the people of God in heaven.

James, however, emphasises that faith without works is dead (James 2:17) giving a wise balance to the teaching of scripture. We must not 'bury our talent' and do nothing, for fear of not using it in a loving way, but neither must we use our talent wrongfully and treat people badly at the same time. The gifts must be used.

More will be said about the exercise of the gifts of the Spirit in ministry in the next volume. But two gifts that merit special mention at this point are the gifts of healing and discernment of spirits. As we have seen in our earlier discussion, the New Testament is quite free in its use of the word healing to include both physical healing and deliverance, so that when Paul talks here about 'gifts of healings' (both words are in the plural in the original) he is clearly referring to a variety of different healing ministries, including deliverance.

In order to do deliverance, however, it is necessary to be able to discern the presence of evil spirits. Hence the need for the exercise of the gift of discernment of spirits, with which it is possible to recognise the presence of the demonic in a person's life and distinguish between that, the human spirit of the person and the Holy Spirit of God.

Wise exercise of this gift is an absolutely vital ingredient in the life of the body of Christ. Without the use of this gift a church can be deceived by the demonic without having any idea of what is happening! In individual ministries to the sick, one can see people going into deeper and deeper despair as ministry after ministry has failed to help them.

So often in these cases the discernment of spirits would have changed the direction of the ministry from praying for physical or emotional healing to deliverance and have given the person hope as they see God at work in their life. The discernment of spirits is probably the least talked about and used gift of the Holy Spirit, and yet it is the one that is so desperately needed if the church is going to rise up in victory over all the works of the enemy.

The Foolish Galatians

There is a thread woven through the whole letter to the Galatian Christians warning them not to become slaves, once again, to evil spirits. In the first two chapters Paul spells out his own testimony, and what it means to be set free from the curse of the law. But it seems as though some of them had fallen once again for the curse of legalism and Paul begins Chapter Three with a graphic question, *"You foolish Galatians! Who has bewitched you?"* (Galatians 3:1). The language he uses directly implies an occultic connection.

In Chapter Four he spells out what it means to be outside of Christ. He says *"we, too, were slaves to the ruling spirits of the universe"*, implying that it was through Jesus they were delivered from their control. And then in verse 9 he asks *"how is it that you want to turn back to those weak and pitiful ruling spirits? Why do you want to become their slaves all over again?"*

Christians have been delivered from the curse of the law, but if we start submitting ourselves to the chains of legalism once again, we are, implies Paul, putting ourselves under demonic control. Those are strong words, but they do help us to understand why it is that so little Holy Spirit life flows from churches whose life and conduct is totally bound by tradition and denominationalism!

In saying that Christians have been delivered from the law Paul is not saying that the obvious sins of the flesh, which were forbidden under the law, can now be indulged in, as we shall see in a moment. No, what he is primarily saying is that it is not obedience to the trappings of religion which brings us freedom to enjoy a relationship with God, and live in fellowship one with another, but the presence and freedom of the Spirit of God in our lives. And if we insist on a legalistic approach to the peripherals of our faith, such as, says Paul, paying too much attention to certain days (4:10), then we are in danger of submitting the affairs of the fellowship to the control of demons! Being in bondage to the legalism of demonic control will undermine true freedom in the Holy Spirit in the life of our church fellowships.

When battling to move a church forward spiritually, it is often necessary to deal with what I now recognise as demonic powers, that have been given a right to control a church through the adherence to religious rules which were given a greater importance to the membership than obedience to the Spirit of God. Such attitudes are a curse on the church and one is tempted to say, with Paul, *"Who has bewitched you?"*, or, more specifically, Who is in control here?

In many cases the answer to that question will not be the present officers of the church, but those who have gone before and left an inheritance to the present membership, not a treasury of good things, but a demonic stranglehold on the spiritual life of the church. We have often seen radical transformations take place in the spiritual atmosphere of a church, and in the freedom to move forward, through spiritual warfare against the otherwise 'weak and pitiful ruling spirits' (Galatians 4:9), which have been given great power by attitudes in the heart of man.

Towards the end of his letter, Paul explains that *"if the Spirit leads you, then you are not subject to the Law"* (Galatians 5:18 GNB). That does not mean we are free to break the law with impunity, but that if we are listening to, and being obedient to, the witness of the Holy Spirit in our hearts then we will not break the commandments that the law introduced, for the Spirit of God can never lead us in a direction that is contrary to God's desires for his people.

In Galatians 5:19 Paul then sums up his arguments by listing the obnoxious consequences of following the desires of the flesh into immorality and witchcraft, drunkenness and the like. These are not things that we would do if we were being obedient to the Holy Spirit. Paul is unequivocal in saying that those who do such things will not possess the Kingdom of God. These are the works of the flesh and, as with the introduction of legalism into the life of the church, so with the introduction of disobedience to the Spirit in the life of the human being - the demonic will be given a free reign to control.

Paul concludes his arguments with strong words indeed to the Galatian Christians, and also to us: *"Do not deceive yourselves; no-one makes a fool of God. A person will reap exactly what he sows. If he sows in the field of his natural desires, from it he will gather the harvest of death; if he sows in the field of the Spirit, from the Spirit he will gather the harvest of eternal life."* (Galatians 6:7-8 GNB).

When ministering to people in need we find that many of them have been sowing in the wrong fields and they have already reaped some of that harvest of death. But I thank God that John was writing to Christians when he said that if we confess our sin God is faithful and just and will forgive (1 John 1:9). Experience proves that Paul's arguments are true, for usually we find that where people have been sowing in the field of their natural desires they have become demonised as a result of their sin, and deliverance has been an essential part of their restoration.

Very, very often we have had to minister to Christians who, many years ago even, truly repented over some sin of the flesh, but are still struggling with both the guilt and the memory of the sin. It is not that the sin has not been forgiven, and usually they have no understanding of why it is they are still in such a mess.

For many it comes as a considerable shock to discover that their problem is the demon that was given access by their sin and which, because the demonic dimension to the ongoing practice of sin has never been properly taught in our churches, was not cast out when repentance took place. The demon keeps on reminding the person of the sin that let it in, and the person eventually becomes thoroughly condemned, even to the point in many cases of doubting their very salvation. They are then convinced that their sin can never be forgiven. Some become rightfully angry at a church which has not used the power and authority that Jesus gave to set the captives free.

Whilst deliverance ministry is, essentially a ministry for individuals, the dimension of deliverance which refers to the needs of a whole church fellowship must not be overlooked. I once attempted to minister deliverance to a lady in a certain church, but found myself struggling in a way that was quite unexpected. The Lord then showed me that there was a ruling spirit over the church with a specific job function to prevent deliverance ministry taking place.

As soon as I bound that spirit from affecting the lady the effect was dramatic. Immediately the demons in her, knowing that their security was now breached, made the lady get up and run from the building as fast as her legs would carry her! I later found out that the leadership of the church did not believe that Christians could be demonised and were, therefore, giving a ruling spirit the right to control their church and keep the members in bondage.

Paul's Advice to the Ephesians - Don't Give the Devil a Chance!

Woven through the text of Paul's letter to the Ephesians is a theme of victory over all the powers of darkness and practical advice about keeping the devil (demons) out of our lives. After the opening chapter, which concludes with one of Paul's supreme statements about the position that Christ holds over all spiritual powers, he begins the second chapter by reminding the Ephesian Christians that before they were Christians they obeyed *"the ruler of the spiritual powers in space, the spirit who now controls the people who disobey God"* (Ephesians 2:2).

This last statement is interesting in that whilst Paul is talking about believers being made free in Christ from these controlling spirits, he does not exclude the possibility of believers disobeying God. By implication, therefore, he does not exclude the possibility of believers being controlled by demons. If that were the only statement in his letter which might encourage one to reach this conclusion, one might be tempted to dismiss its relevance to the present discussion.

However, Paul does not leave the subject alone, for he goes on to say that the different ministries in the church are to stop us from *"being blown about by every shifting wind of the teaching of deceitful men, who lead others into error"* (Ephesians 4:14 GNB). We are not told what these teachings are, but in verse 17 Paul further warns the Ephesians *"not to continue living like the heathen, whose thoughts are worthless and whose minds are in the dark."* So possibly the teachings were such as to allow sinful practices of pre-Christian days to continue in the life of the fellowship.

Paul then hints in the rest of the chapter at various lifestyles which had apparently crept into some sectors of the church, such as lying, wrongful anger, stealing, using harmful words, bitterness, passion, shouting, hateful feelings, sexual immorality, indecency etc. The practice of such things, he warns, will give the devil a chance, foothold, opportunity, or place (depending on which translation you use of verse 27) in your life. He returns to the subject in Chapter Five warning them yet again to *"have nothing to do with the worthless things that people do, things that belong to the darkness"* (Ephesians 5:11).

Now why does Paul go to such lengths to warn the Ephesians in this way? Clearly he was not under the illusion that Christians are unable to sin, otherwise no such warnings would have been relevant or necessary. I believe his concerns were at least sixfold:

1.   Sin grieves the Holy Spirit (Ephesians 4:30)

2.   Sin destroys the credibility of the witness of the Body of Christ (Ephesians 5:8-9)

3.   Sin brings God's anger upon those who do not obey him (Ephesians 5:6)

4.   Sin will jeopardise our inheritance in the kingdom of God (Ephesians 5:5)

5.   Sin will give the devil a foothold (Ephesians 4:27)

6.   There is, as a result, a danger of receiving a wrong spirit into our lives.

The last point is implicit in the whole of Paul's teaching. For example, in his comment about drunkenness I do not believe he was just making a pun on the two types of spirit involved when he said, *"Do not be drunk with wine, which will only ruin you; instead be filled with the Spirit (Holy Spirit)"* (Ephesians 5:18). When he says 'instead, be filled with the Spirit' one has to ask instead of what.

Whilst there certainly is a pun here on the alcoholic spirit in wine, I believe the implication is far deeper. This final injunction comes right at the end of nearly two chapters of various warnings and it seems as though Paul is saying that the practice of all the things he has been talking about will lead to being filled with an evil spirit, that is given a right by the sin; whereas believers should, instead, be constantly being filled with Holy Spirit as a result of living a life that is pleasing to the Father, for *"your life must be controlled by love, just as Christ loved us and gave his life for us, as a sweet-smelling offering and sacrifice that pleases God"* (Ephesians 5:2). Living and moving under the anointing of the Holy Spirit (as opposed to experiencing an anointing at a particular charismatic meeting) is largely a consequence of being obedient. Anointing follows obedience.

This interpretation of Paul's teaching is wholly consistent with experience in ministry. The fact that persistent sin can give entry to the presence of an evil spirit, even in the life of a believer, is daily evidenced as we bring help to those in need. Time and again we find that the powers of darkness have been given rights through the continuing practice of sin, and, once having entered, the evil spirits have carried out a work of devastation in the life of the believer.

For example we never cease to be amazed at the extent of sexual sin there is in the Body of Christ. So often, when people begin to tell their story we find that demonic power, which entered through wrongful sexual relations, has been controlling their lives. The demonic consequences in these cases, however, are not restricted to just the sexual arena. It is not unusual, for example, for spirits of infirmity to enter in this way bringing with them a harvest of physical illness.

In another place Paul warns the Corinthians that if they have sex with prostitutes, for example, then they become one flesh together (1 Corinthians 6:16). In an act of unGodly intercourse it seems as though the demonic has free access to transfer between the partners and people will pick up demons of all types, therefore, from their sexual partners. The demons are certainly not prevented from entering a believer in that sort of situation. Satan (demons) will walk across the welcome mat, whoever puts it down, be the sinner a Christian, a Buddhist, a New Ager or an Atheist.

Satan is no respecter of persons and if Christians give demons rights, they must expect that there will be consequences. The Scriptural principle of sowing and reaping is not discontinued for believers! Rarely, in our experience, has it been that Christians who have entered into sexual sin have not needed deliverance, as well as the experience of deep repentance. Repentance and forgiveness, without the offer of deliverance, will deal with the eternal consequences of the sin, but it will leave the person unhealed and battling with the demons for the rest of their days.

There are many people we have delivered of evil spirits who had lived for years thinking that they had not been forgiven for a sexual indiscretion of their youth. They have had to battle endlessly with lust, guilt and the spiritual, and sometimes, physical consequences of their sin. In practice, they were forgiven of the sin the first time it was truly confessed and repented of, but the demons had not been cast out once the legal ground they were standing on had been removed at the cross.

The healing, and consequential relief that is experienced by those who have been set free, from spirits that had controlled them for much of their lives, has to be seen to be believed. The victory Jesus won for us on the cross is for time as well as eternity. We must set people free in time, therefore, as well as proclaim the forgiveness of God to those who have been trapped into sin.

Those who would, with a measure of smugness, consider themselves 'clean' in the sexual area and believe, therefore, that they cannot be affected by the demonic, should be on their guard. For there are many other ways that demons can enter the believer, it is not only through sexual sin. For example, James tells us that *"if in your heart you are jealous, bitter, and selfish, do not sin against the truth by boasting of your wisdom. Such wisdom does not come down from heaven; it belongs to the world, it is unspiritual and demonic"* (James 3:14-15).

No wonder Paul draws his letter to the Ephesians to a close with that great teaching on the armour of God (Ephesians 6:10-18). He knew the attacks that Satan would, through demons, make on believers. But he knew also that if we stand firm, wearing and using all the protective armour that God himself has provided, then we need not fear the attacks, for with the shield of faith we will be able to put out all the burning arrows shot by the Evil One.

Paul made his understanding of spiritual warfare pretty clear when he said, *"We are not fighting against human beings, but against the wicked spiritual forces in the heavenly world, the rulers, authorities and cosmic powers of this dark age"* (Ephesians 6:12). The war is on and the devil will do all he can to undermine believers and control them through demonisation. Praise God, however, that if we do sin, and confess that sin, not only will God forgive us, but he will also cleanse us from all unrighteousness (1 John 1:9). The deliverance ministry is just one facet of the provision God has made for the cleansing of believers from the consequences of their sin.

The Teachings of Demons

(1 Timothy 4:1-5)

Paul warned Timothy that in the last days some will
abandon the faith, will obey lying spirits and follow the
teachings of demons. He said this was something that the
Holy Spirit had revealed to him (1 Timothy 4:1). Clearly
Paul is talking here about people who were once believers
- they must have been to have abandoned the faith they
once had - but who have come under the control of
demons and are now leading others into error.

Paul obviously had no problems with believing that
believers could become demonised and, as a result,
eventually abandon the faith. For him it was a fact of
experience that he was sharing with his young student of
the Lord, Timothy. The difficulty with this passage is not
so much Paul's assumption that believers could be led
astray in this way, but in the illustrations that Paul uses
to demonstrate the ways in which people have abandoned
the faith.

First he describes them in devastating words as people
who are deceitful liars with dead consciences. One is led
to expect from this that Paul would now tell us the
unspeakable things these people now believe and do. But
the only illustrations Paul gives are of people who teach
that it is wrong to marry or that it is wrong to eat certain
kinds of food! Things which are hardly the most
unforgivable of sins and which, in many quarters, would
hardly raise a Christian eyebrow, especially the question
of not eating certain foods. After all, what is wrong with
vegetarianism, for example? But Paul says here that
everything God created is good and quite categorically
states that no food is to be rejected, and that all should be
eaten after a prayer of thanks!

What I believe Paul is hitting at here is those who would
teach the doctrines of man as a substitute for life in the
Spirit. Ultimately this is idolatry and a form of spiritual
adultery, idolatry because one finishes up worshipping

rules instead of God and spiritual adultery because in obeying such rules one has given the heart to the proponent of the rules, even if that person is oneself! At this point one begins to see the dangers and deceptions of the New Age movement which says that each person already has God within them or, more blatantly by some, we are all gods!

Once religious practice becomes more important than the foundational principles of living the Christian life, then one is on a potentially very slippery slope indeed, with man (or a denomination) proclaiming principles which are of man, as opposed to God. There are then no limits to the dangers of such deception, giving credence and acceptance to a multitude of Christian heresies, which are taught by their proponents as the law of God, as well as false religions which make no attempt whatsoever to make Jesus central to their life and doctrine, and philosophies that owe nothing to the mainstream patterns of Christian belief.

In the myriad of New Age philosophies that abound the devotees submit their lives to an amazing variety of disciplines, which are adhered to with the religiosity of a zealot! One very well known international actor, for example, publicly states that he begins each day with two hours of yoga. There are few Christians who would claim to begin the day with two hours of prayer!

The world is very accepting of all manner of beliefs and practices, excepting, that is, the committed Christian's standpoint that Jesus really is the only way, the only truth and the only life. In the New Age there are no absolutes, only mutual acceptance and respect for whatever set of rules a person wishes to adopt and live by. Hence the plethora of confusing beliefs and practices, all of which set out their stall to attract followers, and all of which effectively proclaim that they are right! Confusion reigns.

Anyone can proclaim a new belief or philosophy and label it, for example, colour therapy, aromatherapy or crystal healing and gain instant acceptance from a gullible world, which seems strangely blinded to the fact that the very existence of so many apparently confusing systems of belief instantly gives the lie to their claims.

Having ministered to many hundreds of people who have dabbled in a huge range of false beliefs, religions and practices, and found that almost universally they needed deliverance from the demons that entered in through their involvement, it is abundantly clear that Satan is behind all such false belief systems and that, to quote Paul again, they are nothing but the deceptions of *"lying spirits and the teachings of demons"* (1 Timothy 4:1) and promoted by evil *"spirits who now control people who disobey God"* (Ephesians 2:2).

There are few Christians who would disagree with the general proposition that demonisation is a likely consequence of involvement in the occult. Paul goes much further than this, however, and implies that demonisation will also be the result of adherence to other religions and even of submitting to the teachings of men (heresies) which are propounded within the broad framework of mainstream Christian belief. He even includes amongst such 'heresies', rules and regulations about what one does or does not eat. So his comments are very far reaching, and, if true, have enormous consequences for the Body of Christ in terms of what we teach, the significance we attach to our denominational peculiarities and of how we minister to those in our care.

One of the hallmarks of Paul's teaching is his constant emphasis on obedience to the Spirit of God as opposed to the rules and regulations of man - a theme that was never far from Jesus's teaching as he battled with the Pharisaism of his day. At this point, therefore, one must ask much more direct questions about whether or not experience lines up with the above interpretations of these scriptures.

I begin by referring back to the quote at the head of this chapter from a report of the Seventh Council of Carthage, in which it was stated that heretics must be exorcised and baptised before being admitted into the church. This statement is interesting on at least two counts.

Firstly, if exorcism (deliverance) was necessary for a heretic, then it was also their experience in the earliest days of the church that demonisation was a consequence of allegiance to heresy. Heresy is deviation from Christian truth, not beliefs that make no pretence at being associated with Christianity. This report would, therefore, lend strong support to Paul's contention that even minor deviations from the teaching of Jesus can be demonic. Not only does the report imply that the demonic is behind heresy, but that adherents to heresy will receive demons into them which have been given a right through wrong beliefs!

Secondly, the report states that both exorcism and baptism are necessary precursors for a heretic to be accepted into the church. No exception is made for heretics who had previously been baptised, but fallen into error. It seems here that a practice had grown up where the cleansing by water was seen as an important step towards the reinstatement of a believer into the main body.

Our experience in ministry would also support and underline both Paul's teaching and the report of the Council of Carthage. We have not only delivered Christians of demons that have entered through their former espousal of false religions such as Buddhism and Sikhism, but also of demons that have been tied to the dictates of every mainstream Christian denomination there is!

One man who had been converted to Christianity from Sikhism some five years before we ministered to him was stunned at the extent of demonic power that he was delivered from, when the false beliefs were fully renounced and the demons addressed directly. There was much violence and anger expressed by the demons as they were challenged and dislodged from their residence.

This particular story underlines how important it is to deliver people of religious spirits when they are converted to Christianity out of false religions or the cults. For example, if a Jehovah's Witness (one of the most legalistic of the modern-day cults) becomes a Christian, not only do they need to renounce their past beliefs and receive Jesus, but they must also be delivered of the demonic spirits that entered them through their espousal of the JW's.

If they are not delivered, then the religious spirits will continue to operate inside the person, doing all they can to distort the new faith with the religious legalism of the JW's. That is why converts from some of the more fanatical cults are often fanatical for Jesus after they are converted. Jesus does not require demonically inspired fanaticism in the Body of Christ, but people who will listen to the gentle voice of the Holy Spirit, instead of the dictates of demons, and be obedient.

Demonically inspired fanaticism will not be a winsome influence in the church, bringing many people into personal faith, but will alienate many who might otherwise be drawn to Christ. We need to heed the words of Jesus to Simon Peter when he tried to oppose what God had planned for Jesus's life and death. Addressing Peter, he said, *"Get away from me, Satan, you are an obstacle in my way"* (Matthew 16:23).

Religious spirits are not only given a right through false religions and the cults, however. Within the confines of the mainstream Christian denominations there is much that is taught as the law of God which, at best, are denominational precepts. Unfortunately, whenever the dictates of a denomination become more important than responsiveness to the Spirit of God, a gateway to demons is made.

We have seen people come into marvellous freedom in Christ through being delivered of Brethren spirits, Anglican spirits, Catholic spirits etc. Satan is a very religious being. After all, he was responsible for worship in heaven before being thrown down to earth, so he is very happy to encourage religion, provided it is devoid of the very breath of God which comes from Jesus being right at the centre and living under the anointing of the Holy Spirit.

Religious spirits are responsible for much bondage inside the church as people stand up for beliefs which are not central to the faith and in so doing create division between believers. Creating division is one of Satan's primary tactics for causing chaos in the Body of Christ. Seeing the consequences of such bondage in the lives of many people, and of how demons will hang on to all religious practices which are peripheral to serving Jesus, helps one to understand the significance of the words that God gave Isaiah to say to Judah, in condemnation of religious practices which are corrupted by the sinfulness of the participants (Isaiah 1:10-20).

Superficially there seems very little difference between all the different clamouring voices of the New Agers, with their different beliefs, and the equally large number of different clamouring voices inside the church implying that they have the only true mandate from God as to how a church should be organised and what it should believe! It is right that Christians should be organised into churches for fellowship purposes, but as soon as any form of exclusive doctrine or practice is proclaimed, which forms part of the basis for membership of that church then we must be on our guard against the dictates of *"lying spirits and the teachings of demons"!*

Discerning the controlling bondage of religious spirits is not always easy, but unless they are discerned and dealt with in a radical way, not only will individuals be subject to the doctrines of demons, but so too will the churches to which they belong. A church fellowship is a corporate entity in its own right, and once demonic power has been given rights through the deceptive teachings of the leadership, over the fellowship, then that demonic power will remain long after the original leadership, which gave access to the fellowship for the demonic, has moved on.

For example, there are many churches which were partially financed in their construction with money from Freemasons. Some even have special masonic foundation stones or symbols built into their designs. Freemasonry is a form of idolatry which always gives access to demonic power. Spirits of freemasonry over a church will be directly opposed to the renewing power of the Holy Spirit and these must be dealt with if the people are to be free to move forward under the anointing of the Holy Spirit.

Returning now to Paul's comment about not eating certain types of food, I remember ministering to a man in whom the demons were manifesting strongly, but initially they would not leave. They appeared to have a legal right to be there. The man had formerly been involved in a New Age household which, through the influence of New Age philosophy, had become vegetarian. After conversion the man renounced all his New Age beliefs, but remained a vegetarian because he thought it made sense.

Whilst ministering to him the Lord drew my attention to this by Word of Knowledge, and I asked him, therefore, if he would renounce vegetarianism also. He declined, the demons would not go and I was unable to minister to him any further. An hour later he was back, realising that if the demons that had come into him through his New Age involvements would not go, because his vegetarianism was giving them a legal right to be there, he would prefer to give up being a vegetarian than continue to be demonised!

Immediately he renounced vegetarianism he was free to be delivered and in a relatively short period of time a large number of spirits left. Refusing to eat all that God had made available for him to eat had given sufficient ground to the enemy for him to be held deeply in bondage, graphically demonstrating the truth of Paul's words to Timothy about the teachings of demons!

I am not saying by the above that in order to be set free we must eat things we do not like - that in itself could be a powerful bondage upon us! But it does seem that if we refuse to eat certain categories of food for pseudo-spiritual reasons, then we are introducing a form of bondage into our lives which Paul describes as a 'doctrine of demons'.

In Conclusion

There are many other passages in the epistles that could be expounded so as to understand the demonic significance of what is being said, but space precludes other than comment on the above sections, which are of particular relevance.

It is clear that for the early church deliverance ministry was a routine and normal part of church life and there are plenty of warnings about the consequences of behaviour patterns that will give grounds for the enemy to attack and invade.

Chapter 12

Demonisation of Christians

Most of this first volume has concentrated on looking at the various passages of New Testament Scripture of particular relevance to the deliverance ministry. The next volume will be devoted to the principles that must be applied in order to minister healing and deliverance and set people free from the powers of darkness.

Before we move on to the practice of deliverance, however, there is one major area which needs to be independently addressed, even though it has already been extensively touched on when commenting on the various passages of scripture that have been analysed in earlier chapters. The threads need to be drawn together so that readers will have a concise understanding of this key issue, which is frequently the source of much discussion and, not infrequently, unnecessary contention.

Can a Christian Have a Demon?

Throughout the text of this book it has been assumed that Christians can be demonised, for the extensive experience of deliverance ministry that I and our team have shared in has been almost exclusively gained when ministering to believing Christians. If Christians cannot be demonised then none of the many thousands of people we have seen delivered of evil spirits, including quite a number of Christian leaders, can have been born again of the Spirit of God! Clearly that is not an acceptable conclusion!

Statements such as the above, however, are not adequate evidence to convince those who are heavily entrenched in the opinion that a Christian cannot be demonised because, they argue, there is no way that the Holy Spirit and an evil spirit can co-exist in the same place. The presence of the Holy Spirit, they say, would automatically preclude the possibility of an evil spirit being present.

Unfortunately this theological viewpoint is considerably at variance with experience. Where theology and experience are at such variance with each other then one must either have the courage to investigate the experiences that others relate and, if necessary, reassess one's theological position as a result; or dismiss the experiences of others as deception and heresy and remain in an entrenched position, not daring to face up to the real world outside. No amount of honest investigation can shake the foundations of true theology.

This whole issue cannot be discussed at the level of finding proof texts to justify one's viewpoint. For, try as you may, and others before me have looked very hard, you cannot come up with any text which uncompromisingly wins the point for either side of the discussion! Nevertheless, I have no doubt, personally, that the balance of Scripture, as I trust is evident from the earlier chapters in this book, gives plenty of support to the belief that Christians can be demonised.

Neither can you, however, find a text that proves one way or the other that Christians can get cancer. Experience, however, indicates very strongly that Christians can, and do, get cancer. Everyone reading this book will know of Christians who have died from the disease.

Jesus died so that all the powers of darkness could be defeated. The consequences of the fall were, therefore, dealt with at the cross. If, as a result, one concludes that Christians must be free from all demons, one also has to conclude that Christians should be free from all sickness. Experience, however, is too much at variance with this conclusion for it to be anything else but vain imagination. Sickness and disease are clearly products of the fall and we have the ministry of Jesus to demonstrate that much sickness can be a direct consequence of the presence of demons. Also, the experience of thousands of practitioners of Christian healing is that Christians *can* be demonised, and, therefore, any theological position that does not allow for this possibility must also be suspect and subject to reappraisal.

I believe there is a clear pathway through this particular theological jungle, but for those who have been entrenched in the theology of 'Christians Have No Demons', it will take a certain amount of courage and humility to traverse it. Especially for those who come from churches for which such a belief is part of the doctrinal basis of their denomination.

Those who hold a dispensationalist conservative viewpoint, which not only rejects the possibility of Christians being demonised, but also questions the practice of the gifts of the Spirit (through which people can be delivered) will have yet greater problems to overcome. It will also not be easy for those who accept the theoretical possibility that Christians can be demonised, but consider it to be a very rare condition and, therefore, not significant within the broad ministry of the Body of Christ.

Can a Christian be Possessed?

I agree one hundred per cent with the view that a born again Christian cannot be possessed by a demon! The word *"possessed"* implies not only occupation, but a total takeover of ownership. It is not a word which appears anywhere in the New Testament with reference to either demons or deliverance. Both the Authorised Version and the New International Version of the Bible wrongfully translate the Greek word (*daimonizomai*), meaning demonised or having a demon, by the word *"possessed"*.

This simple translational error has led to much confusion and misunderstanding. If I possess something I own it, it is mine. When a person receives Jesus Christ as Lord and Saviour they are born again of the Spirit of

God, they are translated out of the kingdom of darkness into the kingdom of light, and ownership of their life has changed hands. From that moment on they are rightfully possessed by the Holy Spirit.

The word which most graphically expresses our salvation is 'redeemed'. The literal meaning of redeemed is 'bought back'. This implies that mankind once enjoyed a direct uninterrupted relationship with God, but that at the fall mankind switched his allegiance to Satan and the powers of darkness, and through the incarnation and the sacrifice of Jesus on the cross, God redeemed those who would believe and receive this salvation. Literally, he bought them back (re-possessed them), and the price paid was the blood of his Son. A price was paid for our redemption.

So when we talk of possession we are talking about ownership, and a Christian can rightfully say, *"I have been bought back from the hands of the enemy and God now possesses me."*

Possession and demonisation are very different. If I buy a house, I possess the land it stands on, the structure of the building and any defects it may have as well! The fact that I possess the house, however, does not mean that it is now totally free from defects that originated during previous ownerships, including, for example, all the woodworm that may be resident in the roof timbers!

That is a far more accurate picture of the process of conversion than one which says the moment a person is born again all the problems and defects that were evident in a person's pre-conversion days are immediately resolved. It is, in fact, the experience of most Christians, especially those who have been converted as mature adults and not as children, that problems can even increase after conversion, as the spiritual battle for occupation of the land, which is now possessed by the Holy Spirit, begins in earnest. At conversion the process which the ancients called sanctification begins, as the

Holy Spirit works in our lives to clean up the mess that has been left behind by the previous owner!

When a house changes hands the woodworm become subject to the new owner also. If at that point, a pest control firm is called in, the house is delivered of its unwelcome occupants. If the new owner ignores the woodworm, however, the chomping of the timbers will carry on uninterrupted until there is a crisis requiring radical action. If when a person is converted the new Christian is not, at that point, delivered of the evil spirits that have previously been in residence, they will continue to operate in the person's life, limit the effectiveness of their Christian life and cause maximum hassle and sickness to the believer.

Jesus never said to the disciples that when people respond to the preaching of the Gospel all the demons will automatically pack their bags and leave. He told them to take action to cast the demons out, as well as preach the Gospel. The practice of deliverance ministry was considered by Jesus to be an essential adjunct to preaching the Gospel.

Ah, but, some might say, the disciples were ministering in pre-Pentecost days, before the Holy Spirit was made available generally to the Body of Christ, and that is why Jesus had to tell the disciples to cast out the demons. Now that Pentecost has come, they argue, and a person has been filled with the Holy Spirit, deliverance ministry is not necessary, because no evil spirit can live within a person at the same time as the Holy Spirit. I will return to a discussion of that particular question in a moment.

But supposing for a moment that the above supposition was a correct one, where do we stand as far as the Great Commission (Matthew 28:19-20) is concerned? As we have already seen, the Commission contained the foundational precepts for the growth and development of the Church. In the Commission Jesus made it very clear that the first disciples were to teach all new disciples to do exactly the same things as Jesus had taught them to do - which, of course, included deliverance.

What he did not say was *"do everything I've taught you to do, except deliverance, for after Pentecost you won't need to cast out demons, because they will then leave automatically when someone gets converted and is filled with the Spirit!"* If deliverance ministry was not going to be relevant for converts to Christianity, it would have been absolutely essential for Jesus to build an exclusion clause into the Great Commission, thus indicating that casting out demons had been a short-term expedient, only of relevance to believers who had followed Jesus during the three short years of his ministry on earth!

Can a Christian Have a Demon?

Not only do I contend that Christians can still have demons in them after conversion, that were there before conversion, but that Christians can receive further demons through the practice of sin and other possible entry points (see next volume). This is not a theoretical view but is based on the extensive experience of deliverance ministry that I and our team at Ellel Grange have shared over a five year period. Our experience has been gained, almost totally, in ministering to believing Christians. If Christians cannot be demonised then none of the many thousands of people we have seen delivered of evil spirits can have been born again of the Spirit of God: or, we were mistaken in thinking that they were being delivered of evil spirits. Clearly, the experience of many people, right across the world, means that neither of these conclusions are acceptable!

Returning to the text of the New Testament, we find that the Greek word associated with the presence of an evil spirit is (*daimonizomai*), meaning, literally, demonised or having a demon. To have a demon is very different from being possessed by a demon.

I see no conflict between the theologically sound perspective that, at conversion, we become possessed of the Holy Spirit and the fact that after conversion people can still be demonised through having a demon which has not yet been cast out through the ministry of deliverance. Much of our work in ministering healing and deliverance to people has been in casting out spirits that have lain dormant in the Christian for many years, some having entered, even, in the womb of the mother.

Each of us is walking towards wholeness in our Christian pilgrimage and as the Holy Spirit exposes darkness, then it is our responsibility to see that the light of Jesus Christ is brought to bear on the demonic and the powers of darkness are cast out. It is as unrealistic to say that once a person is a Christian they will never need any more physical or inner healing as to say that they cannot ever need deliverance ministry.

It is a fact of ministry experience that the greater the gap between conversion and deliverance ministry taking place, the more difficult the ministry often is. It seems as though the demons learn, in time, how to hang on in the Christian with some determination and practice ways of avoiding detection and eviction. But at conversion, or shortly after, the demonic seems to be in such a state of shock at what has happened that, if deliverance ministry follows quickly on conversion, major strongholds can be dealt with relatively easily.

For example, spirits of rejection often lie deeply entrenched and helping Christians in this area of their lives can, sometimes, require extensive and loving ministry. At one of our recent healing services, however, at which we always preach the Gospel of Salvation, a lady gave her life to the Lord and was converted.

Her counsellor not only led her to the Lord but also ministered, immediately, to the whole person. She discerned a deep root of rejection which had come in through the lady's mother. In a matter of minutes the spirit of rejection that had dominated and controlled this lady's life was exposed. She was delivered and the transformation in her life was instant and dramatic. Conversion and deliverance were dealt with naturally, at one and the same time.

I believe this was the normal practice of the early church and that one of the major reasons why deliverance ministry amongst Christians is often so hard, is because the Church has not been ministering the New Testament pattern for salvation, healing and deliverance. As a result years of consequential hurt, pain, and demonic manoevering have to be uncovered and dealt with before the demonic can be fully exposed, identified and cast out.

How Can an Evil Spirit and the Holy Spirit Dwell Within the Same Person at the Same Time?

Propositionally it seems unlikely that an evil spirit and the Holy Spirit could dwell within the same person. It seems even more unlikely, however, that the sinless Son of God could come into a broken and demonised world, that was under the rule of Satan and governed by an army of evil spirits!

The only reason why Jesus did come into such a spiritually hostile environment is summed up by John, in what is arguably the most well known verse in the whole of the Bible, *"For God loved the world so much he sent his son . . ."* (John 3:16). Love is, always has been and always will be the reason why God has conducted himself as he has with reference to the human race.

It was because of love that God sent Jesus; it was because of love that Jesus came; it was love that gave Jesus the determination not to shrink from the cross in the Garden of Gethsemane; it was love that enabled Jesus to give up his life into the hands of cruel soldiers who drove the nails through his hands; love . . , love . . , love. Love is the only force that has ever motivated the heart of God, who is love.

In response to the love of the Father Jesus came to earth. He did enter a world that was sold out to Satan. He did co-exist with Satan and his demons on earth, in spite of being the sinless Son of God. He did not look at the earth, see the ruling spirits in control, and decline to visit the planet. He did not say, 'that place is too demonised for me to get involved'. No, he actually chose to risk everything for the sake of rescuing lost mankind. In the same way the third member of the Trinity, the Holy Spirit, continues the work of rescue, enters people at conversion and begins the process of reclaiming the ground that the enemy has for so long being occupying.

Let me ask another question which may help to clarify confused thinking. Which of the following is more unlikely? That the Holy Spirit will remain inside a person who, by an act of their will, chooses to sin and speak out cursings through consecrated lips; or inside a person who battles against the attacks and temptations of a resident demon, but chooses not to allow his lips to be used sinfully.

James tells us that blessings and cursings can be spoken out of the same lips (James 3:9-10) - lips that belong to converted people in whom the Spirit of God dwells! But, surely the Holy Spirit would be so grieved by the practice of sin that he could not remain inside such a sinner? Not so. John, in speaking to Christians, tells them that if they do sin, God is faithful and just (the price has been paid on the cross) and will forgive them for what they have done (1 John 1:9). He does not say that if they sin it is evidence that the Holy Spirit is not in them.

By the same token, and, to me, equally significantly, one cannot say either that if a person has a demon, it is evidence that the Holy Spirit is not in them. Conversely, and perhaps even more significantly, one cannot say that because a person has the Holy Spirit in them that there cannot also be an evil spirit present.

It is only because of the love of God that, in his mercy, he does not totally withdraw his Holy Spirit from us when we sin. That, to me, is an even greater miracle than that God in his mercy should allow the Holy Spirit to enter and remain inside a person who has not yet been freed from all demonic power. David, after he had committed adultery with Bathsheba, feared on this count (Psalm 51:11) and was grateful for the love and mercy of God.

When a person becomes a Christian the Holy Spirit, having first wooed the person to the point of commitment, then enters by right, because Jesus has been invited to be Lord. But sanctification is not an instant process and it is often many years, (and sometimes it never happens) before a person has come to the point of allowing the Lordship of Jesus to become reality in each and every area of their lives.

We minister to many Christians, for example, who are not infrequently in significant leadership positions, but are still wrestling with major sexual problems. They are embarrassed and guilty about sharing their problem, but it has got to the point when they cannot any longer cope with the guilt of masturbation, and, sometimes, open sexual sin. It is abundantly clear that Jesus is not Lord of their sexuality, even though in every other area of their life their Christian behaviour and witness is often exemplary.

Some such people had never realised that they were not just struggling with the flesh, which we all have to contend with, but a spirit that was occupying the flesh and continually putting them under compulsion to sin. The Lordship of Jesus has certainly not become reality in that area of their life, but if the desire of the person's heart is to be free, it is then possible to minister deliverance so that they can be set free to walk cleanly before God. The real problems in ministry arise when in the heart the person so enjoys the sin that he does not want to be set free!

Thank God that the Holy Spirit does come into our lives and begins his liberating work. If he were to wait until all our demons had been cast out before entering our lives, none of us would either be saved or delivered and we would be destined to a Christless eternity!

Scriptures Often Used to Question the Validity of Deliverance Ministry in Christians

"If the Son sets you free then you will be really free"
(John 8:36)

"If any man be in Christ he is a new creation."
(2 Corinthians 5:17)

The argument runs something like this. When you are converted you are set free from the powers of darkness and you move from the kingdom of darkness into the kingdom of light. If you are now in the kingdom of light then the kingdom of darkness cannot have any further influence on your life and Christians cannot, therefore, be demonised because there are no demons in the Kingdom of light!

The above two Scriptures are often quoted as supporting this viewpoint. Unfortunately the context in which they are quoted usually varies markedly from the context of the original writings. It is easy to be deceived by depending on proof texts, quoted out of context, into adopting a theological position which does not accord with experience. Many have foundered spiritually in this way by trying to fit scripture to their own tunnel visioned theology and have limited the ways in which God is allowed to act in their lives!

No more so is this the case than in the whole area of deliverance ministry. Where theology and experience have become incompatible bedfellows something must be wrong. To pretend that Christians are not being healed through deliverance and to continue to preach and teach that Christians can't be demonised is naive to say the least.

John 8:36 is commented on in detail in Chapter 10, in which it is seen that the whole discourse revolves round Jesus telling some Jewish believers in him that they were still in bondage to their 'father the devil'! They could not cope with the idea that Jesus was expressing and finished up by trying to stone him to death.

The reaction of some sectors of the church today to the idea that Christian believers might be demonised is not dissimilar! They may not use weapons of stone to attack those who do minister deliverance to Christians, but the words that are sometimes spoken betray hearts that are hard as stone towards the work of the Holy Spirit in bringing renewal and freedom to believers, who have formerly been bound by the powers of darkness.

The very people who should be rejoicing at the works of God refuse to acknowledge one of the main ways that God brings healing to his people. I find it hard to understand how people can pray for someone in their church to be healed, and then oppose the ministry of Jesus through which their prayers are answered and that self-same person is eventually healed!

Such opposition from people can be understood in two different lights: either they consider deliverance of Christians to be a naive deception of those conducting the ministry; or they themselves are demonised and are led to oppose the ministry of deliverance by the demonic and so remain in bondage to the enemy! If they genuinely believe the former they are in danger of grieving the Holy Spirit by denying His power to deliver. And I have delivered enough people of religious spirits to believe that there is a distinct possibility of those who oppose deliverance being demonised themselves.

Those who quote *"if any man be in Christ he is a new creation, for the old is past away"* (2 Corinthians 5:17) to support their opposition to deliverance ministry, are confusing the eternal and temporal dimensions to the Gospel. Of course a believer is a new creation in Christ. Their spirit, which was formerly dead to God because of sin, has come back to life and when they are born again they are certainly a new creation.

Using this verse, however, to support the contention that because the new has come people cannot still be demonised, is committing theological suicide! For if the new has come, in this particular way, then there is no way that a Christian can ever again be sick, let alone demonised! Experience, however, would indicate that Christians do get sick, and, therefore, the implied contention that this verse refers to the total renewal of the flesh-life on conversion, must be fallacious.

As has already been stated, the root of the problem lies in the confusion there has been over the word possession. After conversion there has been a change of ownership - the house is under entirely new management. But the house still needs some refurbishment and redecoration (cleansing, healing and deliverance) even though a new owner has taken over.

In Conclusion

Whilst there is no particular scripture that states unequivocally that Christians can have demons, there are many verses which clearly assume that they can. Experience undoubtedly supports this viewpoint and the evidence of many Christians who have been healed through deliverance confirms the supposition.

Not only can born-again Christians be afflicted by the presence of demons, but there is little point in pursuing deliverance ministry with non-believers. For unless a person is born again the demons will seek to return as soon as they can, as Jesus warned in Matthew 12:43-45 and Luke 11:24-26. *"So when it is all over that person is in a worse state than he was at the beginning"* (GNB).

Deliverance ministry is primarily for Christians, described by Jesus in the healing of the Syro-Phoenician woman's daughter as 'bread for the children' (Matthew 15:26). If a church is not involved in deliverance ministry, it is making nonsense of Jesus's command to the disciples, and the whole church, to cast out demons.

Chapter 13

Postscript and Introduction to the Next Volume

Once it has been established that Christians can be demonised (have a demon), it is only a short step to the next conclusion that, when the Holy Spirit (light) exposes the presence of a demon (darkness), deliverance ministry is required. The person is 'sick' because they have a demon and part of the process of healing is to order the demon to leave.

Up to that point it sounds simple, and, essentially, much deliverance ministry is simple to carry out. However, there is one very important stage that cannot be avoided, without which the person is unlikely to be set free. And even if some deliverance ministry does take place, without this they will always be vulnerable to the danger of further demonisation. The legal right to the demon's presence *must* be removed.

Propositionally the legal right to all demons was removed at the cross, so that when a person believes, and receives Jesus for himself, no demon has any right to be there. However, we are living in the dispensation when the writing is on the wall of time for Satan and all his forces, but the battle still has to be taken to the enemy until Jesus comes again. The war is still on even though the outcome is certain.

The war in the Gulf, for example, was planned with meticulous military precision and skill for many months before the decisive strike was made by the allied forces and the Iraqi forces were summarily evicted from Kuwait. The patient build up and preparation for battle removed the foundations on which the enemy's hold on

Kuwait had depended. Kuwait had been illegally occupied. The final strike was the act of deliverance.

Preparation for deliverance ministry and the act of deliverance itself are remarkably similar to this graphic military analogy. Whilst the Iraqi forces certainly occupied the land and caused devastation in the territory, at no time did they possess (own) the land. The legal ownership was never in dispute. In the same way Christians are never possessed by demons, but demons can cause chaos and devastation in the territory they have occupied.

Systematically removing the rights that the demonic has used for the transference of demons into the person receiving ministry, either before or after conversion, is a vital part of deliverance ministry. If this is not done the ministry is unlikely to be either effective or long-lasting. Counselling and consequential 'groundwork ministry' can be vital steps towards healing through deliverance.

In this first volume the scriptural foundations for deliverance ministry have been established. The next volume concentrates on how to prepare a person for ministry by removing the rights that the demonic has claimed and exercise the victory of the cross in a person's life to bring about deliverance and healing.

Outline Contents of the next Volume

1. Foundational Teaching for Healing and Deliverance
2. Observable Symptoms in Demonised People
3. The Major Demonic Entry Routes into Man
4. The Weapons of Ministry Available to Us
5. Counselling and Personal Ministry Guidelines
6. Errors in ministry to be Avoided

I believe I have fairly established in this book that Jesus gave the disciples instructions to cast out demons and that this instruction is implicit within the Great Commission to the church for the whole of time. It is appropriate however, to draw this volume to a close with some lesser known, but equally important, words from John Chapter 3. Jesus is talking about himself when he says, in verse 34, *"He whom God has sent speaks the words of God"* (NKJV). In verse 32 Jesus had shared something of his personal heartbreak over the fact that no-one would accept the truth of his testimony. Then, in verse 33, he explained that accepting the truth of his testimony was an essential part of affirming one's belief in the truth about God.

Clearly, in this reference, Jesus was referring to far more than his teaching about deliverance ministry. Equally, however, his teaching about deliverance ministry was not excluded from his words. One has to conclude, therefore, that not accepting the teaching of Jesus about deliverance ministry is a denial of the truth about God that Jesus declared to us. John expressed this declaration with incomparable words, *"the Word became flesh and dwelt among us, and we beheld his glory, the glory of the only begotten of the Father, full of grace and truth"* (John 1:14 NKJV).

I pray that this book will have confirmed to many people that Jesus's teaching about healing and deliverance is truth that comes from the heart of the Father, and renewed a desire in the hearts of readers to see that same truth lived out today in the life of the Body of Christ.

Bibliography

Bubeck, Mark I. *The Adversary: The Christian Versus Demon Activity*. Chicago USA: Moody Press, 1975

Bubeck, Mark I. *Overcoming the Adversary*. Chicago USA: Moody Press, 1984

Gibson, Noel and Phyl. *Deliver Our Children*. Drummoyne, Australia: Freedom in Christ Ministries, 1989

Gibson, Noel and Phyl. *Evicting Demonic Squatters*. Drummoyne, Australia: Freedom in Christ Ministries, 1987

Green, Michael. *I Believe in Satan's Downfall*. London: Hodder, 1975

Hammond, Frank and Ida Mae. *Pigs in the Parlour: A Practical Guide to Deliverance*. Missouri USA: Impact, 1973

Hobson, Peter. *Christian Deliverance Volumes 1,2 and 3*. Sydney, Australia: Full Salvation Fellowship 1985 to 1988

Koch, Kurt. *Between Christ and Satan*. Grand Rapids USA: Kregel, 1962

Koch, Kurt. *Demonology, Past and Present*. Grand Rapids USA: Kregel, 1969

Koch, Kurt. *Occult Bondage and Deliverance*. Grand Rapids USA: Kregel, 1970

Lewis, C.S.. *The Screwtape Letters*. England: Collins, 1942

McClung, Floyd. *Spirits of the City*. England: Kingsway, 1990

Marshall, Tom. *Foundations for a Healing Ministry*. England: Sovereign World, 1988

Marshall, Tom. *Free Indeed!*. England: Sovereign World, 1980

Parker, Russ. *The Occult: Deliverance from Evil*. England: IVP, 1989

Penn-Lewis, Jessie and Roberts, Evan. *War on the Saints*. England: Diasozo Trust, 1973 (Reprint)

Peretti, Frank. *This Present Darkness (Novel)*. Illinois USA: Crossway Books, 1989 (UK edition: Monarch Publications, 1990)

Peretti, Frank. *Piercing the Darkness (Novel)*. Illinois USA: Crossway Books, 1989 (UK edition: Monarch Publications, 1990)

Powell, Graham and Shirley. *Christian Set Yourself Free*. England: New Wine Press 1986

Prince, Derek. *Blessing or Curse: You Can Choose*. England: Word (UK), 1990

Richards, John. *But Deliver Us from Evil*. London: DLT, 1974

Subritzky, Bill. *Demons Defeated*. England: Sovereign World, 1986

Wagner, C.Peter (Editor). *Territorial Spirits*. England: Sovereign World, 1991

Whyte, H.A.Maxwell. *Demons and Deliverance*. USA: Whittaker House, 1989

Woodworth-Etter, Maria. *A Diary of Signs and Wonders*. Oklahoma USA: Harrison House. (Reprint, originally published 1916)

(A more detailed and annotated bibliography will be provided at the end of the next volume on the practicalities of deliverance ministry)